The Attachment Bond

The Attachment Bond

Affectional Ties across the Lifespan

Virginia M. Shiller

LEXINGTON BOOKS
Lanham • Boulder • New York • London

Published by Lexington Books
An imprint of The Rowman & Littlefield Publishing Group, Inc.
4501 Forbes Boulevard, Suite 200, Lanham, Maryland 20706
www.rowman.com

Unit A, Whitacre Mews, 26-34 Stannary Street, London SE11 4AB

British Library Cataloguing in Publication Information Available

Library of Congress Cataloging-in-Publication Data Available

ISBN 978-1-4985-2253-3 (cloth : alkaline paper)
ISBN 978-1-4985-5173-1 (pbk. : alkaline paper)
ISBN 978-1-4985-5172-4 (electronic)

∞™ The paper used in this publication meets the minimum requirements of American
National Standard for Information Sciences Permanence of Paper for Printed Library
Materials, ANSI/NISO Z39.48-1992.

Printed in the United States of America

To Lukas

Humans wish to be confirmed in their being by other humans, and each wants to have a presence in the being of another. . . . Each looks secretly and shyly for a "yes" for the permission to be—that can come only from one human person to another.

—Martin Buber, *Urdistanz und Beziehung* (*Distance and Relation*), 1951 (translated by Robert Shiller)

Contents

Preface

Like many things in life, the inspiration for this book was multi-faceted. My interest in the myriad ways that attachments shape relationships has roots in my early clinical and research training, in my work with patients for over thirty-five years, and in my teaching and supervision at the Yale Child Study Center. In my research, teaching, and clinical work with children, adults, couples, and families, I have continually been fascinated by the ways people navigate relationships with those with whom they are closest. The profound pleasure of a rich and satisfying connection stands in utter contrast with experiences of aloneness and of rejection, feared or real.

But why *this* book? Recently, while preparing to teach seminars at the Yale Child Study Center on the topics of attachment and early trauma, I read many original research studies as well as books that have been published in the past several decades. It became apparent that while there is a tremendous wealth of knowledge about attachment through the lifespan, there is no single clear, succinct, and scientifically accurate overview of the field. The *Handbook of Attachment: Theory, Research, and Clinical Applications*, now in its third edition, is a wonderful resource for those who want an in-depth understanding of attachment research, but at 1,068 pages it is a daunting "handbook." A number of books have popularized research findings, but they tend to present an overly simplified summary of the field. There seemed a need for a comprehensive yet not overly technical book.

Now, for some history. In 1978, as a young graduate student at the University of Delaware, I searched for a topic for a master's thesis. That very year, the book *Patterns of Attachment: A Psychological Study of the Strange Situation*, authored by Mary Ainsworth and colleagues, was published. "Now, this is *really* interesting research," I remember thinking. Ainsworth had worked as John Bowlby's research assistant in London, and it was she who first employed experimental methods to study infant-mother attachment.

As an aspiring clinical psychologist, I found the work of Bowlby and Ainsworth rich in its clinical significance. Ainsworth's ground-breaking research was able to establish consistent links between mothers' behavior at home during the first year and the way children coped with the stress of a brief separation from their mothers in a laboratory situation. As will be shown in this book, a wealth of home observation data demonstrated that the degree of security in the child's attachment to mother was shaped by the dyad's countless interactions, resulting in different patterns of coping with separations and reunions in the twenty-minute lab procedure Ainsworth devised. Without Mary Ainsworth's laborious and rigorous work to develop valid, reliable ways to assess attachment security in young children, Bowlby might have remained just another theorist with interesting but unproven views.

In 1978, my interest in Mary Ainsworth's "Strange Situation Procedure" was not unique; her procedure was adopted fairly quickly by researchers in other laboratories. And some researchers began to follow children over time, inviting families back to the laboratory and looking at the sequelae of early parent-child relationships. Eventually, a number of these researchers managed to follow children into their teens and twenties. The longest-running study, the Minnesota Study of Risk and Adaption from Birth to Adulthood, today continues to periodically assess study participants, who are now in their forties. As children grew, new methods were developed to assess attachment security and adaptation.

Yet all of this research on the importance of mothers—in fact, it was stay-at-home mothers who were studied by Mary Ainsworth—made attachment theory and research controversial. Early research could easily be interpreted as indicating that children ideally would be blessed with a consistently available, sensitive, and attuned mother. Yet, many women were increasingly eager to unleash their ambitions and establish careers. When I had my first child in 1982, I personally experienced the conflict of wanting to both meet my son's needs and also to work in the field for which I had trained.

In this book, I felt it was especially important to look at the research on the role of fathers, of mother's mental health and life satisfaction, and of the quality of the marital relationship on children's early attachment and later adaptation. Attuned, responsive mothers are most likely to be happy women who feel supported in their role. Women who wish to work outside the home but are unable for one reason or another to do so may well parent differently than women who choose to stay home. It is important to recognize that one study that has never been done, nor ever can be done, is to take a group of women who wish to work outside the home and make them full-time parents, and then compare them and their children with a group of families in which mothers *wish* to be full-time mothers.

In writing this book, I have tried to simplify language when possible, to avoid unnecessary jargon, but still to convey the richness and subtly of research findings. One challenge I encountered was finding ways to integrate sophisticated statistical analyses with descriptive material which brings to life clinically meaningful patterns of behavior. Over the years, journals increasingly have emphasized powerful statistical methods of analysis, with less attention to real-life examples which illustrate research conclusions. Both rigorous analyses and descriptive material have value, and certainly one must be careful not to let colorful but poorly analyzed research findings lead to faulty conclusions. A blend of quantitative and qualitative approaches may be most helpful to many readers.

Leaving graduate school, I chose to work as a clinician rather than a researcher while raising my two sons. As a psychoanalytically oriented psychotherapist, I viewed the relationship that patients developed with me as a key part of the change process. As many of my colleagues believe, and as I have seen repeatedly, individuals who have had problematic relationships with parents can experience a "corrective emotional experience" with a therapist. While many other elements of the therapeutic process also contribute, having the experience of feeling safe and understood by one's therapist has been shown to provide an important foundation for change. Indeed, research data shows that individuals' degree of attachment security can change with new experiences well beyond the childhood years.

This book is not specifically about the many clinical applications of attachment research. Occasionally, I include anecdotes or results of intervention studies, but my main intent is to impart the background needed to understand the many practical applications for which attachment research provides the foundation. In Chapter Eight I do consider some specific practical applications, perhaps most importantly looking at research regarding the impact of child care on children's attachment security and social and emotional development. For other issues, the background research I summarize should place readers in a good position to evaluate diverse applications of attachment research.

Attachment theory grew out of the field of psychoanalysis. John Bowlby, the psychoanalyst who pioneered the study of the impact of attachment, separation, and loss on human development, was for many years at odds with psychoanalytic colleagues for his then-controversial views. Yet today, many say that attachment theory and research has been critical in providing the empirical base needed for psychoanalysis to remain credible. Its legitimacy has come from the work of trained researchers who have found ways to empirically test Bowlby's theories. Solid experimental research in developmental, clinical, and social/personality psychology, as will be reviewed in this book, has provided the methods needed to subject theories to the rigor of scientific evaluation.

While professionals often attribute their interests and views to their work and training experiences, it seems hard to ignore the influence of one's personal, formative relationships. We all grew up with adults who cared for us in one way or another, and who varied in their reliability and sensitivity, with various impacts on later life. My personal interest in attachment undoubtedly has roots in my own childhood experiences. When I was a senior in college, I grappled with challenges related to attachment. After nine months of profound satisfaction with my relationship with the man who was to become my husband, I suddenly found myself critical of him. Should I end this relationship?

Fortunately, the gifted therapist I was then seeing cautioned me to pause. I had been moving towards making a greater commitment to my future husband; what had changed? In therapy, I remembered that when I was six years old, I had felt a deep sense of losing a special place in my father's heart. A combination of my father taking a remote work assignment and the birth of a younger sibling made me feel displaced. In therapy I came to see that fifteen years later, I was fearful of risking the vulnerability that comes with attachment. Empowered by this new insight, I was able to overcome my fears and enter into what has been a very happy forty-year marriage.

This book examines the influence of early life experiences on later personal relationships. But exactly how much continuity should we expect between childhood and later years in security of attachment, in choice of partner, and ultimately in one's approach to parenting one's own children? Longitudinal studies as well as other research help shed light on these important questions.

I do hope that readers will take away at least two messages from this book. First, simply put, both mothers and fathers play a powerful role in shaping the person their child will become. Second, we cannot ask parents to give more than they have been given. The kind of parenting that mothers and fathers are able to engage in is shaped both by their own past experiences and by current circumstances. As a society, we should recognize these two basic facts and invest in the well-being of young families.

Acknowledgments

I am grateful for the many people who provided me with support in expanding my knowledge about attachment and in writing this book. Linda Mayes, head of the Young Child Section of the Yale Child Study Center and now its director, provided mentorship as I and other members of this section developed a curriculum on infant mental health, in partnership with the Anna Freud Centre and, subsequently, with the Austen Riggs Center. As a friend and colleague at Yale, Norka Malberg has been supportive in sharing her wealth of knowledge about the field of attachment. Other members of the Yale Child Study Center, Young Child Section, including Nancy Close, Christiana Mills, Lauren Dennehy, and Megan Lyons, have been valuable colleagues who always have been willing to share their knowledge about attachment as well as their developmental and clinical wisdom.

Further, Peter Dougherty, my husband's editor at Princeton University Press, provided early encouragement and consistent support for this project. Susan Goodman and Laurie Gray read sections of the book and made helpful suggestions. Megan Nelson and Anne Pidano were devoted in reading the manuscript very carefully and offering a good many suggestions to help polish the book. And two editors at Lexington Books, Amy King and Kasey Beduhn, in turn offered thoughtful and patient guidance throughout the long journey as this book moved from being a mere proposal to emerging as a completed manuscript.

My husband, Robert Shiller, not only provided consistent encouragement and support, but also carefully read the entire manuscript and offered numerous valuable comments. I am most grateful for the intellectual companionship as well as the "secure base" he has provided me with for forty years. Finally, I wish to thank two therapists from many years ago, Susan Volpe and Ilda Ficher, for providing the understanding I needed to dare to decide to first fully "attach" and enter this marriage, and then to pursue my dreams of becoming a clinical psychologist.

Chapter One

Nonsense, Common Sense, and (a Little) Research

Birth of the Study of Attachment

In 1914, *Infant Care*, a publication of the Children's Bureau of the US Government Department of Labor, advised parents:

> The rule that parents should not play with the baby may seem hard, but it is without doubt a safe one. A young, delicate, or nervous baby especially needs rest and quiet, and however robust the child much of the play that is indulged in is more or less harmful. It is a great pleasure to hear the baby laugh and crow in apparent delight, but often the means used to produce the laughter, such as tickling, punching, or tossing makes him irritable and restless. It is a regrettable fact that the few minutes of play that the father has when he gets home at night, which is often almost the only time he has with the child, may result in nervous disturbance of the baby and upset his regular habits. [1]

Nine editions of *Infant Care* were published as educational pamphlets between 1914 and 1955[2]; each advised parenting methods that strike the modern reader as severe.

Did parents really adhere to these guidelines? Indeed, some did. But, children's smiles and laughter are so contagious and engaging! It is difficult to imagine caretakers only surreptitiously exchanging timid smiles with the "fragile" creatures under their care, or to think about parents afraid to bring happiness and laughter into their babies' lives. Today, after decades of research on children's psychological development, we know that this engagement and happiness is the foundation not only for a strong, secure parent-child bond, but potentially for a lifetime of sound emotional health.

VIEWS OF CHILD DEVELOPMENT IN
THE FIRST HALF OF THE TWENTIETH CENTURY

Before presenting what we have come to learn about how the significance of the attachment bond, some historical perspective is important. The scientific study of child rearing is barely more than a half-century old. As Robert Sears, Eleanor Maccoby, and Harry Levin note in their seminal work *Patterns of Child Rearing*,[3] even the crudest of scientific approaches to studying human development lagged behind research in other fields.

The lack of research did not prevent "experts" from a variety of backgrounds from offering advice about child rearing. In the early years of the twentieth century, educators, social philosophers, and other professionals (perhaps most notably the psychoanalyst Sigmund Freud) discussed the influence of childhood experience on adult personality and functioning. Before the 1900s, views of infancy and of the nature of the mother-child bond varied over time, with fads and fashions influencing parenting practices, and differing child-care gospels dominating at one period or another.[4] Even when one view was popular, there was diversity in child-rearing practices.[5] Unfortunately, without any significant research on the topic, none of these shifting views of child rearing were based on scientific knowledge.

Certainly, even today, there are a variety of viewpoints offered by different "experts" about the best way to nurture and raise well-adjusted children. Now, we debate topics such as how parents should establish good sleep patterns. Should parents allow the child to "cry it out" as recommended by some?[6] Or are babies who are sensitively responded to when distressed at night more secure and independent in the long run?[7] However, even as these controversies persist, today's parents and children (unlike their grandparents and great-grandparents) have the benefit of a robust body of scientific child development research.

Child Development, Science, and Society

Truly understanding what shapes a child is critical in knowing how best to support parents and children. Researchers must go beyond considering what advice should be provided to parents; they must also study the benefits to society at large, benefits that can be provided once we understand the whole array of factors that influence child development. If children will become the adults they are destined to be by temperament or genetics, then it matters little the emotional, social, and economic conditions in which they live. If, on the other hand, the environment in which the child is raised has a strong influence on his or her destiny, then parents (as well as any other adults who play a role in a child's life) will benefit from understanding current scientific knowledge.

In the twenty-first century, a wide array of individuals play a role in young families' lives. Pediatricians, nurses, day care personnel, mental health professionals, social workers, and teachers are only some of the people who may personally interact with parents and children. In the larger society, judges in family courts, business administrators, and lawmakers who decide on such things as out-of-home placements, parental leave policies, health insurance coverage, and social service benefits all indirectly shape the environment in which children develop.

The purpose of this book is to communicate to a broad audience what we have learned in the last century or so about the factors that shape a growing child. Ultimately, the purpose is to provide a knowledge base for all those whose actions touch the lives of young families. While the goal of this book is not to give in-depth guidance about interventions and social policies, information will be provided along the way about how knowledge can be translated into practices to benefit children. This brief historical review of how psychological science has developed over the past century will provide a foundation for understanding current child development theories and research.

Early Attempts at Scientific Study of Children

In the early decades of the twentieth century, there was a growing desire for child-rearing advice based on scientific knowledge.[8] Concurrently, the nascent field of psychology sought to become more respectable and to be viewed as a true science. There was high hope that scientists could provide information that would improve the care of children.[9] Early psychological studies focused particularly on aspects of development that were easily quantifiable, such as physical growth and intellectual development.[10]

John Watson, an American psychologist who founded the field of behaviorism, responded to the desire for scientifically based recommendations by offering advice in popular as well as professional publications. Research on child development conducted in his laboratory—in particular, showing how habits could be formed by conditioning[11]—served as the basis for his recommendations. Unfortunately, Watson's recommendations went far beyond the findings from his lab,[12] and while he eventually lost the support of many academic psychologists, he maintained a following of parents who were impressed that his views were backed by evidence that sounded scientific.[13]

In his well-known book *Psychological Care of Infant and Child*,[14] Watson loosely translated his theories about conditioning to extend to a variety of areas of child rearing. Controversy was stirred by his firm advice that parents never hug or kiss their children.[15] He argued that infants could only grow up to be responsible, independent adults if they were not coddled. Watson went so far as to say:

Let [the child] learn to overcome difficulties almost from birth. . . . No child should get commendations and notice and petting every time it does something it ought to be doing anyway. If your heart is too tender and you must watch the child, make yourself a peephole so you can see it without being seen, or use a periscope . . . and, finally, learn not to talk in endearing and coddling terms.[16]

The "Watson fad" was embraced by countless parents during the late 1920s and into the 1930s.[17] It was popular at this time in Britain as well as in America, its country of origin.[18] William Kessen, a prominent Yale developmental psychologist,[19] wrote:

It was Watson's dedication to the principle of man's modifiability by experience that made him a child psychologist and changed the tone of child study in the United States for several decades. . . . [This turned out] unhappily for psychology and for children born between 1925 and 1940. . . . Watson's views, cruel and silly as they must have appeared to considerate men at all times, exerted a strong influence on child-rearing procedures, through his own books and articles . . . and through his voice in the Children's Bureau.[20]

So much for science contributing to enlightened child care!

Fortunately, even without scientific support for more reasonable approaches to child rearing, there was a fairly continuous decline in the severity of discipline recommended in the nine editions of *Infant Care*.[21] In 1914, both masturbation and thumb sucking were dangerous habits that were to be stopped by restraint; with masturbation, parents were advised to tie the child's legs to opposite sides of the crib, to avoid a habit that might leave them "wrecked for life." Up until the 1940s, parents were urged to bowel train their children at early ages (in some editions of the pamphlet, it was to be completed by eight months), and weaning and introduction of solid foods was to be done with great firmness. Martha Wolfenstein summarizes the tone of the advice in many of the editions of *Infant Care*: "Successful child training meant winning out against the child in the struggle for domination."[22]

Was America an exception in the Western world? Across the Atlantic, in England in the 1920s, there was a similar emphasis on regimentation of mothering, and a conspicuous absence of references to parental love. Bowel training that was begun very early and feeding that was done by the clock were claimed to be backed by scientific evidence.[23] In fact, any initiative in child care originating in one country typically did not remain confined within its borders, and with international conferences, ideas spread among countries such as Britain, Germany, France, Canada, and America.[24]

In Britain, patterns of child-parent relationships were influenced to some degree by social class. In all social classes, discipline was strict and obedience was highly valued. Corporal punishment was common, most especially among the poor. Working-class parents were emotionally closer to their children, but affection was still typically limited. The most distant and formal parents were those in the upper classes, who left much of the routine child care to nannies.[25]

The view that infants might actually have internal emotional lives received little attention through the first several decades of the twentieth century. Sigmund Freud's writings were certainly an exception, but his emphasis on sexuality made his ideas quite controversial, and his theories were rarely discussed in the realm of child rearing, at least in the United States.[26] Freud spent a good deal of time working to understand how young children's inner lives developed, and he emphasized the importance of the role that innate instincts (particularly sexual and aggressive impulses) and internal fantasies played in shaping children's thoughts and behavior.

Beyond the specific theories he developed, Freud emphasized the general notion that minds were complicated and warranted careful exploration. Importantly, Freud emphasized the existence and significance of the unconscious mind,[27] as well as psychological defenses that relegated painful or otherwise unwanted thoughts and feelings to a place outside of consciousness.

A Move towards Greater Sensitivity

In America, as mid-century approached, parenting guidelines became less rigid, and people were ready to welcome the ideas of someone more sympathetic to the needs of children. Benjamin Spock entered a pediatric internship in 1931, but quickly became disenchanted with the accepted rigid techniques, and was struck by how the prevailing methods of infant care ignored even their simplest emotional needs.[28] Spock's training in psychoanalysis in New York, a field that was still on the fringe of American medicine, offered him new ways to think about infants' emotional lives, e.g., how a baby's "oral drive" leads to his urge to suck as well as to resist weaning.[29]

In 1945, Spock's book *The Common Sense Book of Baby and Child Care*[30] was published, and it went on to become one of the best-selling books of all time.[31] While Freud's ideas pervaded the book, Spock did not mention him, but instead translated Freud's theoretical ideas into simple, practical advice for parents, writing in a friendly, non-condescending manner.[32] Early in the book, Spock suggests things such as "Enjoy your baby. He isn't a schemer. He needs loving. . . . A little gentle rocking may actually be good for him."[33]

Progress at Mid-Century: A Science of Child Development Begins

In 1957, Robert Sears, Eleanor Maccoby, and Harry Levin, working in the Laboratory of Human Development at Harvard University, published the most extensive systematic study of child rearing to date in their book *Patterns of Child Rearing.* In the introductory chapter, the authors wrote that "it is high time for the behavioral sciences to use research methods to replace common sense (or nonsense) fancies with demonstrable facts."[34] This groundbreaking study included almost 400 mothers with children in kindergarten. Through semi-structured interviews, mothers provided information about both current and past child-rearing practices. Questions probed their disciplinary practices, degree of permissiveness, the severity of training techniques they used, and how they worked to encourage more mature behaviors while discouraging unwanted ones. The researchers also asked about the mothers' own temperaments. Questions were worded sensitively to encourage openness in responses; for example, "Do you ever find time to play with Johnny just for your own pleasure?" The goal was to obtain information about the effects of various types of child-rearing practices on the developing personalities and behaviors of young children, as well as to learn something about the temperament and social relationships of mothers who engaged in various kinds of child-rearing practices.[35]

Sears and co-authors' theoretical foundation for their work was learning theory. For example, they ascribed the infant's desire for mother to the learned association between mother and the pleasure of having hunger drives satisfied when mother provided milk through breast or bottle.[36] Consistent with social learning theory, this team of researchers looked to see if "reinforcement" of behaviors such as crying and clinging would result in more instances of such behavior. However, despite their inclination to look for the influence of learning, these researchers thoughtfully considered a variety of possible underlying causes for behavior.

Sears and co-authors found in their study that 20 percent of mothers reported that their children had had prolonged periods of appetite loss at some point during their first five years. In analyzing their findings, they first considered whether these symptoms might result from feeding practices, such as whether the infant was breast-fed, the age of the child when weaning was started, whether infant feeding was scheduled or on-demand, or whether the child was emotionally upset over weaning. No correlations were found between these practices and later loss of appetite.[37]

Next, Sears and his colleagues considered whether emotions such as fear or anger, or a child's desire to rebel against parental harshness, might explain the feeding problems. And indeed, they found that children who had had feeding problems were more likely to have had negative experiences such as severe toilet training and frequent physical punishment. In addition, when children had had significant loss of appetite, their mothers more often reported having strongly discouraged expression of aggression towards parents. They also discouraged expressions of dependency by, for example, responding angrily when children clung or demanded attention.[38] Thus, emotions, rather than learned behaviors, seemed to underlie the feeding difficulties.

This study was limited by the fact that all information came from mothers themselves. No direct observations of the children were made. Yet, this was an ambitious, careful beginning to the scientific study of the impact of parenting behaviors on child development.

BIRTH OF THE STUDY OF ATTACHMENT:
ENTER JOHN BOWLBY

Mid-century, John Bowlby ushered in a new era of thinking about children's innate needs, the influence of parenting, and the ways in which the social environment contributed to child development. His theorizing has led to a vast amount of research, which has provided a solid body of scientific knowledge to support recommendations for child-rearing practices. Research inspired by Bowlby's theories, conducted by hundreds of researchers on a number of continents, provides the foundation for the understanding of life-span development and emotional adjustment that will be summarized in this book.

How did Bowlby come to discover and introduce a radical new theory of human development? As a psychotherapist, I find it hard to ignore the possible contribution of formative personal experiences. Born in Britain in 1907, Bowlby's parents raised him in the manner common in well-off British families in the early twentieth century. As noted earlier, at that time and within that socio-economic class, reserved interactions with parents were the norm.[39] Most of the caretaking was left to nursemaids, and young John and his five siblings visited with their mother one hour daily and saw their father for a few hours on Sunday. "Minnie" was John's favorite nursemaid until she left the family when he was about four. While Bowlby at one point claimed he had never experienced any significant separations in his childhood, he did write in 1958: "But for a child to be looked after entirely by a loving nanny and then for her to leave when he is two or three, or even four or five, can be almost as tragic as the loss of a mother."[40]

In fact, in 2004, in a new introduction of the book *The Making and Breaking of Affectional Bonds*, Bowlby's son Richard wrote:

> When he [my father] was young he was cared for by an affectionate and playful young nanny called Minnie, but she left the family when he was about four. He told me that he was very attached to Minnie and felt the pain of separation when their affectional bond was broken. . . . Losing a very important attachment figure and working out the importance of an enduring relationship was, I think, a large part of his motivation for a lifetime study of the

affectional bond that forms between a child and his primary attachment figure.[41]

In 1918, during the last year of World War I, ten-year-old Bowlby and his
eleven-year-old brother were sent away to boarding school.[42] During one of
his holiday visits home, he attended a soccer game in which his godfather
played. Tragically, the godfather dropped dead on the field.[43] It is not clear
whether John received any support in grieving this death, or whether he was
simply sent back to boarding school. In 1990, Bowlby stated in an interview
that he didn't think boarding school was a good idea for younger children[44]
and he advised that children younger than thirteen not be sent away to
school.[45] Perhaps the cumulative effect of the loss of his nanny, followed by
the time spent living apart from family, not to mention his witnessing his
godfather's sudden death, left him uniquely sensitive to the possibility that
separation and loss experiences may leave their mark.

Bowlby's Academic and Real-World Experiences

There are two major trends in Bowlby's work and experiences that seem
central in inspiring his pathbreaking work on the importance of parent-child
attachment. First, and perhaps most importantly, Bowlby had a keen interest
in understanding how social influences affected children's emotional development. Second, he had a strong interest in the sciences, including evolution,
biology, and animal behavior.

At Cambridge University, Bowlby focused on both of these topics. He
began his studies in the natural sciences, with an emphasis on evolutionary
biology. Then, he spent one year working in the fields of philosophy and
psychology. During his time at Cambridge he became interested in psychoanalysis, which was very much in vogue. It is noteworthy, however, that his
principal teachers believed neither in extreme behaviorism nor in dogmatic
Freudian theory. Bowlby's studies at Cambridge taught him the importance
of careful observations and experiments in settings that were close to real-life
situations.[46]

After leaving Cambridge, Bowlby had a variety of professional experiences that impressed upon him the importance of children having a solid,
consistent, and loving relationship with a parent or parent figure. As a teacher at a progressive school, he had an opportunity to work closely with a group
of "difficult" children; at least some of these youngsters were known to have
had significant separations or problematic relationships with parents or caregivers. Two children particularly intrigued him: one was an isolated, affec-
tionless teenager with a history of theft—Bowlby described him as a "very,
very emotionally frozen character"—who had a history of having had no
stable mother figure.[47] The second was an anxious boy of seven or eight who

followed Bowlby around and was known as his shadow.[48] Bowlby later asserted that his experiences at this school were a significant factor in kindling his decision to focus on the emotional and behavioral problems resulting from separations of children from parents.[49]

Developing a New Theory

While Bowlby focused much of his writing on the impact of child-parent separations, he was also concerned about difficulties in parent-child emotional interactions. In a paper published in 1940, he outlined environmental factors operative during a child's early years which influenced the development of the child's character. Among these factors, he included

> the general colour of the mother's emotional attitude to her child . . . including her handling of feeding, weaning and toilet-training; for the way in which a mother (or nurse) handles these questions is dependent far more upon her unconscious attitude both to these things in herself and to the child as a person, than upon any conscious method she adopts. The handling of feeding, weaning and habit-training can thus be regarded to a great extent as a function of a mother's character.[50]

Later, Bowlby explained that he chose to focus on the effects of actual separation as opposed to problematic parent-child relationships because of intense controversy, in psychiatry, psychoanalysis, and with the general public, regarding the idea that parents' treatment of children could be the cause of later difficulties.[51]

Indeed, Bowlby's interest in the impact that childhood experiences might have on later adjustment—whether actual separations or troubled parent-child relationships—was at odds with prevailing cultural views. In a 1979 interview, Bowlby asserted: "The idea [that painful experiences were undesirable for children and would mold their characters] was totally alien to the culture of the time, you know." Bowlby further noted: "The principle was formulated that the more you gave a child affection and attention, the more he'd grow up to be a selfish brat—which of course is the exact opposite of the truth."[52]

Bowlby's interest in exploring the impact of major separations during the early years eventually lead him to conduct a study regarding delinquency and mental disturbance. "Forty-Four Juvenile Thieves" summarized his study of the case histories of forty-four youngsters with histories of stealing. These youngsters were compared with forty-four non-thieves, who were receiving psychiatric services at a child guidance clinic and hence were assumed to be suffering from "some form of mental disturbance." In this paper, he reported that many more of the juvenile thieves, compared with youngsters with other

forms of psychological difficulty, had had separations of six months or longer from major caregivers during their first five years. [53]

At that time, a sick child's stay in a hospital often meant a long separation
from his or her parents. Most hospitals had very strict rules against family
visits. Hospital staff viewed parents as carriers of germs, and felt their visits
only left children distressed when visiting hours ended. Children's distress
following their parents' departure was interpreted as evidence that children
were upset by visits and hence better off without them. In the 1940s and
1950s, the issue of parents visiting their children during hospitalizations was
hotly debated in the British medical journal *The Lancet*, as well as among
professionals in papers and lectures. [54] Around the same time, there was also
increasing attention to the problems of children placed in foster and institu-
tional care.

Harnessing the Power of Film

Two films which vividly showed children's grief and loneliness when separated from parents helped bring attention to this issue. In 1947 in the United
States, René Spitz produced a silent black-and-white film titled *Grief: A
Peril in Infancy*. This film featured a baby named Jane who changed from a
happy, approachable child to a withdrawn one within weeks of placement in
a foundling home. When this film was shown to psychoanalysts and physi-
cians, the response was one of shock and disbelief. In fact, it is said that
Spitz's film "shook the ground of psychologists in the U.S." [55]

A second film was made in London a few years later by James Robertson,
whom Bowlby, then head of the Department for Children and Parents at the
London Tavistock Clinic, had hired as a research assistant. In 1948, Robertson began observing children separated from parents during hospitalizations,
and he tried to communicate to professionals his concern about the serious
emotional problems these children experienced. Eventually, he became exas-
perated with the unending resistance he met during presentations. [56]

In 1952, Robertson decided he might best convince people of the seriousness of separation symptoms if he made a film of a child's experience.
Bowlby, anticipating that Robertson might be accused of a biased presentation, insisted that Robertson be careful to choose the child by a random
process. [57] *A Two Year Old Goes to Hospital* [58] showed a little girl named
Laura who underwent a nine-day hospitalization, and in the process went
from being a charming child to a silent and unresponsive one. The power of
the film was undeniable, but when shown to an audience of pediatricians and
nurses, it was met with intense hostility. Accusers hotly asserted that this was
an "atypical child of atypical parents in an atypical ward," that the film had
slandered pediatrics, and that it should be withdrawn. [59]

A Pivotal Report: Maternal Care and Mental Health

In 1950, two years before the making of the Robertson film, Bowlby had been recruited by the World Health Organization (WHO) to do a report on the problems of children left homeless after World War II. In gathering data for this report, Bowlby visited a number of European countries as well as the United States, speaking with experts and learning about the most recent advances in studies on parental deprivation.[60] His monograph *Maternal Care and Mental Health* summarized his findings. He concluded "the evidence is now such that it leaves no room for doubt regarding the general propositions—that the prolonged deprivation of the young child of maternal care may have grave and far-reaching effects on his character and so on the whole of his future life." [61]

When Bowlby first presented his conclusions, they were met with a great deal of skepticism and hostility. Some interpreted his findings as suggesting mothers should never leave their children, even to go to the cinema.[62] Bowlby himself eventually addressed this view, providing reassurance to parents that short-term care by individuals familiar to the child was not harmful.[63]

But Bowlby stood by his conclusion that longer separations, particularly from caregivers with whom the child lacked a strong attachment, were indeed harmful. A paperback abridgement of the WHO monograph, entitled *Child Care and the Growth of Love*, was published two years later, and it quickly became an international bestseller.[64] Overall, Bowlby's WHO report eventually had a major influence on public opinion and led to changes in the institutionalized care of children in many countries.[65]

Understanding the Impact of Maternal Deprivation

Based on the observations James Robertson, together with his wife, Joyce Robertson, had made of children undergoing hospitalizations, Bowlby and the Robertsons identified three phases commonly seen when a young child is cared for by unfamiliar people in unfamiliar setting. First, children show *protest*, as they attempt to recover the mother. Second comes *despair* of recovering mother, along with depression, and third, *emotional detachment*.[66] These three phases have become classic in the literature on separation.

After finishing the report for the World Health Organization, Bowlby felt he lacked a comprehensive theoretical explanation for the severe impact of maternal deprivation. As he wrote in volume one of his trilogy on attachment, separation, and loss:

> As more than one reviewer pointed out, the report had at least one grave limitation. Whereas it had much to say about the many kinds of ill effect that evidence shows can be attributed to maternal deprivation and also about prac-

tical measures that may prevent or mitigate these ill effects, it said very little indeed about the processes whereby these ill effects are brought into being. How does it come about that one or another of the events included under the general heading of maternal deprivation produces this or that form of psychiatric disturbance? What are the processes at work?[67]

In thinking about these questions, Bowlby was not satisfied with the prevailing psychoanalytic view that love of mother derives from sensuous oral gratification. He also did not agree with social learning theory's claim that dependency was based on the association of mother with feeding.[68] So, he actively sought evidence that would allow him to build a new theory.[69] To accomplish this, he had to go outside the fields of psychiatry and psychoanalysis.

Delving into Ethology: Learning from Animals

In 1951, Bowlby began to pursue the second major avenue that led to his pathbreaking work. In that year he was introduced to Konrad Lorenz's studies of animal behavior (ethology), which had been conducted in the 1930s.[70] In his now-famous experiments, Lorenz showed that if goslings were hatched in an incubator, with no exposure to adult geese, they would instinctively "imprint" (a term coined by Lorenz) onto the first human they saw. Thereafter, these geese would react to this human as they would have reacted to their bird parents, by flocking and following them.[71] In fact, even when these birds were later introduced to other geese, they did not accept them. Lorenz showed that the young gosling's susceptibility to forming a bond with another individual—whether animal or human—lasted for a very brief time, but once the bond was formed, it was totally irreversible. Lorenz argued that this indicated that the bond was based on an instinctual response rather than some kind of associative learning.

Bowlby was very intrigued by this account of "imprinting" in geese. In this theory, social bond formation had nothing to do with feeding. He also appreciated the ethological method of observing animals in their natural environment, as this was consistent with the methods Robertson had developed at the Tavistock research unit.[72]

Robert Hinde was a second ethologist who had a significant influence on Bowlby, and was likely the person who introduced Bowlby to the concept of the "environment of evolutionary adaptedness."[73] Bowlby used this concept to explain how humans adopted attachment behavior as a survival strategy.[74] Knowledge gained from the field of ethology encouraged Bowlby to think about a species-specific genetic susceptibility to attachment. With input from and discussions with Lorenz, Hinde, and other ethologists, Bowlby developed a solid theoretical foundation for his theory of attachment.

One other individual who influenced Bowlby's development of his new theory was the American psychologist Harry Harlow. Across the Atlantic, Harlow was conducting experiments which supported the ethological viewpoints that Bowlby had embraced. In his now-classic studies, Harlow showed that orphaned infant monkeys preferred to cling to cloth-covered mother "surrogates" that had no milk to offer, rather than to wire surrogates which offered milk but no soft surface to which to cling.[75]

The cloth mother surrogates were viewed as providing the young monkeys with a source of security, and Harlow and Zimmerman noted that this role was seen "with special clarity when mother and child are in a strange situation."[76] In an unfamiliar room containing objects which would arouse the curiosity of young monkeys and entice them to explore, the baby monkeys initially rushed to the cloth mother and clutched her. However, after a few sessions the babies began to use the soft mother surrogate as a "source of security, a base of operations," and they would explore the objects and then return to the mother before again adventuring out for further exploration.[77]

When the cloth mothers were absent from the room, the babies' behaviors were quite different; frequently they would freeze in a crouched position or run rapidly from object to object, screaming and crying. In coming chapters, as we trace the development of Bowlby's theory and how it was supported (and sometimes modified) by research with human infants, Harlow's observations should be remembered as an early view into the power of the child's attachment to a comforting figure to provide security in an unfamiliar environment.

PSYCHOANALYSIS AND ATTACHMENT THEORY

Attachment theory grew out of the field of psychoanalysis, and much of Bowlby's work had a foundation in the field Sigmund Freud and colleagues had created. Freud and his followers produced a model in which adults' mental problems are explained by their adverse emotional experiences during childhood.[78] Freud had enormous influence in promoting the idea that what parents do with children when they are young contributes a great deal to those children's development and to their adult personalities.[79]

Freud's views also challenged the strict discipline that was common in areas of infant training, particularly early toilet training. Writing in 1978, Elizabeth Lomax and co-authors summarized the positive impact of Freud's writings as they related to the practice of child care as follows: "Implicit in his theories, at least from the American viewpoint, was the promise that, if a child's early experiences were pleasurable and if he suffered a minimum of frustration and was given a maximum of encouragement and understanding, he would develop into a well-adjusted person."[80]

One of the most controversial of Freud's theories, and one that contributed eventually to a rift between Bowlby and Freud's followers, was Freud's
emphasis on the importance of internal fantasies rather than on real-life experiences. Early in his work, Freud had attributed adult problems, particularly
"hysteria,"[81] to seduction in early childhood, usually by the father. By 1897
he changed his view, concluding that rather than being true memories of
childhood trauma, hysterical patients were expressing fantasies.[82]

Freud developed his theories about child development not from observing
children, but from conversations with middle-class adult patients.[83] Freud's
"laboratory" was his consulting room, where he listened carefully to the
thoughts, fantasies, and dreams of adult patients during psychoanalysis, and
sought clues to understand the basis for psychological symptoms.

Parting Ways with Traditional Psychoanalysis

Unlike Freud, Bowlby believed in the importance of direct observation of
infants and children. Also, unlike other psychoanalysts, he sought information from a variety of fields. In weekly research seminars at the Tavistock
Clinic that focused on cases of mother-child relationships,[84] Bowlby demonstrated his inclination to learn from a variety of theoretical viewpoints. These
seminars included the ethologist Robert Hinde, psychoanalysts from two
schools of thought, a Hullian learning theorist, a Skinnerian learning theorist,
a Piagetian, an "anti-psychiatrist" (Ronald Laing), and a psychiatric social
worker.[85]

Despite retaining his allegiance to psychoanalysis, Bowlby challenged a
number of widely accepted viewpoints in the field, arousing the ire of
many.[86] Bowlby maintained that he aimed only to "rewrite psychoanalysis in
the light of ethological concepts," but his views were seen as a threat to
Freudian theory.[87] Bowlby's focus on real-life experiences rather than inner
fantasies and conflicts was only one of a number of major sources of difference.[88]

Bowlby himself felt that the divergence in his work from that of traditional psychoanalysis was less significant than many of his detractors believed.
When Bowlby was in his seventies, he reflected in an interview on the
difficulties he had with his colleagues in earlier years, and noted that he got
"an awful battering" from an audience of psychoanalysts when he first presented his theories integrating ethology with psychoanalytic concepts. To his
peers, a theory of child development based on the "clinging" instinct seen in
a variety of young mammals was simplistic. In reflecting upon this time,
Bowlby said, "But the reason I decided to concentrate on these very elemen-
tal factors of attachment and separation was because to attempt to deal with
the other influences which parents have on children was at that time just too
difficult and controversial."[89]

Freud never engaged in systematic scientific research, and for many years psychoanalysts following in his footsteps did not test psychoanalytic conjectures empirically.[90] The failure of the field of psychoanalysis to rigorously test theories and treatments has made it vulnerable to criticism throughout much of the twentieth century.[91] Bowlby anticipated this criticism, asserting, "If psychoanalysis is to attain full status as one of the behavioral sciences, it must add to its traditional method the tried methods of the natural sciences."[92]

Finding Common Ground and Mending Fences

Beginning in the last decade of the twentieth century, there has been a rapprochement between attachment theorists and psychoanalytic theories, as changes within each area of thought have opened up more common ground and shared language.[93] As attachment theorists have placed more emphasis on individuals' *representations* of attachment (i.e., internal models of relationships with significant attachment figures) and less on purely behavioral signs of attachment, the two areas of study have increasingly found common ground.

Mary Ainsworth, and other researchers who followed her, generally worked within a psychoanalytically oriented framework. However, in 1987, several decades after Ainsworth began her work, two social psychologists, Cindy Hazan and Phillip Shaver, conducted research using social psychology methods to investigate Bowlby's theoretical ideas. They published a landmark study that proposed that romantic love could be thought of as an attachment process.[94] Since this 1987 publication, a very extensive literature has developed within the social psychology field which has deepened our understanding of attachment bonds across the lifespan.[95]

As advances have been made in neuroscience, researchers in this field are actively investigating the biological underpinnings of the attachment relationship. Bowlby had anticipated that brain structures involved in the attachment system would someday be identified.[96] Given the extensiveness of this topic, this book is only able to include occasional references to work in this area. Interested readers can learn more from resources such as the *Handbook of Attachment: Theory, Research, and Clinical Applications*[97] or *The Developing Mind: How Relationships and the Brain Interact to Shape Who We Are*.[98] As Bowlby had a strong interest in biology, we can imagine he would be extremely pleased with these new developments.

OUTLINE OF THE REST OF THIS BOOK

In the next chapter, I will introduce Mary Ainsworth, who began working in Bowlby's research lab in 1950,[99] and with whom Bowlby eventually had a life-long collaboration, ending with Bowlby's death in 1990. It was Mary Ainsworth who spearheaded the effort to find ways of putting Bowlby's ideas to experimental test. A short laboratory assessment procedure she devised, the "Strange Situation Procedure," turned out to reveal a great deal about a child's history of interaction with his or her mother in the first year of life. Gaining a clear understanding of the patterns of attachment security Ainsworth identified and the parenting behaviors observed to be associated with these patterns will help readers understand research discussed in later chapters.

Ainsworth's work, along with that of her students as well as many others who were intrigued by Bowlby's theories and Ainsworth's methods, has succeeded in fulfilling Bowlby's desire to see psychoanalytic notions being subjected to experimental examination. In the process, a solid and comprehensive science of child development and parent-child relationships has been developed.

Chapter Three delves into the question as to how attachment security lays the groundwork for future development. Bowlby theorized that children begin to build internal "working models": cognitive structures that guide children in anticipating what to expect when interacting with others. More recent theorists have proposed that attachment security not only lays a groundwork for expectations, but also provides the basis for affect regulation. Chapter Three also introduces an important debate about the degree to which continuity versus discontinuity in attachment security is expected as children grow. To what extent are experiences in infancy carried forward, into the preschool years and beyond? How much flexibility do children show if circumstances in their lives change? While these questions will continue to be addressed throughout the book, the third chapter provides preliminary data as well as recent theory and findings about on-going brain plasticity.

In Chapter Four, I introduce four longitudinal studies spearheaded by researchers in three countries that began following "Child Veterans" of the Strange Situation Procedure beyond infancy. We will find that attachment security in infancy significantly predicts observations of children's adjustment in the toddler and preschool years. Children with different attachment histories vary in important areas, including social competence, independence, language skills, empathy, and even in the tendency to bully others. However, predictions from infancy turn out to be imperfect, and the issue of continuity versus discontinuity continues to be examined.

Chapter Five takes us on a detour to consider attachment security in *parents*. Researchers became curious about the thought processes of the adults who behave in different ways with their children. Mary Ainsworth's student Mary Main developed the Adult Attachment Interview (AAI) to probe parents' general thoughts regarding attachment. This complex interview procedure yields rich information about adults' "states of mind with respect to attachment." Research using the AAI shows us that parents' states of mind are clearly linked with children's attachment security.

In Chapter Five I also provide a brief introduction to another tradition of research regarding adult attachment styles. In the late 1980s, social psychologists became intrigued with the notion that Bowlby's theories about attachment might offer a great deal to our understanding of adult romantic relationships. Using self-report questionnaires, social psychologists' approach to assessing attachment styles has yielded somewhat different kinds of information about adult attachment, but it has led to a voluminous literature focusing on adult relationships.

In Chapter Six we return to following the Strange Situation Veterans through middle childhood and into adolescence. Does attachment insecurity early in life predict behavior problems as the child grows older? What about social competence, self-confidence, and ability to cope with conflict? Different studies yield somewhat different results regarding continuity in adaptation through the years, but some intriguing links are found. In this chapter we also focus on outcomes for children whose attachment behavior is described as disorganized. This pattern turns out to predict some worrisome behaviors as children move into middle childhood.

Chapter Seven brings us to adulthood, when attachment bonds have shifted from parents to romantic partners and friends. We look at how adult security, as assessed by the Adult Attachment Interview as well as by self-report measures, influences individuals' choices of partners, how they handle conflict, and the success of romantic relationships over time. Ways in which partners can buffer the insecurities of their significant others are explored, and we examine whether new, more secure relationships can help insecure individuals move towards security.

In Chapter Eight we focus on three practical applications of attachment theory and research. First, we look at the philosophy termed "attachment parenting" and consider whether research data support some of its key tenets. Second, we look at the research on non-maternal child care, and what is known about the short- and long-term impact of child care when it varies in quality as well as quantity. Third, we look at the area of divorce and custody and consider the impact for infants and toddlers of having regular overnight stays in two homes.

Finally, in the Conclusion we summarize some of the main themes and most significant findings of the book. The implications of attachment security for marital success, mental health, and even for physical health are reviewed. We also consider evidence that the early mother-infant attachment relationship may contribute to different patterns of affect regulation which may lead to altered patterns of stress physiology that can be assessed later in life. Finally, we come full circle and look at attachment security in relationships at the end of life, when daughters have become caretakers to their disabled mothers.

NOTES

1. West, *Infant Care*, 59–60.
2. Sears, Maccoby, and Levin, *Patterns of Child Rearing*.
3. Ibid.
4. Lomax, Kagan, and Rosenkrantz, *Science and Patterns of Child Care*; Davis, "Government Intervention in Child Rearing"; Urwin and Sharland, "From Bodies to Minds in Childcare Literature," 177–178.
5. Kessen, *The Child*.
6. E.g., Ferber, *Solve Your Child's Sleep Problems*.
7. Sears et al., *The Baby Sleep Book*.
8. Bigelow and Morris, "John B. Watson's Advice on Child Rearing."
9. Cunningham, *Children and Childhood in Western Society since 1500*, 176–77; Senn, "Insights on the Child Development Movement in the United States," 11.
10. Ibid., 6.
11. Ivan Pavlov introduced the idea of conditioning, by which he meant that the pairing of one stimulus with another that naturally caused a certain behavior would result in the new stimulus eventually evoking the original behavior. Pavlov demonstrated this with dogs, who would salivate when food was presented, and eventually salivated to the ringing of a bell that had been paired with food presentation.
12. Kessen, *The Child*; Bigelow and Morris, "John B. Watson's Advice on Child Rearing."
13. Lomax, Kagan, and Rosenkrantz, *Science and Patterns of Child Care*, 126.
14. Watson, *Psychological Care of Infant and Child*.
15. Lomax, Kagan, and Rosenkrantz, *Science and Patterns of Child Care*, 81–82.
16. Watson, *Psychological Care of Infant and Child*, 84–85.
17. Senn et al., "Insights on the Child Development Movement in the United States."
18. Urwin and Sharland, "From Bodies to Minds in Childcare Literature," 180.
19. Mandler, "Obituary."
20. Kessen, *The Child*, 229–31.
21. Wolfenstein, "Trends in Infant Care."
22. Ibid., 121.
23. Urwin and Sharland, "From Bodies to Minds in Childcare Literature," 177–78.
24. Cunningham, *Children and Childhood in Western Society since 1500*, 178.
25. Hendrick, *Children, Childhood and English Society, 1880–1990*, 27.
26. Maier, *Dr. Spock*, 134.
27. Ellenberger, *The Discovery of the Unconscious*.
28. Maier, *Dr. Spock*, 85–87.
29. Ibid., 91.
30. Spock, *Common Sense Book of Baby and Child Care*.
31. DeLoache and Gottlieb, "If Dr. Spock Were Born in Bali," 20.
32. Maier, *Dr. Spock*, 131.
33. Spock, *Common Sense Book of Baby and Child Care*, 19–20.
34. Sears, Maccoby, and Levin, *Patterns of Child Rearing*, 7.
35. Ibid., 27.
36. Ibid., 66; Cassidy, "The Nature of the Child's Ties," 3.
37. Sears, Maccoby, and Levin, *Patterns of Child Rearing*, 95–96.
38. Ibid., 97.
39. van der Horst and van der Veer, "The Ontogeny of an Idea," 17; van Dijken, *John Bowlby*, 21.
40. Bowlby, *Can I Leave My Baby?*, 7.
41. Bowlby, *The Making and Breaking of Affectional Bonds*, xi.

42. Hunter, "John Bowlby."
43. van Dijken, *John Bowlby*, 34.
44. Hunter, "John Bowlby."
45. Hunter, 1990, unpublished interview, cited by van Dijken, *John Bowlby*, 34.
46. van Dijken et al., "Bowlby before Bowlby," 249.
47. Dinnage, "John Bowlby."
48. Bretherton, "The Origins of Attachment Theory," quoting unpublished manuscript, Ainsworth, 1974.
49. Bowlby, "Perspective."
50. Bowlby, "The Influence of Early Environment in the Development of Neurosis and Neurotic Character," 157–58.
51. Bowlby, "Perspective," 2.
52. Dinnage, "John Bowlby," 323.
53. Bowlby, "Forty-Four Juvenile Thieves," 108.
54. van der Horst, *John Bowlby: From Psychoanalysis to Ethology*, 35–43.
55. Ibid., 63.
56. Ibid., 64.
57. Ibid., 64.
58. Robertson, *A Two Year Old Goes to Hospital.*
59. Robertson and Robertson, *Separation and the Very Young*, 44.
60. van der Horst, *John Bowlby*, 50; Karen, *Becoming Attached*, 61–62.
61. Bowlby, *Maternal Care and Mental Health*, 46.
62. Dinnage, "John Bowlby," 324.
63. Bowlby, *Can I Leave My Baby?*
64. Karen, *Becoming Attached*, 68.
65. Lomax, Kagan, and Rosenkrantz, *Science and Patterns of Child Care*, 80.
66. Robertson, "Some Responses of Young Children to the Loss of Maternal Care"; Bowlby, *Attachment and Loss.*
67. Bowlby, *Attachment and Loss: Vol. 1*, xiii.
68. Bretherton, "The Origins of Attachment Theory," 762.
69. van der Horst, *John Bowlby*, 76.
70. van der Horst, van der Veer, and van IJzendoorn, "John Bowlby and Ethology," 323; Bretherton, "The Origins of Attachment Theory," 762.
71. Lorenz, "The Companion in the Bird's World," 262–63.
72. Bretherton, "The Origins of Attachment Theory," 762.
73. cf. Bowlby, *Attachment and Loss: Vol. 1.*
74. van der Horst, van der Veer, and van IJzendoorn, "John Bowlby and Ethology," 327.
75. Harlow and Zimmerman, "The Development of Affectional Responses in Infant Monkeys."
76. Ibid., 503.
77. Ibid., 504–5.
78. van der Horst, *John Bowlby.*
79. Karen, *Becoming Attached*, 25.
80. Lomax, Kagan, and Rosenkrantz, *Science and Patterns of Child Care*, 64.
81. Hysteria referred to symptoms with no apparent organic pathology, which were believed to result from emotional distress, anxiety, or some other psychological cause.
82. Lomax, Kagan, and Rosenkrantz, *Science and Patterns of Child Care*, 46.
83. Ibid.
84. Hinde, "Q. & A. Robert A. Hinde," 582.
85. Hinde, "Q. & A. Robert A. Hinde"; van der Horst, *John Bowlby*, 89.
86. Freud, "Discussion of Dr. John Bowlby's Paper"; Schur, "Discussion of Dr. John Bowlby's Paper"; Spitz, "Discussion of Dr. John Bowlby's Paper"; Fonagy, "Psychoanalytic Theory from the Viewpoint of Attachment Theory and Research."
87. van Dijken et al., "Bowlby before Bowlby."
88. Fonagy, "Psychoanalytic Theory from the Viewpoint of Attachment Theory and Research."

89. Dinnage, "John Bowlby."
90. Fonagy, "Psychoanalytic Theory from the Viewpoint of Attachment Theory and Research," 615.
91. Bornstein, "Psychoanalysis in the Undergraduate Curriculum."
92. Bowlby, *Attachment and Loss: Vol. 1*, 9.
93. Fonagy, Gergely, and Target, "Psychoanalytic Constructs and Attachment Theory and Research."
94. Hazan and Shaver, "Romantic Love Conceptualized as an Attachment Process."
95. Mikulincer and Shaver, *Attachment in Adulthood.*
96. Bowlby, *Attachment and Loss: Vol. 1*, 9.
97. Cassidy and Shaver, *Handbook of Attachment: Theory, Research, and Clinical Applications.*
98. Siegel, *The Developing Mind.*
99. Bretherton, "The Roots and Growing Points of Attachment Theory."

REFERENCES

Bigelow, Kathryn M., and Edward K. Morris. "John B. Watson's Advice on Child Rearing: Some Historical Context." *Behavioral Development Bulletin* 10, no. 1 (2001): 26–30.
Bornstein, Robert F. "Psychoanalysis in the Undergraduate Curriculum: The Treatment of Psychoanalytic Theory in Abnormal Psychology Texts." *Psychoanalytic Psychology* 5, no. 1 (1988): 86–90.
Bowlby, John. "The Influence of Early Environment in the Development of Neurosis and Neurotic Character." *The International Journal of Psycho-Analysis* 21 (1940): 154–78.
———. "Forty-Four Juvenile Thieves: Their Characters and Home-Life." *The International Journal of Psycho-Analysis* 25 (1944): 107–28.
———. *Maternal Care and Mental Health, Vol. 2.* Geneva: World Health Organization, 1952.
———. *Can I Leave My Baby?* London: National Association for Mental Health, 1958.
———. *Attachment and Loss: Vol. 1. Attachment.* New York: Basic Books, 1969/1982.
———. *The Making and Breaking of Affectional Bonds.* London: Tavistock, 1979.
———. "Perspective: A Contribution by John Bowlby." *Bulletin of the Royal College of Psychiatrists* 5, no. 2 (1981): 2–4.
Breger, Louis. *Freud: Darkness in the Midst of Vision.* New York: John Wiley & Sons, 2000.
Bretherton, Inge. "The Roots and Growing Points of Attachment Theory." In *Attachment across the Life Cycle*, edited by Colin M. Parkes, Joan Stevenson-Hinde, and Peter Marris, 9–32. London/New York: Tavistock/Routledge, 1991.
———. "The Origins of Attachment Theory: John Bowlby and Mary Ainsworth." *Developmental Psychology* 28, no. 5 (1992): 759–75.
Cassidy, Jude. "The Nature of the Child's Ties." In *Handbook of Attachment: Theory, Research, and Clinical Applications*, edited by Jude Cassidy and Phillip R. Shaver, 3–20. New York: The Guilford Press, 1999.
Cunningham, Hugh. *Children and Childhood in Western Society since 1500.* Upper Saddle River, NJ: Pearson Education, 2005.
Davis, Robert A. "Government Intervention in Child Rearing: Governing Infancy." *Educational Theory* 60, no. 3 (2010): 285–98.
DeLoache, Judy S., and Alma Gottlieb. "If Dr Spock Were Born in Bali." In *A World of Babies: Imagined Child Care Guides for Seven Societies*, edited by Judy S. DeLoache and Alma Gottlieb, 1–27. Cambridge University Press, 2000.
Dinnage, Rosemary. "John Bowlby." *New Society*, 10 (1979): 323–25.
Ellenberger, Henri F. *The Discovery of the Unconscious: The History and Evolution of Dynamic Psychiatry.* New York: Basic Books, 1970.
Ferber, Richard. *Solve Your Child's Sleep Problems: New, Revised, and Expanded Edition.* New York: Simon and Schuster, 2006.

Fonagy, Peter. "Psychoanalytic Theory from the Viewpoint of Attachment Theory and Research." In *Handbook of Attachment: Theory, Research, and Clinical Applications*, edited by Jude Cassidy and Phillip R. Shaver, 595–624. New York: The Guilford Press, 1999.

Fonagy, Peter, George Gergely, and Mary Target. "Psychoanalytic Constructs and Attachment Theory and Research." In *Handbook of Attachment: Theory, Research, and Clinical Applications, Second Edition*, edited by Jude Cassidy and Phillip R. Shaver, 783–810. New York: The Guilford Press, 2008.

Freud, Anna. "Discussion of Dr. John Bowlby's Paper." *The Psychoanalytic Study of the Child*, 15 (1960): 53–62.

Harlow, Harry F., and Robert R. Zimmermann. "The Development of Affectional Responses in Infant Monkeys." *Proceedings of the American Philosophical Society* 102, no. 5 (1958): 501–9.

Hazan, Cindy, and Phillip Shaver. "Romantic Love Conceptualized as an Attachment Process." *Journal of Personality and Social Psychology* 52, no. 3 (1987): 511–25.

Hendrick, Harry. *Children, Childhood and English Society, 1880–1990*. Vol. 32. Cambridge University Press, 1997.

Hinde, Robert A. "Q. and A. with Robert A. Hinde." *Current Biology* 18, no. 14 (2008): R581–82.

Hunter, Virginia. "John Bowlby: An Interview." *Psychoanalytic Review* 78, no. 2 (1991): 159–75.

Karen, Robert. *Becoming Attached: Unfolding the Mystery of the Infant-Mother Bond and Its Impact on Later Life*. New York: Warner Books, 1994.

Kessen, William. *The Child*. New York: John Wiley & Sons, 1965.

Lomax, Elizabeth M. R., Jerome Kagan, and Barbara G. Rosenkrantz. *Science and Patterns of Child Care*. San Francisco: W. H. Freeman and Co., 1978.

Lorenz, Konrad Z. "The Companion in the Bird's World." *The Auk* 54 (1937): 245–73.

Maier, Thomas. *Dr. Spock: An American Life*. New York: Harcourt, Brace & Co., 1998.

Mandler, George. "Obituary: William Kessen (1925–1999)." *American Psychologist* 55, no. 7 (2000): 758–59.

Mikulincer, Mario, and Phillip R. Shaver. *Attachment in Adulthood: Structure, Dynamics, and Change*. New York: The Guilford Press, 2007.

Robertson, James. *A Two Year Old Goes to Hospital*. Robertson Films, 1952.

———. "Some Responses of Young Children to Loss of Maternal Care." *Nursing Times*, April 18 (1953): 382–86.

Robertson, James, and Joyce Robertson. *Separation and the Very Young*. London: Free Association Books, 1989.

Schur, Max. "Discussion of Dr. John Bowlby's Paper." *The Psychoanalytic Study of the Child* 15 (1959): 63–84.

Sears, Robert. R., Eleanor E. Maccoby, and Harry Levin. *Patterns of Child Rearing*. Evanston, Illinois: Row, Peterson and Co., 1957.

Sears, William, Robert Sears, James Sears, and Martha Sears. *The Baby Sleep Book: The Complete Guide to a Good Night's Rest for the Whole Family*. Boston: Little, Brown and Co., 2008.

Senn, Milton J. E., William Kessen, L. J. Borstelmann, G. Stanley Hall, John Dewey, Caroline Zachry, Lawrence K. Frank et al. "Insights on the Child Development Movement in the United States." *Monographs of the Society for Research in Child Development* 40, no. 3/4 (1975): 1–107.

Siegel, Daniel J. *The Developing Mind, Second Edition: How Relationships and the Brain Interact to Shape Who We Are*. New York: Guilford Publications, 2015.

Spitz, René, A. "Discussion of Dr. Bowlby's Paper." *The Psychoanalytic Study of the Child* 15 (1959): 85–94.

Spock, Benjamin. *Common Sense Book of Baby and Child Care*. New York: Duell, Sloan, & Pearce, 1945.

Urwin, Cathy, and Elaine Sharland. "From Bodies to Minds in Childcare Literature: Advice to Parents in Inter-War Britain." In *In the Name of the Child: Health and Welfare, 1880–1940*, edited by Roger Cooter, 174–99. New York and London: Routledge.

van der Horst, Frank C. P. *John Bowlby: From Psychoanalysis to Ethology.* West Sussex: Wiley-Blackwell, 2011.

van der Horst, Frank C. P., and René van der Veer. "The Ontogeny of an Idea: John Bowlby and Contemporaries on Mother-Child Separation." *History of Psychology* 13, no. 1 (2010): 25–45.

van der Horst, Frank C. P., René van der Veer, and Marinus H. van IJzendoorn. "John Bowlby and Ethology: An Annotated Interview with Robert Hinde." *Attachment & Human Development* 9, no. 4 (2007): 321–35.

van Dijken, Suzan. *John Bowlby, His Early Life: A Biographical Journey into the Roots of Attachment Theory.* London: Free Association Books, 1998.

van Dijken, Suzan, René van der Veer, Marinus van IJzendoorn, and Hans-Jan Kuipers. "Bowlby before Bowlby: The Sources of an Intellectual Departure in Psychoanalysis and Psychology." *Journal of the History of the Behavioral Sciences* 34, no. 3 (1998): 247–69.

Watson, John Broadus. *Psychological Care of Infant and Child.* New York: W. W. Norton and Co., 1928.

West, Mrs. Max. *Infant Care.* Washington, D.C.: Government Printing Office, 1914.

Wolfenstein, Martha. "Trends in Infant Care." *American Journal of Orthopsychiatry* 23, no. 1 (1953): 120–30.

Chapter Two

First Bonds

Infants and Parents

The nine-month-old little boy spent virtually all of his time with his mother. His mom breast-fed him whenever he wanted. Yet he was an extremely fussy baby. While the boy's mother kept him with her physically, she was invariably preoccupied with other things and not very attentive towards her son. She did not get along with the child's father, who did not help with his son's care, and mother seemed quite anxious.

What should we expect for the future development of this little boy? He was extremely fussy, and we could consider a variety of reasons for this. Some might speculate that he was temperamentally irritable, and wonder whether his mother might have kept him with her physically to try to calm him. Alternatively, his mother's preoccupation and inattentiveness might have contributed to his fussiness. Perhaps tension between the parents contributed to his irritability.

This vignette is actually based upon a description of a boy named Muhamidi whom Mary Ainsworth carefully observed in Uganda, where she worked for several years following her time as a research assistant for Bowlby in London. Ainsworth was trained as a developmental psychologist, and her graduate study provided her with skills which allowed her to devise ways of putting Bowlby's theories to experimental test. She first became intrigued by her observations of mothers and children in Uganda, and eventually conducted a more rigorous study of mother-child interaction in the United States.

MARY AINSWORTH: A NEW RESEARCH PARADIGM

Understanding how Mary Ainsworth began her quest to test Bowlby's ideas sets the stage for understanding her groundbreaking discoveries. Because of her work and that of hundreds of scientists who were inspired by her research over the past sixty years—and who have replicated and extended her findings—we now understand a great deal about the significance of infant-parent interactions.

Working with Bowlby in London between 1950 and 1954, Ainsworth was very impressed by James Robertson's observational studies of children undergoing hospitalization, and she decided that when she had an opportunity to do her own study, it would be an observational study of mother-child interaction in the natural environment.[1] That opportunity arrived in 1954, when Ainsworth's anthropologist husband decided to take a position in Uganda. While Mary was not enthusiastic about leaving London and following her husband to Africa, the move turned out to be fortuitous. In Uganda, Ainsworth believed she had an unusual opportunity to study the effects of infants undergoing separation from their mothers under conditions that weren't confounded with the effects of a depriving institution or traumatic illness. It was said that according to ancient custom, Ugandan mothers would wean their babies abruptly and send them to grandmothers or other relatives to be reared. By observing children first during the time they lived with their mothers, Ainsworth planned to study the effects of separation.[2]

As Ainsworth began working with a group that was to include twenty-eight children, she learned that abrupt weaning was actually *not* the norm. Meanwhile, she had been observing infant-care practices and infant-mother interaction and felt she was gaining information about the development of attachment that had not previously been reported in the scientific literature.[3]

At that point, despite her considerable exposure to Bowlby's theories, she still held to the traditional view that a baby becomes attached to mother because she provides life-sustaining milk. Reflecting upon these views, Ainsworth later wrote, "Although I was intrigued with Lorenz's imprinting studies, I myself was so brainwashed by psychological theories of the day that I felt uneasy. . . . To me at that time, it seemed self-evident that a baby becomes attached to his mother because she fulfills his basic needs or drives."[4] In Uganda, observing a society that was entirely new to her, Ainsworth found it easier to be objective, and it took only a matter of weeks of observation before she concluded that the "self-evident" view which she had held for so long did not square with what she saw. Instead, Bowlby's ethological approach seemed to better explain her observations.

In her study, Ainsworth visited parents and children in their homes for two hours every two weeks, over a period of nine months. While she no longer expected to observe many instances of abrupt and traumatic separations, more mundane separation experiences seemed an obvious place to look for evidence of attachment. Ainsworth carefully observed and inquired about a child's response when mother left the room. Many children showed separation distress by crying, trying to follow, clinging and trying to prevent mother leaving, or clinging to her when she returned. However, Ainsworth noted "there were some babies who seemed clearly attached to their mothers, who did not dependably cry, follow, or cling when their mothers seemed about to leave them."[5] Ainsworth initially questioned whether these children were less attached than children who clung to their mothers and tried to prevent them from leaving, or conversely, if they might actually be more secure.

Of the twenty-eight children she observed, Ainsworth decided that five, whose parents were absent a great deal or who hardly responded to them, were "non-attached" and seven, including Muhamidi, were "insecurely attached." The insecurely attached children could not tolerate any distance from mother, needed virtually continual contact with her, yet remained fussy even when held by her. In Uganda, Ainsworth was beginning to develop theories as to why children like Muhamidi might show the fussy, clingy behaviors they displayed, but she had no firm data to explain insecure attachments.

The Baltimore Study

The next stop for Mary Ainsworth and her husband was John Hopkins University in Baltimore, Maryland. There, Ainsworth planned a more rigorous study of mothers and children during their first year of life. During eighteen home visits in the first year of life, trained graduate students sat for four hours at a time, making careful observations of mother-child interactions in middle-class homes.[6] At times they would offer a helping hand to mothers, thus working to blend into the environment they were carefully observing.

Even with the rich home observations, Ainsworth wanted to get a clearer idea of what made for a secure versus an insecure attachment. Compared to the children in Uganda, American babies were more accustomed to mothers leaving the room, and would not immediately cry and try to follow her. Ainsworth felt that in Baltimore she had not seen much of the kind of "attachment stress" aroused in Ugandan children when mothers were out of sight. So, Ainsworth and colleagues developed a twenty-minute laboratory procedure, appropriate for children twelve to eighteen months of age, which included a series of play episodes, separations, and reunions. An idea that was sketched out in a mere half hour went on to become one of the most widely used psychology measures ever developed.

What came to be known as the "Strange Situation Procedure" has provided invaluable information about how we as humans connect with others, from infancy onward. The power of this procedure comes in part because

Ainsworth's earlier extensive home observations of parenting behaviors during the first year proved to have impressive ability to predict how children would cope with the stress of this short laboratory test. More surprisingly, it turns out that a child's behavior in this procedure relates, at least to some degree, to how he or she will develop and will interact with others in the next two, four, six, ten, and twenty or more years. What a powerfully predictive test!

About the Strange Situation Procedure

The Strange Situation assesses children's ability to use their mother (or in later research, their father) as a "secure base"—both to explore and to receive comfort from when distressed. Besides a free-play period in an unfamiliar laboratory play room, the child meets a stranger, and then experiences two separations from mother. Ainsworth found that the most telling part of the Strange Situation Procedure was not how distressed the child became when mother left, but instead how effectively the child used his or her parent for comfort when reunited.

Careful analyses showed that a one-year-old child's behavior during two reunion episodes in the laboratory, each three minutes in length, tells a lot about the kind of relationship the child has had with mother over the first year. Ainsworth's home observations showed that the child who historically had had his or her needs met consistently, sensitively, and appropriately may cry and want to be picked up when mother returns, but he or she calms down fairly easily. In the Strange Situation Procedure, these children are termed "secure." Other children show less harmonious behavior in reunions, and are termed "insecurely attached."

Ainsworth and colleagues divided the insecurely attached children into two categories (the securely attached children occupied a third category, "Group B"). Children identified as insecurely attached and placed in "Group A" showed conspicuous avoidance of proximity to or interaction with mother during reunion episodes. Casual observations of the reunion behavior of these children might suggest that they were simply inclined to be more independent. But, at home, they hadn't acted this way; instead they often seemed angry with their mothers. Ainsworth's observations showed, for example, that these children would get upset when mothers put them down—unlike the securely attached children, who when set down would cheerfully move away and become engaged in play.

Based on all of the information available about these children, Ainsworth and colleagues concluded that Group A children's attachment behavior was indeed strongly activated in the separation episodes, but they tended not to show their distress overtly.[7] Ainsworth classified these children as "insecure-avoidant." Perhaps one way we can think of avoidant infants is that under the stress of the Strange Situation they nonetheless maintain a "stiff upper lip."

At this point, it is important that readers understand that there are many diverse behaviors that indicate insecure attachment, i.e., difficulty using mother as a "secure base" to allow soothing. The Strange Situation Procedure is a sophisticated assessment tool that requires a good deal of training to determine attachment patterns. This book does not provide a guide that would allow the reader to accurately identify children's attachment pattern in real-life situations. The take-away message here is simply that children, over the first year of life, are already developing coping styles to deal with stressful experiences with those they do love dearly.

The second group of children who showed insecure attachment were placed into "Group C." In the original description of Group C children, Ainsworth and co-authors stated, "The baby displays conspicuous contact- and interaction-resisting behavior; he shows moderate-to-strong seeking of proximity and contact . . . so that he gives the impression of being ambivalent to his mother; he shows little or no tendency to ignore his mother in the reunion episodes."[8] In general, Group C children are difficult to calm during reunion, perhaps alternating between seeking to be picked up and clinging, then resisting contact. Resistance is demonstrated either through angrily pushing mother away, or more passively resisting comforting.

The insecurely attached children in Group C have been described as "insecure-resistant," "insecure-ambivalent," and "anxious-resistant." The fundamental characteristic of these children is that they alternate between seeking consolation and contact and then resisting it. For simplicity, I will refer to these children as "insecure-resistant." Essentially, these children resist consolation, even when they are quite upset.

Over the past few decades, thousands of children have been observed in the Strange Situation—first in Ainsworth's laboratory and later in other research playrooms in the United States and around the world—and some of these children have been followed over time to watch their development.[9] Subsequent chapters will describe these children's behavior at later points in time, and the significance of attachment security and of the different patterns of attachment identified by Ainsworth in the Strange Situation will be a theme followed throughout this book. Hopefully, I have intrigued the reader to want to know more about what contributes to the development of different attachment patterns, and how these patterns may influence the way that children relate to others as they grow.

Before moving on, however, it is important to put security of attachment in perspective. While it is considered "normative" (i.e., more common than insecure attachment), subsequent research in Western societies with large numbers of children has shown that approximately 65 percent of children develop secure attachments. The next most common category is insecure-avoidant, with about 21 percent of children, and approximately 14 percent receive an insecure-resistant designation.[10] Thus, it must be appreciated that insecure attachments are not rare, and do not in themselves indicate serious deviance.

Parenting Behaviors that Matter

Mary Ainsworth studied mothers, with the assumption that it is mother who plays the primary role in infant care.[11] However, a father, grandparent, foster parent, or other reliable adult could occupy the role of primary caregiver for a young child. So, readers should understand the term "mother" to be relevant to the primary caregiver, whether or not that person is also the child's biological mother.

The rich observations of mothers' home behavior that Ainsworth's students had gathered proved most useful when condensed into four areas. These areas included 1) the mother's *sensitivity* to the baby's signals, 2) her *acceptance versus rejection* of the baby and the impact of having the baby on her life, 3) her *cooperation versus interference* with the desires of her child, and 4) her emotional *accessibility* to the baby.

Mothers who scored highest in Ainsworth's ratings of parenting behavior were able to consistently rise to caregiving challenges. Optimally *sensitive* mothers generally managed to be alert to their babies' signals, understood what their children were communicating, and generally met their needs. In contrast, *insensitive* mothers' interactions with their babies were more timed to their own wishes or activities. Highly *accepting* mothers typically responded well even when their babies were angry or didn't respond happily to them, despite their best efforts; *rejecting* mothers grumbled about the ways the child interfered with their lives, frequently scolding their children.

In terms of cooperation, highly *cooperative* mothers strove to work with their children's moods, while *interfering* mothers tried to control babies and shape their behavior. And highly *accessible* mothers attended to their babies' signals and communications, unlike *ignoring* mothers who might be so preoccupied with their own thoughts and activities that they didn't notice babies wanting their attention.

Readers, whether they are professionals or not, may have strong feelings about these descriptions. Those who are young parents may worry that they do not live up to the high standards for optimal parenting. Older parents may look back at their children's early years, regretful that stresses kept them from being the kind of parents they ideally wanted to be. And readers of any age may wonder what it was like for themselves when they were young and in the care of their parents.

I do not want to fall into the company of the many psychologists who have engaged in mother-blaming.[12] Before going further, it is important to consider the enormity of the task of parenting. With the birth of a child, mothers are suddenly responsible for a helpless but demanding baby who cries when they themselves are tired and who wants attention when they are longing to exercise, talk to a friend, or watch a television show. To respond well, parents must be able to put aside their own needs, again and again. The job of parenting requires a great deal of emotional strength and tolerance. While the emphasis of Ainsworth's work was on the behavior of the mother, mothers unquestionably have an easier time parenting when they receive strong support from partners, family, and friends.

However, while recognizing how hard mothers must struggle to meet their children's needs, based on the research that will be reviewed in this book, plus my own experience working with children and families, I nonetheless do believe that the way in which a parent cares for a child is awfully important for the child's well-being. As noted earlier, this book is meant to provide a guide for those who work with young families and want to know how best to support and improve the well-being of children. It is also hoped that this book can help parents who aspire to do better, as well as for adults who want to improve their relationships with partners, friends, grown children, and even grandchildren. Knowing the behaviors that hinder optimal connections can be a first step in finding ways to change and improve.

Links between Home and Laboratory

Mary Ainsworth's painstakingly careful observations succeeded in showing a clear link between the way parents handled their child at home and children's reaction to the stress of the Strange Situation. Mothers of children who showed secure attachment behaviors scored higher in all four parenting areas described above. In general, at home these mothers had been faster to pick children up when they cried, were inclined to hold them longer, and appeared overall to take more enjoyment in parenting. They received the highest scores in *sensitivity, acceptance, cooperation,* and *accessibility.*[13]

Mothers of the insecurely attached children (both avoidant and resistant) scored lower on the four rating scales. Mothers of the insecure-avoidant children (i.e., those who seemed to maintain a "stiff upper lip" following separation) had been the least accepting, most rejecting of their children. Compared to mothers of securely attached babies, they tended to be abrupt and interfering (sometimes even rather rough) when they picked up their children, and they more often used forcible physical interventions to back up verbal commands.[14] These mothers actually did hold their babies as much as others, but observers noted a clear aversion—something only a few mothers openly acknowledged—regarding physical contact. Ainsworth's observers felt that mothers communicated their aversion to their babies, who consequently found being held an unpleasant, sometimes even downright painful, experience. [15]

Mothers of the insecure-avoidant children at home had shown their discomfort with physical contact in a variety of ways. They might stiffen while holding the child, or actually withdraw when their child was approaching them. One mother stated that she had always had an aversion to physical contact with other people. Other mothers made comments such as "You know I hate to have you crawling on me" or "Don't touch me!" [16] In a study in which mothers and babies were videotaped, some mothers of these insecure-avoidant children were observed expressing anger by mocking their children or speaking sarcastically to them. One mother actually expressed irritation when her child spilled imaginary tea! [17]

Mothers of the insecure-resistant babies (those who resisted consolation following separation) at home had had trouble responding in a loving, attuned, and consistent way, particularly when their children were demanding or distressed. In general, they showed less affection, spoke to their children less often, and more often seemed inept in their handling of the baby during close physical contact. At home, these babies protested if the mother's pick-up was badly timed, especially if they were not picked up when they wanted to be, or were put down when they wanted to be held. [18]

When observed during feeding times, some of the mothers of babies in this group resisted any effort the child made to feed himself, which resulted in meals being unhappy and occasions for struggle. [19] With at least some mothers, their difficulties seemed to be related to lack of knowledge and understanding, with the result that they were not reliably responsive. However, unlike mothers of the insecure-avoidant children, these mothers showed no dislike of close bodily contact. [20]

Good research can be replicated, and dozens of studies over several decades have confirmed the link between sensitive, responsive parenting and children's attachment security. Ainsworth's findings have generally withstood the test of time, and by and large have been shown to hold true across cultures. [21, 22]

Putting Mothers' Behavior in Context

As one reads Ainsworth's findings about parenting behaviors that matter, it is easy to view mothers' parenting styles as reflecting fixed character traits. While this may be to some extent true, the role of social supports in the environment should not be overlooked. Indeed, one of Ainsworth's observations that has received little attention should be highlighted. During her year of Baltimore home observations, Ainsworth observed a couple of instances where mothers who had been very sensitive with their babies abruptly became less responsive or even rejecting when marital difficulties or a family crisis arose.[23] This observation suggests that "insensitive" or "rejecting" mothers might better be viewed as mothers in need of help with the burdens they bear.

Subsequent research has broadened our understanding of the factors that help children feel safe and secure in their first, formative relationships. Mothers (at least most) do not parent in a vacuum, and research has shown that support from others can be critical to their maintaining patience and emotional availability. Fathers develop their own relationship with their children, and their importance must not be overlooked. Finally, it must be remembered that children come into the world with in-born strengths as well as vulnerabilities that may make it more or less challenging for parents to give them sensitive attention.

One New Attachment Category

In the 1980s, a new attachment pattern termed "disorganized/disoriented" was identified by researchers at Berkeley who were protégés of Mary Ainsworth.[24] It turns out that this attachment classification (which I will henceforth refer to as simply "disorganized") is a very important category. Children in this group at age one are at particular risk of significant behavioral and emotional difficulties as they grow older.[25]

Ainsworth's doctoral student Mary Main, along with *her* student Judith Solomon, led the way in describing this attachment pattern. Before the "disorganized" category was developed, these children had been a bit of a puzzle. They showed aspects of the three major attachment patterns (secure, insecure-avoidant, insecure-resistant), so researchers tried to place them in the best-fitting group. Yet, some of the behaviors of these children were quite odd and contradictory, and the children seemed more disturbed than children in the insecure categories.

These children did not resemble one another in coherent, organized ways. Instead, they shared a tendency to have bouts of behavior that appeared to lack a clear goal, intention, or explanation. For example, when mother returned after the brief laboratory separation, they might act in seemingly contradictory ways such as approaching their mother, but with face averted, or they might act disoriented, perhaps taking on an anomalous posture, stopping all movement, or appearing dazed.[26] Many of these children seemed fearful in approaching their mothers.

As an example, one child classified as disorganized hunched her upper body and shoulders when she heard her mother's call, then broke into extravagant laugh-like screeches and excitedly moved forward. Then, without taking a new breath, her loud laughter became a cry, and with a distressed look on her face, she hunched forward further. Finally, her face suddenly lost all expression.[27] Like this particular girl, children described as disorganized

showed a wide variety of behaviors suggesting they had no organized strategy to deal with the stress of separation.

Origins of Disorganized Attachment

It was soon discovered that in studies in which children had experienced
maltreatment, up to about three-quarters of children were classified as disorganized.[28] What does maltreatment consist of? While it is defined differently
in different studies, it is often identified based on the fact that parents were
reported to child protection agencies or were referred to intervention programs for families believed to be "at risk." In such families, maltreatment
might consist of abusive behavior such as regular hitting, bruising, or even
bone fractures. Maltreatment also covers various forms of neglect, such as
lack of supervision and failure to feed children properly or to seek medical
care when needed. Sometimes, mothers might be included in groups of "maltreating" families if there were inconsistencies in the care of children that
raised concerns from professionals interacting with these families, even if
clear abuse or neglect was not identified.[29]

With these children, highly problematic attachment is understandable.
Parents who maltreat children may directly frighten them with physically
violent acts or by failing to protect them from dangers, and as a group
maltreating parents also use highly inadequate and inconsistent forms of
discipline.

Even if there has been no documented history of maltreatment, children in
families with multiple risk factors also show high levels of disorganized
attachment. Factors that emerge as conferring risk include low income, low
education, substance abuse, ethnic minority status, single parenthood, and
adolescent parenthood.[30]

However, disorganized attachment is also found in one of six or seven (15
to 18 percent) of children from more affluent families, who are considered
low risk because maltreatment is not believed to have occurred and social
and economic stress is lower.[31] Initially, it was difficult to understand why
disorganized attachment would be found in low-risk community samples.
One clue that emerged is that parents of children who show disorganization
often have a history of personal loss or trauma, and these parents have been
observed to act in frightened or frightening ways with children.

Frightened or frightening episodes with mothers could be quite subtle or
more blatant. When acting in a frightened way, the mother might suddenly
freeze or might interact with the child as if the child were in control. In a
frightening episode, a parent might loom close to the infant or use a haunted-
sounding voice. Or, in a situation that was not clearly intended to be playful,
parents might "stalk" their infant on all fours, exposing their teeth, hissing, or
making deep growls at the young child.[32]

While these parental behaviors sound quite odd, frightened or frightening behaviors are believed to occur because parents are themselves feeling very fearful about their own past traumatic experiences.[33, 34] Individuals who continue to relive traumatic experiences may have episodes of dissociation in which they become detached from their surroundings and fail to monitor what is going on within themselves and around them. During such dissociative episodes, odd, scary behaviors may emerge without parents' conscious awareness. Children who have been cared for by traumatized parents logically might show disorganized, contradictory behaviors after a separation, for in their daily lives they are unsure whether parents will be a source of safety or of alarm. If something scary happens in the environment, should the child move towards the caregiver or flee? Given the uncertainty that these children feel, poorly organized behaviors make sense.[35]

Additional Causes of Disorganized Behavior

Researchers are still working to probe other possible reasons for disorganized attachment in children from low-risk samples. One study found that a subgroup of these children had shown difficulties with emotional regulation when they were newborns,[36] leading the researchers to conclude that this subgroup of children may have started out with compromised emotional regulation abilities at birth.[37] In some studies, it appears that disorganized behavior, particularly as manifested by such things as anomalous postures or abrupt falling to the floor, may reflect the fact that children have been overstressed by *the Strange Situation itself.*[38]

The Strange Situation Procedure was designed to mildly stress children's attachment system. Researchers have found that if the Strange Situation is used in a way that elicits more-than-mild stress, higher rates of disorganized behavior are found. For example, if repetitions of the Strange Situation occur too close in time, children may become extremely stressed and unable to utilize their typical ways of responding to parents' unavailability.

In a recent study that re-analyzed tapes from a 1986 research project that had found very high rates (about 40 percent) of disorganized attachment, it was discovered that two factors related to the way the Strange Situation Procedure was used increased the likelihood of disorganized behavior. Children who returned for a repetition of the laboratory procedure (the first with father, the second with mother) within a relatively short period (ranging from four days to one and a half months), *and* who became very distressed during separation and were allowed to cry hard for a full minute, were more likely to act in a disorganized manner.[39] In fact, about two-thirds of children who experienced both closely spaced lab visits and high levels of distress during separations were classified as disorganized.

Disorganized Attachment: Caution with Interpreting Findings

Mary Main and colleagues have expressed concern that there is a widespread perception that disorganized attachment in the Strange Situation Procedure indicates maltreatment.[40] Indeed, in a 2012 paper that appeared in the *Journal of Social Work Practice*, it was argued that child protection workers should be trained to assess disorganized attachment since *"disorganized attachment is not just associated with child maltreatment but is indicative of it"* (italics added).[41] It is certainly reasonable to consider the possibility of hidden abuse or neglect, but given that other reasons for disorganized attachment behavior—including the experience of the Strange Situation itself—have been identified, assumptions of maltreatment are clearly not warranted.

An additional situation where caution must be used in interpreting findings is in custody evaluations and legal proceedings. There are suggestions that the Strange Situation be used as part of an assessment by those making recommendations about custody for young children with divorcing parents. In situations where a comparison is sought between the quality of one parent-child relationship with that of another, as might occur in an acrimonious custody contest, the timing of repetitions of the procedure must be considered carefully.[42]

Finally, it is important to recognize that the meaning of children's behavior in the Strange Situation Procedure originally was derived from a study of American children. In the United States, as in many Western cultures, children are accustomed to at least occasional separations from parents. As a consequence, children acquire and practice strategies for dealing with the stress of separation. If the child lives in a culture that does not include occasional separations in the context of sensitive parenting, then the Strange Situation Procedure may provide misleading information about that child's likely home experiences with his or her parents.[43]

BEYOND THE MOTHER-CHILD DYAD

Ideally, mothers are surrounded by supportive others—partners, parents, and friends—who give them respite, provide help with daily tasks, and bolster them emotionally. All of these things can help mothers rise to the task at hand and to react sensitively to their infants' needs. Conversely, stress caused by a lack of needed support may diminish the sensitivity of a parent who, in easier circumstances, might be better able to meet her child's needs.

Fathers develop their own relationship style with their children. Typically, it is a somewhat different kind of relationship than the one the child has with mother. In fact, the parenting behaviors of fathers that are linked to a secure attachment in children aren't as easy to identify as they are for mothers. Observations of how fathers behave during *routine* caregiving interactions do not predict nearly as much about how their child will interact with them in the Strange Situation as is true with mother. [44]

Studies indicate that a father's sensitivity to his child is best observed during play. At least in homes with two parents of different genders, father's play sensitivity appears important to the quality of the father-child relationship. Working in Germany, Karin and Klaus Grossmann and colleagues have for many years studied how fathers interact with children to promote attachment security. They have observed that fathers of securely attached children often sit back when children are focused and happily playing. But, once children seem to be losing interest or looking unhappy, they step in and help children sustain interest. [45]

Fathers of the insecure-avoidant children (i.e., those who maintain a "stiff upper lip" in the Strange Situation) behave quite differently. They tend to join the child in play when he or she is already engaged, interfering by offering a toy or redirecting the child's attention. Often, children will not be happy with this interference and will stop playing. Then, when children stop playing and become fussy, these men more often than not pull back and leave children alone, waiting for them to get over their upset. [46]

Despite the different ways in which sensitive caregiving is shown by mothers and fathers, young children are equally likely to have a secure attachment with their fathers as with mothers in the Strange Situation. Interestingly, though, a fair number will show a secure attachment with one parent and an insecure attachment with the other. Some children will reunite with fathers in a manner that shows no hesitation in seeking comfort, even if they show insecure behaviors with their mother. So, even children as young as twelve or eighteen months have established different kinds of relationships with each parent. [47]

What is the significance of a child having a secure attachment with father? In later chapters we will consider what security—or conversely, insecurity—of attachment in infancy with both mother and father heralds for the growing child. Not surprisingly, a secure attachment to father does indeed make a contribution to how well the child fares in later years. [48]

Family Systems, Couple Relationships, and Child Attachment

Almost twenty years after Ainsworth and colleagues published *Patterns of Attachment*, in which they put forth detailed descriptions of how mothers' parenting behaviors at home were related to children's attachment security, a prominent psychologist named Philip Cowan wrote an article in which he criticized the attachment field's primary focus on mothers. Cowan, who along with his wife Carolyn Pape Cowan have spent decades studying how couple and family relationships influence the parenting of mothers and fathers, argued in a 1997 article that "the pervasive focus on mothers has serious negative consequences both for attachment theory and for what is conveyed by researchers to the general public."[49]

This criticism did not go unheeded; there is now beginning evidence that the quality of the couple relationship plays a significant role in the path towards infant security.[50] In one careful study that sought to identify the family components contributing to attachment security, it was found that better couple functioning contributed to better family functioning, which was conceptualized as including good skills in areas such as problem solving, communication, emotional responsiveness, emotional involvement, and behavior control. In turn, better family functioning was related to greater likelihood of children having secure attachments with mothers.[51] Another study found that better co-parenting relationships contributed to children (particularly boys) having more secure attachments with their fathers.[52]

Challenges for Young Families

Without doubt, the early years of parenting are a stressful time for couples. With the birth of a child, marital satisfaction typically decreases and negative emotional interactions increase between spouses.[53] The couple relationship shifts during the postpartum period, often resulting in dramatically increased conflict, changes in the division of labor and roles outside of the family, and reduced couple companionship and sex.[54] Of note, however, is the fact that 20 or 30 percent of couples experience a rise in marital satisfaction after having a baby.[55]

An in-depth investigation of contributions to child attachment security was directed by Jay Belsky, a psychologist who headed the Pennsylvania Infant and Family Development Project. Studies within this project followed families beginning in the last trimester of pregnancy through the transition to parenthood, tracking marital satisfaction during the first year. While the researchers documented a general decline in marital satisfaction during the first few months after babies arrived, beginning at about four months post-delivery the majority of mothers managed to gather the resources necessary to maintain a loving relationship with spouses and satisfaction with their marriages. This eventually led to the development of secure infant-mother attachment relationships. It was the mothers of children eventually classified as insecure who more often experienced a pronounced and continuing decline in couple relationship quality over the first year.[56]

Vignette from Clinical Practice

The kinds of vulnerabilities that can interfere with marital happiness and optimal parenting are well-illustrated with a couple who sought marital therapy with me when their children were one and three years. Brett and Kimberly had had a fragile but reasonably satisfactory relationship before the birth of their first child. Their marital conflict increased significantly after their daughter was born, and even more so with the arrival of a son two years later. Both partners worked demanding jobs and were exhausted by their multiple responsibilities. Additionally, Brett and Kimberly had each grown up in families where parents gave limited attention to their emotional needs and little personal affirmation, and they both desperately wanted their spouses' attention and concern at the end of the work day. Yet, housework and parenting responsibilities limited their emotional availability to each other, and old wounds were re-opened.

With therapy, Brett and Kimberly developed better way of communicating their needs and of feeling heard and understood by each other. This was a challenging process; at the point when they sought therapy, they were both very defensive, and their quarrels easily escalated during sessions. However, as therapy progressed they increasingly felt heard and understood by each other, and they reacted less quickly to perceived slights. As they learned to better acknowledge each other's emotional needs, the quality of their interactions improved, and they reported that their young children seemed less anxious and clingy.

THE ROLE OF TEMPERAMENT

After Ainsworth's findings began circulating widely, some prominent researchers challenged her conclusions that differences in behaviors in the Strange Situation reflected the quality of parenting they had received during the first year. Instead, they believed that temperamental differences could explain at least some of the differences.[57] For example, Stella Chess and Alexander Thomas, well-known for their work distinguishing different patterns of temperamental organization,[58] wrote in 1982 that "We ourselves would certainly consider that the items of the infant's behavior in the Ainsworth Strange Situation could be appropriately rated under the temperamental categories of approach/withdrawal, adaptability, quality of mood, and intensity."[59] Chess and Thomas' cautions were not without merit. They were concerned that Ainsworth's findings would encourage anxiety and guilt in mothers, and wanted to offer reassurance that children whose signals were not easily understood were not doomed to an unhealthy parent attachment.[60]

Ainsworth did not discount the importance of possible temperamental differences in babies. In fact, she asserted that her group was convinced that different mothers behaved differently because they were responding to infants with different characteristics. Her measures of sensitivity were geared to infant cues, so if babies acted in different ways, mothers *should* respond differently.[61]

Researchers have found no consistent evidence that temperament (rather than parenting styles) explains differences in Strange Situation attachment patterns. One review article looking at over fifty published studies of children from the general population revealed inconsistent and occasionally contradictory findings regarding temperament factors. The authors of this review article concluded that security and insecurity in attachment in the general population could not be explained by temperament constructs based on the major temperament approaches. [62]

Stress, Temperament, and Maternal Sensitivity

The inconsistent and contradictory findings about temperament actually begin to make sense if one takes into consideration the fact that different studies focus on different groups of parents—parents who are likely to experience varying levels of stress from any number of factors. As it turns out, infants who are more "difficult" and who cry and fuss more than the average child appear to evoke insensitive caregiving only when there are other risk factors in the picture. Risks could be increased as a result of economic stress that leaves mothers tired and depleted, or alternatively because mothers are predisposed to depression or anger because of difficult childhood experiences or current stress with their partner. When additional risks beyond difficult temperament are not present, there is evidence that mothers may be *more* sensitive to their irritable infants. [63]

An interesting example of the effect of context and stress comes from a study looking at how infants who show high levels of distress fare when mothers have different lengths of maternal leave. Only the mothers of four-month-olds who perceived their infants as being more prone to distress *and* who took shorter (e.g., six weeks rather than twelve weeks) maternity leave were observed to be less sensitive and responsive. When infants had easy temperaments, length of leave was not associated with less sensitive interactions. [64]

Social support—as may be provided by spouses, extended family, other children, friends and neighbors, and professionals—is another factor that has been shown to influence how skillfully mothers can respond to the needs of children with irritable temperaments. One study showed that when young mothers of irritable infants reported greater support, their babies were no more likely to be insecurely attached than infants who were not irritable. However, when social support was low, insecure attachment was more likely. [65]

Parental personality characteristics and quality of marital relationships are an additional factor that have been shown to influence whether children who start out as irritable infants remain high on negative emotionality. When mothers *or* fathers reported higher self-esteem before children were born, observations made first at three months and again at nine months showed that the more irritable children became less irritable during this time period. In contrast, when parents reported lower self-esteem, their children remained high in negative emotionality over the first year. Better marriages also predicted less irritability over time; when mothers had reported significantly less conflict and ambivalence in their marriages during prenatal interviews, children were more likely to become less irritable over the first year. [66]

Nature and Nurture Entwined

Teasing out the relative influence of parenting practices and temperament becomes further complicated by the fact that responsive parenting actually begins to influence brain functioning and child behavior in the early months. How and to what extent this occurs is a topic that will be discussed in later chapters. Suffice it to say, by the second half of the first year, the behavior children show, and even the physiological measures underlying behavior, reflect the interplay of genetic and environmental factors. [67] Thus, we have a "chicken or the egg" problem: it is hard to determine in a parent-child dyad whether temperament or parenting behaviors are causal or consequential.

Help for Parents of Irritable Infants

One important study conducted in the Netherlands showed that mothers of irritable infants can be coached to adjust their actions to their children's unique personalities. [68] Before the coaching began, observers found that irritable infants were less attentive and responsive to their mothers, and seemed to enjoy interacting with them less than did babies who did not have an irritable temperament. Not surprisingly, mothers whose infants were irritable increasingly withdrew from their children, becoming more inactive and passive. The reason for this is not entirely clear, but they may well have been uncertain as to how to interact with their more challenging infants.

In the coaching intervention, which occurred in the home during three two-hour visits scheduled between the ages of six and nine months, mothers were taught to attend to their infants' signals. For example, they were encouraged to imitate their children's behaviors, and to be silent when the baby turned his or her gaze away, thus respecting the child's need to have a break from stimulation. Mothers gained skill in observing their infants, in understanding the importance of responding to both positive and negative communications from their child, and in learning to anticipate changes in infant behavior. Adapting the coaching to the needs of each mother-child pair was important; some babies liked close physical contact and some did not, so mothers were offered a number of ways to soothe their children.

This intervention was highly successful, with improvements in both mothers' and infants' behavior. Compared to mothers of irritable infants who were not given the intervention, mothers who had the opportunity to be coached were more responsive, stimulating, and visually attentive to their child's behavior. Their children were more sociable, better at self-soothing, more sophisticated at exploring their surroundings, and cried less. And, at twelve months, they were significantly more likely to be securely attached in the Strange Situation. In fact, the differences between groups were quite striking; 62 percent of infants of mothers who received the coaching intervention were securely attached, while only 28 percent of infants whose mothers were not coached received a secure attachment classification.

SUMMING UP AND LOOKING FORWARD

Revolutions do not occur in the academic world without creating major ripples. When Mary Ainsworth's research was being disseminated to her psychology colleagues, many were skeptical or downright critical of her research. At the time, behaviorism dominated the field.[69] Behaviorists believed that behaviors that were reinforced, i.e., rewarded, would be seen more frequently, while those that received little response would fade away.[70] Behaviorists were not concerned with what infants felt, or the meaning underlying their actions, but instead focused on counting directly observable behaviors to determine what the child was learning through experience.

This conceptualization of attachment was squarely at odds with Ainsworth's viewpoint. In understanding the parent-child relationship, Ainsworth felt that developing measures that captured *how* parents interacted with their children was more important than counting how often they performed a certain action. As noted earlier, she found that mothers of the insecure-avoidant babies held their babies as much as did mothers of those judged securely attached, but they held their babies in ways that were less comforting and more intrusive compared to mothers of securely attached babies.[71]

The Netherlands intervention program provides an example of how knowledge gained from research about the parenting behaviors that matter most for children's emotional development can have practical applications. This coaching intervention was successful in helping mothers learn to more sensitively read and respond to their temperamentally at-risk children. Intervention programs have now been developed and shown to be effective with children who are at-risk for a variety of reasons, including because their mothers are young, disadvantaged, lacking sensitivity, suffer from depression, or have unstable marriages.[72]

In the twenty-first century, research methods have become more sophisticated and we have begun to understand some of the physiological processes and neurological pathways that underlie attachment-related behaviors and affect the structure and wiring of the developing brain.[73] While a review of findings from current neuroscientific research is beyond the scope of this book, it is important to appreciate that without the careful observations of Mary Ainsworth and those inspired by her research, technologically advanced methods, such as functional magnetic resonance imaging that allows us to "look inside" the brain, might not be guided by a sophisticated understanding of human behavior. In fact, attachment theory and attachment research are seen as a model of how clear conceptualizations and penetrating research can work hand in hand, allowing scientists to zero in on important concepts and gather pertinent data.[74]

In the next chapter, we will consider ways in which attachment experiences begin to shape children's expectations, or working models, about close relationships. We will also look at theories about how attachment-related experiences influence children's capacity for emotional regulation. As we consider the issue of how early experiences may start to have an influence on the developing brain, we will confront the important, and still controversial, question: When and to what extent do early experiences start to become "wired in" to the developing brain, and to shape later development?

NOTES

1. Karen, *Becoming Attached*, 131.
2. Ainsworth, "Mary D. Salter Ainsworth."
3. Ainsworth, *Infancy in Uganda*.
4. Ainsworth, "Mary D. Salter Ainsworth," 209.
5. Ainsworth, *Infancy in Uganda*, 331–32.
6. Ainsworth et al., *Patterns of Attachment*.
7. Ibid., 319.
8. Ibid., 62.
9. Mesman, van IJzendoorn, and Sagi-Schwartz, "Cross-Cultural Patterns of Attachment"; Grossmann, Grossmann, and Kindler, "Early Care and the Roots of Attachment and Partnership Representations"; Sroufe et al., *The Development of the Person*; Main, Hesse, and Kaplan, "Predictability of Attachment Behavior and Representational Processes at 1, 6, and 19 Years of Age."
10. van IJzendoorn and Kroonenberg, "Cross-Cultural Patterns of Attachment."
11. Kotila, Schoppe-Sullivan, and Kamp Dush, "Time in Parenting Activities in Dual-Earner Families at the Transition to Parenthood."
12. Caplan and Hall-McCorquodale, "Mother-Blaming in Major Clinical Journals."
13. Ainsworth et al., *Patterns of Attachment*.
14. Ibid., 147, 317.
15. Ibid., 154, 316–17; Ainsworth, "Attachment as Related to Mother-Infant Interaction," 34.
16. Main and Stadtman, "Infant Response to Rejection of Physical Contact by the Mother," 302.
17. Main and Weston, "Avoidance of the Attachment Figure in Infancy," 46.
18. Ainsworth et al., *Patterns of Attachment*, 315.
19. Ibid., 146.
20. Ibid.; Cassidy and Berlin, "The Insecure/Ambivalent Pattern of Attachment."
21. Pederson et al., "Understanding Sensitivity."

22. Mesman, van IJzendoorn, and Sagi-Schwartz, "Cross-Cultural Patterns of Attachment."

23. Ainsworth et al., *Patterns of Attachment*, 242.

24. Main and Solomon, "Discovery of an Insecure-Disorganized/Disoriented Attachment Pattern"; Main and Solomon, "Procedures of Identifying Infants as Disorganized/Disoriented During the Ainsworth Strange Situation."

25. van IJzendoorn, Schuengel, and Bakermans-Kranenburg, "Disorganized Attachment in Early Childhood"; Carlson, "A Prospective Longitudinal Study of Attachment Disorganization/ Disorientation"; Fearon et al., "The Significance of Insecure Attachment and Disorganization in the Development of Children's Externalizing Behavior."

26. Main and Solomon, "Discovery of an Insecure-Disorganized/Disoriented Attachment Pattern"; Main and Solomon, "Procedures of Identifying Infants as Disorganized/Disoriented During the Ainsworth Strange Situation."

27. Main and Solomon, "Discovery of an Insecure-Disorganized/Disoriented Attachment Pattern"; Main and Solomon, "Procedures of Identifying Infants as Disorganized/Disoriented During the Ainsworth Strange Situation."

28. van IJzendoorn, Schuengel, and Bakermans-Kranenburg, "Disorganized Attachment in Early Childhood."

29. Crittenden, "Maltreated Infants"; Lyons-Ruth et al., "Infants at Social Risk."

30. Carlson et al., "Disorganized/Disoriented Attachment Relationships in Maltreated Infants"; Cyr et al., "Attachment Security and Disorganization in Maltreating and High-Risk Families."

31. van IJzendoorn, Schuengel, and Bakermans-Kranenburg, "Disorganized Attachment in Early Childhood"; Groh et al., "The Significance of Insecure and Disorganized Attachment for Children's Internalizing Symptoms."

32. Main and Hesse, "Parents' Unresolved Traumatic Experiences Are Related to Infant Disorganized Attachment Status"; Hesse and Main, "Frightened, Threatening, and Dissociative Parental Behavior in Low-Risk Samples."

33. Main and Solomon, "Procedures of Identifying Infants as Disorganized/Disoriented During the Ainsworth Strange Situation."

34. Madigan et al., "Unresolved States of Mind, Anomalous Parental Behavior, and Disorganized Attachment."

35. Sroufe et al., *The Development of the Person*.

36. Emotional regulation difficulties were found on the Neonatal Brazelton Assessment Scale (NBAS, Brazelton, 1973), which looks at infants' early adaptive responses and possible vulnerabilities.

37. Padrón, Carlson, and Sroufe, "Frightened versus Not Frightened Disorganized Infant Attachment."

38. Main, Hesse, and Hesse, "Attachment Theory and Research," 441; Granqvist et al., "Prior Participation in the Strange Situation and Overstress Jointly Facilitate Disorganized Behaviours."

39. Granqvist et al., "Prior Participation in the Strange Situation and Overstress Jointly Facilitate Disorganized Behaviours."

40. Main, Hesse, and Hesse, "Attachment Theory and Research."

41. Wilkins, "Disorganised Attachment Indicates Child Maltreatment," 16.

42. Main, Hesse, and Hesse, "Attachment Theory and Research," 450–51.

43. Granqvist et al., "Prior Participation in the Strange Situation and Overstress Jointly Facilitate Disorganized Behaviours."

44. van IJzendoorn and de Wolff, "In Search of the Absent Father."

45. Grossmann et al., "The Uniqueness of the Child-Father Attachment Relationship"; Grossmann, Grossmann, and Kindler, "Early Care and the Roots of Attachment and Partnership Representations."

46. Grossmann and Grossmann, "Attachment Quality as an Organizer of Emotional and Behavioral Responses in a Longitudinal Perspective," 99.

47. Main and Weston, "The Quality of the Toddler's Relationship to Mother and to Father"; Grossmann et al., "German Children's Behavior towards Their Mothers at 12 Months and Their

Fathers at 18 Months in Ainsworth's Strange Situation"; Steele, Steele, and Fonagy, "Associations among Attachment Classifications of Mothers, Fathers, and Their Infants."

48. Grossmann et al., "The Uniqueness of the Child-Father Attachment Relationship."

49. Cowan, "Beyond Meta-Analysis," 602.

50. Belsky and Fearon, "Precursors of Attachment Security."

51. Dickstein, Seifer, and Albus, "Maternal Adult Attachment Representations across Relationship Domains and Infant Outcomes."

52. Brown et al., "Observed and Reported Supportive Coparenting as Predictors of Infant-Mother and Infant-Father Attachment Security."

53. Cowan and Cowan, "Normative Family Transitions, Normal Family Processes, and Healthy Child Development"; Cowan et al., "Becoming a Family."

54. Cowan and Cowan, "Interventions to Ease the Transition to Parenthood."

55. Cowan et al., "Becoming a Family."

56. Belsky, "Attachment Theory and Research in Ecological Perspective"; Belsky and Isabella, "Maternal, Infant, and Social-Contextual Determinants of Attachment Security," 76–79.

57. Kagan, *Psychological Research on the Human Infant*; Chess and Thomas, "Infant Bonding."

58. Thomas, Chess, and Birch, *Temperament and Behavior Disorders in Children.*

59. Chess and Thomas, "Infant Bonding," 220.

60. Ibid., 221.

61. Ainsworth, "Attachment as Related to Mother-Infant Interaction," 45.

62. Vaugn, Bost, and van IJzendoorn, "Attachment and Temperament."

63. Crockenberg and Leerkes, "Infant Negative Emotionality, Caregiving, and Family Relationships."

64. Clark et al., "Length of Maternity Leave and Quality of Mother-Infant Interactions."

65. Crockenberg, "Infant Irritability, Mother Responsiveness, and Social Support Influences on the Security of Infant-Mother Attachment."

66. Belsky, Fish, and Isabella, "Continuity and Discontinuity in Infant Negative and Positive Emotionality."

67. Crockenberg and Leerkes, "Infant Negative Emotionality, Caregiving, and Family Relationships," 59.

68. van den Boom, "The Influence of Temperament and Mothering on Attachment and Exploration."

69. Karen, *Becoming Attached*, 167.

70. Dollard and Miller, *Personality and Psychotherapy.*

71. Ainsworth et al., *Patterns of Attachment.*

72. Letourneau et al., "Narrative and Meta-Analytic Review of Interventions Aiming to Improve Maternal-Child Attachment Security"; Berlin, Zeanah, and Lieberman, "Prevention and Intervention Programs to Support Early Attachment Security."

73. Schore, "Attachment, Affect Regulation, and the Developing Right Brain"; Schore and Sieff, "On the Same Wave-Length."

74. Cassidy and Shaver, "Preface."

REFERENCES

Ainsworth, Mary D. Salter. *Infancy in Uganda: Infant Care and the Growth of Love.* Baltimore: John Hopkins Press, 1967.

———. "Attachment as Related to Mother-Infant Interaction." *Advances in the Study of Behavior* 9 (1979): 1–51.

———. "Mary D. Salter Ainsworth: An Autobiographical Sketch." In *Models of Achievement: Reflections of Eminent Women in Psychology*, edited by Agnes N. O'Connell and Nancy F. Russo, 201–19. New York: Columbia University Press, 1983.

Ainsworth, Mary D. Salter, Mary C. Blehar, Everett Waters, and Sally N. Wall. *Patterns of Attachment: A Psychological Study of the Strange Situation.* New York and London: Psychology Press, 1978/2015.

Belsky, Jay. "Attachment Theory and Research in Ecological Perspective: Insights from the Pennsylvania Infant and Family Development Project and the NICHD Study of Early Child Care." In *Attachment from Infancy to Adulthood: The Major Longitudinal Studies*, edited by Klaus. E. Grossmann, Karin Grossmann, and Everett Waters, 71–97. New York: The Guilford Press, 2005.

Belsky, Jay, and R. M. Pasco Fearon. "Precursors of Attachment Security." In *Handbook of Attachment: Theory, Research, and Clinical Applications, Second Edition*, edited by Jude Cassidy and Phillip R. Shaver, 295–316. New York: The Guilford Press, 2008.

Belsky, Jay, Margaret Fish, and Russell A. Isabella. "Continuity and Discontinuity in Infant Negative and Positive Emotionality: Family Antecedents and Attachment Consequences." *Developmental Psychology* 27, no. 3 (1991): 421–31.

Belsky, Jay, and Russell A. Isabella. "Maternal, Infant, and Social-Contextual Determinants of Attachment Security." In *Clinical Implications of Attachment*, edited by Jay Belsky and Teresa Nezworski, 41–94. New York and London: Routledge, 1988.

Berlin, Lisa J., Charles H. Zeanah, and Alicia F. Lieberman. "Prevention and Intervention Programs to Support Early Attachment Security: A Move to the Level of the Community." In *Handbook of Attachment: Theory, Research, and Clinical Applications, Third Edition*, edited by Jude Cassidy and Phillip R. Shaver, 739–58. New York: The Guilford Press, 2016.

Brazelton, Thomas Berry. *Neonatal Assessment Scale.* Philadelphia, PA: Lippincott, 1973.

Brown, Geoffrey L., Sarah J. Schoppe-Sullivan, Sarah C. Mangelsdorf, and Cynthia Neff. "Observed and Reported Supportive Coparenting as Predictors of Infant–Mother and Infant–Father Attachment Security." *Early Child Development and Care* 180, no. 1–2 (2010): 121–37.

Caplan, Paula J., and Ian Hall-McCorquodale. "Mother-Blaming in Major Clinical Journals." *American Journal of Orthopsychiatry* 55, no. 3 (1985): 345–53.

Carlson, Elizabeth A. "A Prospective Longitudinal Study of Attachment Disorganization/Disorientation." *Child Development* 69, no. 4 (1998): 1107–28.

Carlson, Vicki, Dante Cicchetti, Douglas Barnett, and Karen Braunwald. "Disorganized/Disoriented Attachment Relationships in Maltreated Infants." *Developmental Psychology* 25, no. 4 (1989): 525–31.

Cassidy, Jude, and Lisa J. Berlin. "The Insecure/Ambivalent Pattern of Attachment: Theory and Research." *Child Development* 65, no. 4 (1994): 971–91.

Cassidy, Jude, and Phillip R. Shaver. "Preface." In *Handbook of Attachment: Theory, Research, and Clinical Applications, Third Edition*, edited by Jude Cassidy and Phillip R. Shaver, x–xvi. New York: The Guilford Press, 2016.

Chess, Stella, and Alexander Thomas. "Infant Bonding: Mystique and Reality." *American Journal of Orthopsychiatry* 52, no. 2 (1982): 213–22.

Clark, Roseanne, Janet Shibley Hyde, Marilyn J. Essex, and Marjorie H. Klein. "Length of Maternity Leave and Quality of Mother-Infant Interactions." *Child Development* 68, no. 2 (1997): 364–83.

Cowan, Carolyn Pape, and Philip A. Cowan. "Interventions to Ease the Transition to Parenthood: Why They Are Needed and What They Can Do." *Family Relations: Journal of Applied Family & Child Studies* 44, no. 4 (1995): 412–23.

Cowan, Carolyn Pape, Philip A. Cowan, Gertrude Heming, and Nancy B. Miller. "Becoming a Family: Marriage, Parenting, and Child Development." In *Family Transitions*, edited by Philip A. Cowan and E. Mavis Hetherington, 79–109. Hillsdale, NJ: Erlbaum, 1991.

Cowan, Philip A. "Beyond Meta-Analysis: A Plea for a Family Systems View of Attachment." *Child Development* 68 no. 4 (1997): 601–3.

Cowan, Philip A., and Carolyn Pape Cowan. "Normative Family Transitions, Normal Family Processes, and Healthy Child Development." In *Normal Family Processes: Growing Diversity and Complexity*, edited by Froma Walsh, 424–59. New York: The Guilford Press, 2003.

Crittenden, Patricia M. "Maltreated Infants: Vulnerability and Resilience." *Journal of Child Psychology and Psychiatry* 26, no. 1 (1985): 85–96.

Crockenberg, Susan. "Infant Irritability, Mother Responsiveness, and Social Support Influences on the Security of Infant-Mother Attachment." *Child Development* 52, no. 3 (1981): 857–65.

Crockenberg, Susan, and Esther Leerkes. "Infant Negative Emotionality, Caregiving, and Family Relationships." In *Children's Influence on Family Dynamics: The Neglected Side of Family Relationships*, edited by Ann C. Crouter and Alan Booth, 57–78. Mahwah, NJ: Lawrence Erlbaum and Associates, 2003.

Cyr, Chantal, Eveline M. Euser, Marian J. Bakermans-Kranenburg, and Marinus H. van IJzendoorn. "Attachment Security and Disorganization in Maltreating and High-Risk Families: A Series of Meta-Analyses." *Development and Psychopathology* 22, no. 1 (2010): 87–108.

Dickstein, Susan, Ronald Seifer, and Kathleen E. Albus. "Maternal Adult Attachment Representations across Relationship Domains and Infant Outcomes: The Importance of Family and Couple Functioning." *Attachment & Human Development* 11, no. 1 (2009): 5–27.

Dollard, John, and Neal E. Miller. *Personality and Psychotherapy: An Analysis in Terms of Learning, Thinking, and Culture*. New York: McGraw-Hill Book Co., 1950.

Fearon, R. Pasco, Marian J. Bakermans-Kranenburg, Marinus H. van IJzendoorn, Anne-Marie Lapsley, and Glenn I. Roisman. "The Significance of Insecure Attachment and Disorganization in the Development of Children's Externalizing Behavior: A Meta-Analytic Study." *Child Development* 81, no. 2 (2010): 435–56.

Granqvist, Pehr, Erik Hesse, Mari Fransson, Mary Main, Berit Hagekull, and Gunilla Bohlin. "Prior Participation in the Strange Situation and Overstress Jointly Facilitate Disorganized Behaviours: Implications for Theory, Research and Practice." *Attachment & Human Development* 18, no. 3 (2016): 235–49.

Groh, Ashley M., Glenn I. Roisman, Marinus H. van IJzendoorn, Marian J. Bakermans-Kranenburg, and R. Pasco Fearon. "The Significance of Insecure and Disorganized Attachment for Children's Internalizing Symptoms: A Meta-Analytic Study." *Child Development* 83, no. 2 (2012): 591–610.

Grossmann, Karin, Klaus E. Grossmann, Elisabeth Fremmer-Bombik, Heinz Kindler, and Hermann Scheuerer-Englisch. "The Uniqueness of the Child–Father Attachment Relationship: Fathers' Sensitive and Challenging Play as a Pivotal Variable in a 16-Year Longitudinal Study." *Social Development* 11, no. 3 (2002): 301–37.

Grossmann, Klaus E., Karin Grossmann, Franz Huber, and Ulrike Wartner. "German Children's Behavior towards Their Mothers at 12 Months and Their Fathers at 18 Months in Ainsworth's Strange Situation." *International Journal of Behavioral Development* 4, no. 2 (1981): 157–81.

Grossmann, Karin, Klaus E. Grossman, and Heinz Kindler. "Early Care and the Roots of Attachment and Partnership Representations: The Bielefeld and Regensburg Longitudinal Studies." In *Attachment from Infancy to Adulthood: The Major Longitudinal Studies*, edited by Klaus. E. Grossmann, Karin Grossmann, and Everett Waters, 98–136. New York: Guilford, 2005.

Grossmann, Klaus E., and Karin Grossman. "Attachment Quality as an Organizer of Emotional and Behavioral Responses in a Longitudinal Perspective." In *Attachment across the Life Cycle*, edited by Colin M. Parkes, Joan Stevenson-Hinde, and Peter Marris, 93–114. New York: Routledge, 1991.

Hesse, Erik, and Mary Main. "Frightened, Threatening, and Dissociative Parental Behavior in Low-Risk Samples: Description, Discussion, and Interpretations." *Development and Psychopathology* 18, no. 2 (2006): 309–43.

Kagan, Jerome. *Psychological Research on the Human Infant: An Evaluative Summary*. WT Grant Foundation, 1982.

Karen, Robert. *Becoming Attached: First Relationships and How They Shape Our Capacity to Love*. New York: Oxford University Press, 1998.

Kotila, Letitia E., Sarah J. Schoppe-Sullivan, and Claire M. Kamp Dush. "Time in Parenting Activities in Dual-Earner Families at the Transition to Parenthood." *Family Relations* 62, no. 5 (2013): 795–807.

Letourneau, Nicole, Panagiota Tryphonopoulos, Gerald Giesbrecht, Cindy-Lee Dennis, Sanjit Bhogal, and Barry Watson. "Narrative and Meta-Analytic Review of Interventions Aiming to Improve Maternal-Child Attachment Security." *Infant Mental Health Journal* 36, no. 4 (2015): 366–87.

Lyons-Ruth, Karlen, David B. Connell, Henry U. Grunebaum, and Sheila Botein. "Infants at Social Risk: Maternal Depression and Family Support Services as Mediators of Infant Development and Security of Attachment." *Child Development* 61, no. 1 (1990): 85–98.

Madigan, Sheri, Marian J. Bakermans-Kranenburg, Marinus H. van IJzendoorn, Greg Moran, David R. Pederson, and Diane Benoit. "Unresolved States of Mind, Anomalous Parental Behavior, and Disorganized Attachment: A Review and Meta-Analysis of a Transmission Gap." *Attachment & Human Development* 8, no. 2 (2006): 89–111.

Main, Mary, and Erik Hesse. "Parents' Unresolved Traumatic Experiences are Related to Infant Disorganized Attachment Status: Is Frightened and/or Frightening Parental Behavior the Linking Mechanism?" In *Attachment in the Preschool Years: Theory, Research, and Intervention*, edited by Mark T. Greenberg, Dante Ciccetti, and Mark E. Cummings, 161–82. Chicago: University of Chicago Press, 1990.

Main, Mary, Erik Hesse, and Siegfried Hesse. "Attachment Theory and Research: Overview with Suggested Applications to Child Custody." *Family Court Review* 49, no. 3 (2011): 426–63.

Main, Mary, Erik Hesse, and Nancy Kaplan. "Predictability of Attachment Behavior and Representational Processes at 1, 6, and 19 Years of Age: The Berkeley Longitudinal Study." In *Attachment from Infancy to Adulthood: The Major Longitudinal Studies*, edited by Klaus. E. Grossmann, Karin Grossmann, and Everett Waters, 245–304. New York: The Guilford Press, 2005.

Main, Mary, and Judith Solomon. "Discovery of an Insecure-Disorganized/Disoriented Attachment Pattern." In *Affective Development in Infancy*, edited by Thomas Berry Brazelton and Michael W. Yogman, 95–124. Norwood, NJ: Ablex, 1986.

Main, Mary, and Judith Solomon. "Procedures of Identifying Infants as Disorganized/Disoriented During the Ainsworth Strange Situation." In *Attachment in the Preschool Years: Theory, Research, and Intervention*, edited by Mark T. Greenberg, Dante Ciccetti, and Mark E. Cummings, 121–60. Chicago: University of Chicago Press, 1990.

Main, Mary, and Jackolyn Stadtman. "Infant Response to Rejection of Physical Contact by the Mother." *Journal of the American Academy of Child Psychiatry* 20, no. 2 (1981): 292–307.

Main, Mary, and Donna R. Weston. "The Quality of the Toddler's Relationship to Mother and to Father: Related to Conflict Behavior and the Readiness to Establish New Relationships." *Child Development* 52, no. 3 (1981): 932–40.

Main, Mary, and Donna R. Weston. "Avoidance of the Attachment Figure in Infancy: Descriptions and Interpretations." In *The Place of Attachment in Human Behavior*, edited by Colin M. Parkes and Joan Stevenson-Hinde, 203–17. New York: Basic Books, 1982.

Mesman, Judi, Marinus H. van IJzendoorn, and Abraham Sagi-Schwartz. "Cross-Cultural Patterns of Attachment: Universal and Contextual Dimensions." In *Handbook of Attachment: Theory, Research, and Clinical Applications, Third Edition*, edited by Jude Cassidy and Phillip R. Shaver, 852–77. New York: The Guilford Press, 2016.

Padrón, Elena, Elizabeth A. Carlson, and L. Alan Sroufe. "Frightened versus Not Frightened Disorganized Infant Attachment: Newborn Characteristics and Maternal Caregiving." *American Journal of Orthopsychiatry* 84, no. 2 (2014): 201–8.

Pederson, David R., Heidi N. Bailey, George M. Tarabulsy, Sandi Bento, and Greg Moran. "Understanding Sensitivity: Lessons Learned from the Legacy of Mary Ainsworth." *Attachment & Human Development* 16, no. 3 (2014): 261–70.

Schore, Allan N. "Attachment, Affect Regulation, and the Developing Right Brain: Linking Developmental Neuroscience to Pediatrics." *Pediatrics in Review* 26, no. 6 (2005): 204–17.

Schore, Allan N., and Daniella Sieff. "On the Same Wave-Length: How Our Emotional Brain Is Shaped by Human Relationships." In *Understanding and Healing Emotional Trauma: Conversations with Pioneering Clinicians and Researchers*, edited by Daniella F. Sieff, 11–136. London: Routledge, 2015.

Sroufe, L. Alan, Byron Egeland, Elizabeth A. Carlson, and W. Andrew Collins. *The Development of the Person: The Minnesota Study of Risk and Adaptation from Birth to Adulthood*. New York: The Guilford Press, 2005.

Steele, Howard, Miriam Steele, and Peter Fonagy. "Associations among Attachment Classifications of Mothers, Fathers, and Their Infants." *Child Development* 67, no. 2 (1996): 541–55.

Thomas, Alexander, Stella Chess, and Herbet G. Birch. *Temperament and Behavior Disorders in Children.* New York: New York University Press, 1968.

van den Boom, Dymphna C. "The Influence of Temperament and Mothering on Attachment and Exploration: An Experimental Manipulation of Sensitive Responsiveness Among Lower-Class Mothers with Irritable Infants." *Child Development* 65, no. 5 (1994): 1457–77.

van IJzendoorn, Marinus H., and Pieter M. Kroonenberg. "Cross-Cultural Patterns of Attachment: A Meta-Analysis of the Strange Situation." *Child Development* 59, no. 1 (1988): 147–56.

van IJzendoorn, Marinus H., Carlo Schuengel, and Marian J. Bakermans-Kranenburg. "Disorganized Attachment in Early Childhood: Meta-Analysis of Precursors, Concomitants, and Sequelae." *Development and Psychopathology* 11, no. 02 (1999): 225–50.

van IJzendoorn, Marinus H., and Marianne S. Wolff. "In Search of the Absent Father—Meta-Analyses of Infant-Father Attachment: A Rejoinder to Our Discussants." *Child Development* 68, no. 4 (1997): 604–9.

Vaughn, Brian E., Kelly K. Bost, and Marinus H. van IJzendoorn. "Attachment and Temperament: Additive and Interactive Influences on Behavior, Affect, and Cognition during Infancy and Childhood." In *Handbook of Attachment: Theory, Research, and Clinical Applications, Second Edition*, edited by Jude Cassidy and Phillip R. Shaver, 192–296. New York: The Guilford Press, 2008.

Wilkins, David. "Disorganised Attachment Indicates Child Maltreatment: How Is This Link Useful for Child Protection Social Workers?" *Journal of Social Work Practice* 26, no. 1 (2012): 15–30.

Chapter Three

How Do Attachment Relationships Lay the Groundwork for Future Development?

In the 2015 box-office hit movie "Inside Out," 11-year-old Riley angrily gets on a bus to leave her parents in San Francisco and return to her old life in Minnesota. However, animated characters with personalities based on distinct emotions work in a "control tower" (symbolizing the control functions inside Riley's brain) to look out for her best interests, and as Riley boards the bus "Joy" urges "Sadness" to take the controls. With "Sadness" now determining Riley's emotional experience, she begins to long for the lost loving times with her parents. She abruptly gets off the bus to return home, where she is reunited with parents, who warmly embrace her.

In a *New York Times* review of *Inside Out*, emotion researchers Dacher Keltner and Paul Ekman, who served as scientific consultants in the making of the film, asserted that the movie theme fits with the current view of emotions. Contrary to past models of emotion, researchers now believe that emotions organize, rather than disrupt, our social lives. In making this point, Keltner and Ekman wrote that "Studies have found . . . that emotions structure (not just color) such disparate social interactions as *attachment between parents and children*, sibling conflicts, flirtations between young courters and negotiations between rivals [italics added]."[1]

So, in this captivating movie that entertains adults as well as children, the public is actually being educated about the role emotions play in organizing human relationships! But, exactly how *do* emotions come to organize social interactions? What role might differences in attachment during infancy play in shaping how emotion systems develop? How do patterns of attachment begin to organize our experiences?

49

Figure 3.1.   (Left) Anger, Disgust, Joy, Fear, & Sadness controlling Riley's thoughts. © 2015 Disney.Pixar. This image is reprinted with permission of Disney Enterprises, Inc.
Figure 3.2.   (Right) Riley embracing with her parents after "Sadness" motivates her to return home. © 2015 Disney.Pixar. This image is reprinted with permission of Disney Enterprises, Inc.

EMOTIONS AS ORGANIZERS AND REGULATORS

Let's return briefly to the story line in *Inside Out*. When Sadness takes the controls, it is noteworthy that this "emotion character" has a pretty easy time motivating Riley to return home. Riley had had a happy life in Minnesota, and her earlier positive experiences with her mom and dad, shown throughout the movie as memories of precious moments with caring parents, have given her a store of positive memories she can readily access at this time of crisis.

In attachment theory terms, Riley has internalized largely positive "working models" of her parents. Accumulated experiences from babyhood onward have led her to develop "representations" (a term essentially synonymous with internal models) of each of her parents as responsive caregivers. Her positive working models of parents allow her to anticipate that they will welcome her back home.

The character Sadness is also able to easily influence Riley because Riley's defenses against experiencing painful emotions are not rigid. She has only recently begun to develop a "stiff upper lip" to deal with the family stresses, but the movie gives us a sense that throughout most of her life she has been able to turn to her parents for comfort, without fear of rebuff. Things might have played out differently if Riley had had repeated experiences where revealing her emotional needs resulted in rejection, distancing, or ridicule by her parents. In that case, she would likely have developed a wall (i.e., strong defenses)[2] against consciously experiencing, and then act-ing upon the sad feelings that prompted her to return home. Her parents' earlier warmth and responsiveness had helped her develop the ability to smoothly and easily access her emotions.

Finally, Riley shows the ability to organize her behavior to accomplish goals in a reasonably deliberate manner. She did not resort to intentionally self-harming activities, as some young women do when struggling to control strong emotions that seem impossible to tolerate.[3] While her decision to leave home and board a bus to Minnesota may have been rash, she was able to develop a plan to buy a bus ticket and get herself on board the bus. Then, when she came to regret this decision, she managed to slip off the bus and quietly make her way home.

Riley's fictional but very plausible life story offers a starting point to consider how attachment experiences influence emotional development. Consideration of this youngster's life trajectory during her first eleven years allows us to contemplate the role of both early and later experiences in shaping an individual's personality. Questions to ponder include:

- To what extent might Riley's attachment experiences with parents during infancy have shaped the course of her development?
- Are there periods when social and emotional experiences have a particu-larly important, or even critical impact on personality development?
- When family stress mounted during her eleventh year, how might her earlier positive experiences have influenced the way she coped with ten-sion and disappointment?

We now have the benefit of a wealth of information mined from careful study of what I will call "Child Veterans" of the Strange Situation Procedure, who have been followed by researchers beyond infancy, and in some cases until late adolescence or even adulthood. By following children over time, researchers have gathered evidence to address these and other important questions. But, before reviewing research findings, it is useful to consider some important concepts in attachment theory and to discuss some proposed frameworks for understanding patterns of attachment and reasons for differ-ent paths children may take during development.

Working Models

Bowlby's concept of working models describes how individuals come to develop expectations that guide their behavior. In his 1973 book *Separation: Anxiety and Anger*, he wrote:

The states of mind with which we are concerned can conveniently be described in terms of representational or working models . . . it is plausible to
suppose that each individual builds working models of the world and of himself in it, with the aid of which he perceives events, forecasts the future, and
constructs his plans. In the working model of the world that anyone builds, a
key feature is his notion of who his attachment figures are, where they may be
found, and how they may be expected to respond. Similarly, in the working
model of the self that anyone builds a key feature is his notion of how accept-
able or unacceptable he himself is in the eyes of his attachment figures. [4]

Working models of relationships are seen as structures that aid in predicting and constructing plans. Internal working models are theorized to direct
feelings and behavior, as well as attention, memory, and cognition. They
often operate outside of conscious awareness, and they assist in acting as gate
keepers for access to emotions. [5]

Working Models in the Strange Situation

Children's attachment behaviors when they reunite with parents in the
Strange Situation are believed to reflect the influence of early working models about the availability of caretakers. [6] Securely attached children expect
parents will comfort them, while insecurely attached children anticipate that
parents may not be a source of security and reassurance.

If we imagine a securely attached young boy having an unfamiliar, somewhat frightening experience, as occurs with the Strange Situation, we assume
the child feels fear or uneasiness. Based on a working model of mother as
comforting, this boy has no reason to squelch his emotions, and he becomes
distressed and promptly goes to her when she returns.

An insecure-avoidant little girl (one who appears to maintain a "stiff-
upper-lip" in the Strange Situation) in a frightening situation would feel fear,
but her working model causes her to expect that mother won't be a source of
comfort. So, she squelches her feelings. Insecure-avoidant children are less
likely to cry during laboratory separation episodes than are securely attached
children. When mother returns, they show their characteristic avoidance behavior, and interestingly, the more they avoid, the less they show obvious
angry behavior such as angry crying, hitting, batting away toys, or open
petulance.

Do we have evidence that insecure-avoidant children are truly squelching
their emotions? Two studies that measured heart rate changes in children
during the Strange Situation have provided some evidence for this notion. In
general, increases in heart-rate in aversive situations may or may not occur
along with distress behavior, but such increases do suggest emotional arousal, even when arousal isn't evident in behavior.

A German study that measured heart rate changes during the Strange Situation found that children in the insecure-avoidant group did not overtly show much distress during separation, but their heart rates did increase. In fact, in this study heart rate elevations were even higher than with securely attached children, who were likely to act distressed. A second, more recent study also found a lack of concordance between overt displays of distress and heart rate elevations during the Strange Situation separation episode in the insecure-avoidant group.[7]

In this second study, researchers theorized that behavioral reactions of distress seemed to be habitually inhibited for this group. They speculated that this could lead to impulsive release of the "bottled up" negative emotions, and could also undermine the child's ability to recognize distress in other people.[8]

In the German study, measurement of a stress hormone (cortisol) after the Strange Situation Procedure indicated that the laboratory procedure was *more* stressful for avoidant than for secure babies. But, unlike secure babies, insecure-avoidant children did not turn to their mothers when heart rate measures showed they were highly aroused.[9]

Given that mothers of insecure-avoidant children typically reject children's display of attachment behaviors, the expression of emotions such as anger, sadness or distress may be risky, as they may alienate the attachment figure. In the Strange Situation, avoidance is theorized as a way for a child to control his or her expression of anger regarding separation, as might be stimulated by close contact. If a child focuses on objects in the environment, he or she is better able to maintain organization, control, and flexibility in behavior. It has been theorized that the insecure-avoidant pattern may be a sort of necessary strategy for keeping an insensitive or rejecting caregiver minimally accessible, thereby maintaining to some degree the protective function of the attachment relationship.[10]

What working models do the "consolation resistant" (insecure-resistant) babies bring to the Strange Situation? Their mothers have been minimally or inconsistently available,[11] and it is theorized that their expectation is that they must show exaggerated and fairly chronic negative emotions to keep the attention of the attachment figure. If the insecure-resistant child were to allow himself to relax and be soothed, he runs the risk of losing contact with the parent.[12]

Working Models beyond Infancy

Bowlby allowed for the possibility that working models of both self and of attachment figures could gradually be updated in response to changes in the way the child is treated.[13] More recent theorists have strongly argued that working models should be understood as *developing representations* as opposed to fixed entities.[14] This view emphasizes the possibility for growth and change in the years past infancy.

With older children, adolescents, and adults, a variety of assessment tools have been developed to probe working models. Interviews, storytelling in response to pictures or pretend scenes with doll props, and other "projective" techniques can evoke individuals' representations of parents, peers, romantic partners, and importantly, of themselves. The Strange Situation is useful for nonverbal children who can only provide evidence of their working models in behavior, but beyond infancy researchers have developed creative approaches that allow us a window into individuals' sense of themselves and the social world in which they live.

Emotion Regulation and Dysregulation

It would be misleading to end this section with the notion that emotions *always* play an organizing role in social relationships and individual functioning. Emotions are organizing when they allow us to respond to challenges quickly, with minimal deliberation, and when they provide a drive to seek out things that are good for us and avoid those that are harmful.

Impairment of emotion regulation is called dysregulation. When dysregulation is brief and transient, it results in anxiety or pain, behavioral tantrums, or withdrawal. When chronic, dysregulation results in psychopathology. Conditions such as conduct disorder and depression can be thought of as failure in the behavioral and/or affective regulation of the emotion system.[15]

Parents play an important role in helping children develop emotion regulation in at least two ways. First, they help teach strategies that children can use to regulate difficult emotions. Second, they can help provide an environment with a relatively low degree of stress that allows children's nervous systems to develop in a way that leads to skillful emotion regulation. There is evidence that children growing up in harsh, threatening conditions develop altered autonomic nervous system functioning, and subsequently they are likely to be emotionally reactive to challenges.[16]

Attachment and the Regulation of Emotions

Theory and research now support the idea that an additional function of attachment relationships is to support the development of emotion regulation skills.[17] Indeed, a child's skill in the regulation of emotions, or what is more commonly referred to as "affect regulation," turns out to be closely linked to attachment security.

Allan Schore, a prominent neuropsychologist and attachment theorist, described in an interview his view of the connection between attachment and affect regulation as follows:

The attachment drive evolved partly because infants needed to remain close to their mothers for protection from predators and partly because infants cannot regulate either their bodily functions or their emotional states and need a caregiver to do this for them. The role of regulation is so important that I now see attachment theory primarily as a theory of emotional and bodily regulation. Typically an attuned caregiver will minimize her infant's discomfort, fear and pain, and as importantly, create opportunities for the child to feel joy and excitement. She will also mediate the transitions between these emotional states. [18]

In the early months of an infant's life the caregiver works to regulate the child's affect by interpreting his or her signals and striving to satisfy the child's needs. Over time, however, parents begin to influence how children themselves cope with emotionally arousing events. Sensitive parenting, particularly sensitivity in response to distress, is an important vehicle that helps children to learn to self-regulate. A sensitive mother helps promote self-soothing in her infant by such means as providing security objects, gently shifting attention by providing something interesting to look at, or modeling and encouraging adaptive responses to problems. [19]

Sensitive parenting both teaches children coping strategies and ensures that children spend less time in states of frustration or distress. Thus, they have more opportunities to experience the world positively, as well as for their nervous systems to develop in an optimal fashion. Pioneers such as Allan Schore and Daniel Siegel[20] have articulated ways in which caregiving experiences contribute to the early shaping of the architecture of the brain. In writing about what he terms "interpersonal neurobiology," Siegel asserts, "By altering both the activity and the structure of the connections between neurons, experience directly shapes the circuits responsible for such processes as memory, emotion, and self-awareness."[21]

The possibility that early experiences become in some way "programmed" in the brain is an intriguing one. However, investigators are still uncertain about when sensitive periods for neurodevelopment in humans may occur.[22] Caution is warranted before too quickly concluding that early experiences become set in stone.

PATHS OF CONTINUITY AND DISCONTINUITY

A critical question is to what extent infants' experiences with mother during the first year, leading to a secure, insecure, or disorganized attachment, lay a foundation that contributes to a child's successful adjustment in subsequent years. In thinking about the development of internal working models and about how early experiences may help to shape the architecture of the brain, one may wonder whether the nature of these early experiences has a critical influence on later adjustment. In theory, a case can be made as to why we should expect to find at least some degree of continuity in adaptation over time. However, arguments can also be made to support the possibility for change and discontinuity.

The Case for Continuity in Adjustment

Attachment theorists have hypothesized that children's interactions with early caregivers coalesce into patterns of attachment and communication that eventually become established modes of behavior. Children's perceptions of themselves and other people, as well as patterns in their thoughts, feelings, and behaviors may begin to influence on-going experiences. Children who have developed positive working models of self and others based on affirming experiences with their parents will enter new situations with the expectation that relationships will be rewarding and that people will like them.

Confidence in the ability to act independently when navigating new terrain is a closely related concept that would contribute to continuity in good adjustment. A key concept in attachment theory is that the attachment figure provides a "secure base from which to explore." If children feel assured of their caretaker's ready availability in case of need, they can explore with greater zest.[23] In infancy, exploration can mean simply crawling away from mother and investigating toys, and in later years it can indicate a willingness to take on intellectual challenges or novel social interactions.

Additionally, children who have good affect regulation skills gained through positive interactions with a sensitive caregiver should be better prepared to cope with limits imposed by teachers or frustrating situations with peers. If children have the capacity to act with age-appropriate self-control, they will fare better outside the home. Being prepared to be a cooperative, patient playmate and a rule-abiding citizen who is able to delay gratification gives one an advantage when entering the wider world.

The Case for Discontinuity in Adjustment

Quite possibly, a family's circumstances may change, and these changes may be either beneficial or detrimental to the child's adjustment. It seems plausible that improved family circumstances after infancy can mitigate, at least to some degree, the negative effects of early experiences. Alternatively, new stresses could disrupt a path of good adjustment.

Common sense suggests that the one-year-old child's knowledge about the world and his experiences with mother and father aren't captured in a bubble that will entirely insulate him or her through every trial to come. One parent may withdraw emotionally or leave the family. Siblings may be born, grandparents may relocate, parents may gain or lose jobs, and illness or financial hardship may strike. More auspiciously, fathers may become more supportive of their partners and mothers may overcome depression or grow fonder of and more comfortable with the job of motherhood.

Controversy Regarding Expectations for Continuity

Early on, as research on attachment was beginning to produce findings that early attachment security in the Strange Situation predicted better child adjustment in later years, this research was criticized for neglecting to investigate the role of the rearing environment later in the child's life, when these children's adjustment was being re-evaluated.[24] Criticisms focused on the notion that a child's attachment classification—secure or insecure—can be considered an enduring characteristic that will have an automatic or inevitable impact on the course of children's future development, regardless of later events.[25]

Regrettably for the field, there is some validity for these criticisms.[26] A good many studies that concluded that attachment security predicts better later adjustment did not fully investigate the reasons for these findings. Given that there are theoretical reasons to believe that there would be continuity in adjustment, it has been easy for some to suggest that attachment security in infancy is a pathway for success in later life.

However, any student of logic will tell you that correlation does *not* necessarily imply causation; a third factor could be responsible for both findings. Neglecting this possibility is commonly referred to as the "post hoc fallacy." In the case of attachment, it could well be that good outcomes for securely attached children can be attributed to the fact that caregivers who earlier were sensitive have *continued to be* sensitively supportive.[27]

The criticism that attachment researchers too easily attribute later good adjustment to earlier security is in no way a fair critique of the whole field. Prominent researchers and attachment theorists have warned that it is a major misconception that Bowlby's attachment theory implies that there is a critical period for developing attachment security, and that the secure and the two insecure categories are fixed patterns.[28] Further, attachment researchers have asserted that a secure attachment does not "inoculate" a child from the effects of less sensitive parenting and other detrimental experiences that may arise later in life.[29]

Investigating Reasons for Continuity and Discontinuity

Some well-designed longitudinal studies have carefully sought to take into account the impact of changes in family circumstances and maternal sensitivity. These studies provide data regarding factors that result in what is termed "lawful discontinuity."[30] By lawful discontinuity, researchers refer to in-

stances in which changes in children's functioning can be explained by observed factors in the social and emotional environment.

A particularly informative study, conducted by the National Institute of
Child Health and Human Development, included over 1,000 economically
and racially diverse mother-child pairs.[31] Researchers had information about
the children's Strange Situation attachment security at fifteen months, their
mothers' sensitivity when interacting with children at twenty-four months,
and children's social competence, behavior problems, and language skills at
three years. In this study it was presumed that children's security of attachment at one year was indicative of mother's sensitivity around the time of the
Strange Situation Procedure. Not surprisingly, children who were securely
attached at one year and also had sensitive parenting at twenty-four months
had better developmental outcomes at three years, and those who were insecurely attached at one year and were observed to have relatively insensitive
parenting at the two-year assessment showed poorer developmental outcomes when aged three.

While continuity in sensitivity of parenting was found more often than
discontinuity, some inconsistencies over time were observed. This study was
unique in being able to compare the three-year-old adjustment of two groups
of children who—between the ages of one and two—had contrasting experiences with changing parental sensitivity, and ultimately showed different
patterns of attachment security. In the first group, children were securely
attached at fifteen months but then experienced insensitive parenting at age
two; in the second group, children were insecurely attached at fifteen months
but then experienced sensitive parenting at age two.

Changes in mothers' sensitivity, for better or worse, were predictable
from a survey of stressful events experienced by the family. The survey
included reports of entrances and exits of individuals from the household,
illness or job loss of a relative or close friend, moves, mother's job loss, and
financial stress. Mothers also reported their levels of depressive symptoms.
Changes in life stress and maternal depression accompanied changes in
mothers' sensitivity, with decreased stress resulting in greater sensitivity and
increased stress and depression accompanying lower sensitivity. Indeed, this
study clearly illustrated when "lawful discontinuities" occur.

When looking at whether children with early attachment security (and
presumed sensitive parenting) followed by later insensitive parenting did
better or worse at three years than children with the opposite developmental
history, the results were clear-cut. Children who had early insecure attachment followed by later sensitivity had more positive developmental outcomes when aged three than did children with early attachment security
followed by later insensitive care. Not surprisingly, children with inconsis-
tency in their experiences fell in between the two consistent groups when
looking at developmental outcomes at three years.

Clearly, secure attachment at age one did not buffer a child from the effects of later insensitive caregiving. In this study, continuity of development clearly depended on continuity in caregiving, and children who had earlier experienced insecure attachments were able to benefit from improved maternal sensitivity.

CHILDHOOD AND THE DEVELOPING BRAIN

As discussed earlier, individuals such as Allan Schore and Daniel Siegel have proposed that early attachment experiences have an impact on the developing brain. But, how significant and formative are these early influences on the brain, compared to experiences that come later in life?

Human brain development is uniquely slow.[32] Children are dependent on caretakers for many years, and they continue to experience significant brain growth for a very long time, compared with any other species. Researchers have pondered possible reasons for this prolonged childhood, and evolutionary theory provides a framework for considering the survival advantages of an extended period of immaturity.

Evolution and Attachment Theory

Bowlby introduced the concept of the "environment of evolutionary adaptiveness" in his discussion of attachment behaviors.[33] His view was that many aspects of infants' and mothers' behaviors were likely shaped by natural selection.[34] Bowlby concluded that anxiety over actual or threatened separation from mother and security in maintaining proximity to her must have been adaptive for infants.

The theoretical writings of Bowlby and Ainsworth focused on the evolutionary goal of ensuring an individual's survival through early childhood, and did not place much emphasis on other behaviors that would increase adult humans' fitness and ability to successfully reproduce.[35] In reading some of the attachment literature, a secure attachment comes across as representing the optimal preparation for a child's successful growth and development, and the impression is often that a secure attachment may be the best outcome for all children.[36] However, the reality is more complex.

While a secure attachment may be best for mental health, more recent evolutionary theories focus on how different parenting styles, leading to varying patterns of attachment, may be important in different environments. Robert Hinde, one of the ethologists who influenced Bowlby, has speculated about how particular parental styles may have evolved:

> In the longer term, we might expect natural selection to have shaped offspring
> to use parental styles as cues to the environmental conditions they will have to

face in their turn. For example, if maternal rejection is induced by a competitive social situation, those of her offspring who develop aggressive, non-altruistic temperaments may do better than those who do not. On the other hand, infants brought up in an equable social environment might do better to develop propensities for reciprocal altruism and cooperation.[37]

The notion that evolution has planned that mothers should not provide ideal infant and child care under all circumstances, but rather to adapt and adjust their investment depending on changing conditions, is an important one.[38]

In the early 1990s, the attachment researcher Jay Belsky, along with co-authors, made similar arguments about how patterns of child rearing can be seen as resulting from the general environment in which parents reside.[39] They proposed that rearing strategies reflect parents' attempts, made consciously or unconsciously, to prepare their children for the world that they are likely to encounter as adults. If parents live in a harsh environment and are beset by stressors, they will likely parent in an insensitive, rejecting, or inconsistent way. As a result, their children will develop an insecure attachment, and the working models they build of others will prepare them for a world in which the people around them cannot be relied upon.

In contrast, if parents experience less stress and have abundant resources, they are more likely to parent in a sensitive, nurturing way. Belsky and co-authors speculated that these offspring will grow up trusting others, mate cautiously, delay childbearing, and will form satisfactory and stable marriages. In a supportive environment, where parents can reasonably expect all of their children to survive into adulthood, it would make evolutionary sense to have a smaller number of children and to invest more heavily in each one.[40]

More recently, evolutionarily minded developmentalists pointed out the importance of considering whether the effects of different environmental conditions might affect the rate at which young people mature sexually and begin to have children. Greater harshness in the environment, as well as more unpredictability, would make it optimal for individuals at risk of dying before reaching reproductive age to develop faster, mature earlier, and engage in sexual activity sooner rather than later.[41]

Indeed, there is some evidence linking maternal harshness with earlier onset of menstruation (menarche) in girls. Mothers who scored high in harsh control on a questionnaire when their children were four and a half years old had daughters who reached menarche at an earlier age. Earlier menarche was associated with greater sexual and other risk taking. On the questionnaire, mothers with higher scores for harsh control reported that they spanked their children for wrong-doing, expected their child to obey without asking questions, expected the child to be quiet and respectful when adults were around, regarded respect for authority as the most important thing for the child to learn, believed praise spoiled the child, and did not give many hugs and kisses.[42] While security of attachment was not assessed, these parenting behaviors would likely result in insecure attachments.

Ethologists caution that it is important to recognize that behaviors that were adaptive in our "environment of evolutionary adaptiveness" are not necessarily adaptive today. Additionally, rearing behaviors that are best for the ultimate mental health of offspring may be different from behaviors that increase reproductive success. Sensitive mothering may produce happy, well-adjusted children, but relaxed, trusting children may not always have had the best reproductive success, at least during earlier periods of human evolution.[43]

Evolution and Our Prolonged Childhood

In an evolutionary framework, the pace of development would be the one that best prepared an individual to survive, reproduce, and successfully bring up a new generation. Researchers have theorized that longer developmental periods may provide more time for young children to develop better skills in a variety of areas, including being able to differentiate individuals and their motivations. Also, a longer period of childhood makes it more likely that a child will encounter multiple caregivers, which would result in a richer and more complex social environment.[44]

An additional evolutionary explanation for a prolonged period of development is that this would allow for humans to have great potential for adaptation to a changing environment.[45] The longer the period over which learning occurs, the better attuned the individual should be to his or her environment.[46]

We know very little about the kind of social structure and relationships that existed in our "environment of evolutionary adaptiveness." Thus, we can only speculate about the evolutionary processes that contributed to the different attachment patterns we find in children and to the variations in styles of parent-child interaction we observe today. However, if the ability to adapt to changing circumstances is optimal for humans to survive and prosper, then the observed changes in children's behavior following shifts in parental sensitivity that were discussed earlier in this chapter make good sense.

Given the importance of the capacity for change, it is perhaps no surprise that children can change their attachment patterns if caregivers change their behavior. In fact, it could be problematic if children did *not* adapt their behavior to changes in caregiving. In subsequent chapters, as we consider the research data as to how parenting behaviors—whether stable or changing—shape children's development and attachment patterns beyond infancy, it is useful to keep evolutionary theory in mind.

Attachment and Plasticity in the Brain

"Plasticity" refers to the brain's ability to change in response to learning. In essence, plasticity means that the brain is not constructed in an inflexible way, but can be molded and shaped by experience. Indeed, researchers have argued that "Behavior will lead to changes in brain circuitry, just as changes in brain circuitry will lead to behavioral modifications."[47] Plasticity is viewed as a basic, intrinsic property of the brain. While neural systems tend to be more plastic earlier in development than later,[48] this capacity is retained through the lifespan. Up to at least age thirty, important development continues in at least some regions of the brain.[49]

Researchers are only beginning to probe mechanisms in the brain that may contribute to attachment experiences. In thinking about areas in the brain where plasticity may be important for attachment, those that specialize in emotion processing are important to consider. One small region of the brain, the amygdala, is seen as important because it mediates many of the emotional difficulties seen in individuals who experience adversity in early life. Additionally, the amygdala is rich with stress hormone receptors, particularly during very early infancy.

There is a significant difference in the kinds of connections the amygdala has with higher brain regions during childhood compared to adolescence and adulthood.[50] The change to the adult forms of connectivity occurs at about ten years of age; before this age it is believed that there may be a sensitive period when modifications occur more easily.[51]

One pioneering study investigating reactivity of the amygdala looked at whether pictures of mother, or her actual presence, had an influence on amygdala functioning. A group of children aged ten and under, and another group of adolescents, were put into a magnetic resonance imaging (MRI) machine and asked to quickly push a button when they saw a smiling face, but not to react to sober faces. Photos of the child's mother and of a stranger were then shown. One can imagine that the experience of being alone inside an MRI machine provoked a certain amount of stress during the task.

Researchers found that children showed less reactivity in the amygdala when doing a performance task involving pictures of their mothers than when doing the task with photos of a stranger. This finding was interpreted as showing that the photo reminders of mother successfully "buffered" a potential stress reaction in the amygdala. And, intriguingly, children who benefitted more from the "maternal buffering" effect when in the MRI machine were those who reported a greater sense of security in their attachment with mother.[52]

Adolescents did not show a difference in response to photos of mother and stranger. The authors theorized that the maternal buffering effect may become internalized by adolescence. In childhood, caregivers may serve an external regulatory role while the neural circuitry supporting emotion regulation develops in childhood.

While we are only beginning to understand how the brain might allow for change in working models and emotional responses during the course of development, there are intriguing findings regarding brain development in children who have been raised for a period of time in orphanages, before being adopted. Children in orphanages, which are still found in some countries, typically have *no* stable caregiving figure to whom they can develop an attachment of any sorts, whether it be secure, insecure, or disorganized. Therefore, these children are deprived of a "species-expected" attachment figure; that is to say, they lack the consistent caregiver that our species evolved to expect during early childhood.

Previously institutionalized children show a number of differences in amygdala activity, and compared to other children they also show faster development of connections between the amygdala and higher cortical areas.[53] This finding has been interpreted as indicating that this sensitive period is prematurely shortened in children who have entirely lacked an attachment figure in early life.

Are Early Experiences Relevant to Later Development?

Given the fact that the prolonged period of childhood in humans provides opportunity for shaping and reshaping children's brains and behaviors, we can wonder whether parent-child interactions during the first year and resulting infant attachment patterns have any influence at all on later adjustment. Is it reasonable to expect that early positive working models and skills in affect regulation gained during the infancy might contribute *some* advantage to the child as he or she grows, even if families later go through hard times?

In the example of Riley presented at the beginning of this chapter, hard times did not arise until late childhood, and the solid parenting she received during her first ten years arguably gave this fictional character a significant advantage in weathering the storms that her family encountered when she was eleven. This is, of course, only one of the many possible life trajectories that a child may experience. One child may have a sensitive environment for the first year, followed by ten years of greater harshness; another may live five, ten, or fifteen years with supportive caregiving before the family encounters hardship. And, of course, children may start out living with adversity, but at some point their rearing environment may improve significantly. Research studies cannot investigate every possible life trajectory, but they can probe some general patterns.

In Chapter Four, when we begin considering findings from longitudinal studies that have followed the Child Veterans of the Strange Situation for a number of years, we will carefully examine findings regarding the influence of early attachment patterns on later development. Is there evidence for continuity in at least some aspects of development? Theories can guide research, but ultimately research must either support or discredit them.

NOTES

1. Keltner and Ekman, "The Science of 'Inside Out.'"
2. Attachment theory incorporates psychoanalytic thinking about the importance of defenses in relegating thoughts and feelings to the unconscious mind.
3. Perroud et al., "Functions and Timescale of Self-Cutting in Participants Suffering from Borderline Personality Disorder."
4. Bowlby, *Separation, Anxiety, and Anger*, 203.
5. Main, Kaplan, and Cassidy, "Security in Infancy, Childhood, and Adulthood," 67–69.
6. Ibid., 77.
7. Zelenko et al., "Heart Rate Correlates of Attachment Status in Young Mothers and Their Infants."
8. Ibid.
9. Spangler and Grossmann, "Biobehavioral Organization in Securely Attached and Insecurely Attached Infants."
10. Main and Weston, "Avoidance of the Attachment Figure in Infancy," 50–52; Cassidy, "Emotion Regulation," 235.
11. Ainsworth et al., *Patterns of Attachment*; Belsky, Rovine, and Taylor, "Pennsylvania Infant and Family Development Project."
12. Cassidy, "Emotion Regulation," 241.
13. Bowlby, *A Secure Base*, 130.
14. Thompson, "The Legacy of Early Attachments," 176.
15. Dodge and Garber, "Domains of Emotion Regulation," 9.
16. Thompson, "Socialization of Emotion and Emotional Regulation in the Family," 176.
17. Cassidy, "Emotion Regulation"; Schore, "Attachment, Affect Regulation, and the Developing Right Brain."
18. Schore and Sieff, "On the Same Wave-Length."
19. Leerkes, Blankson, and O'Brien, "Differential Effects of Maternal Sensitivity to Infant Distress and Nondistress on Social-Emotional Functioning," 763.
20. Schore, "Attachment, Affect Regulation, and the Developing Right Brain"; Siegel, "Attachment and Self-Understanding." (See also Center for the Developing Child, internet resource.)
21. Siegel, *The Developing Mind*, 4.
22. Gee et al., "Early Developmental Emergence of Human Amygdala–Prefrontal Connectivity after Maternal Deprivation," 9.
23. Ainsworth et al., *Patterns of Attachment*.
24. Lamb et al., "Security of Infantile Attachment as Assessed in the 'Strange Situation.'"
25. Lewis, Feiring, and Rosenthal, "Attachment over Time."
26. Waters et al., "Is Attachment Theory Ready to Contribute to Our Understanding of Disruptive Behavior Problems?"
27. Belsky and Fearon, "Early Attachment Security, Subsequent Maternal Sensitivity, and Later Child Development."
28. Sroufe, "The Role of Infant-Caregiver Attachment in Development," 24.
29. Waters et al., "Is Attachment Theory Ready to Contribute to Our Understanding of Disruptive Behavior Problems?"
30. Belsky, Fish and Isabella, "Continuity and Discontinuity in Infant Negative and Positive Emotionality."
31. Belsky and Fearon, "Early Attachment Security, Subsequent Maternal Sensitivity, and Later Child Development."

32. Tottenham, "The Importance of Early Environments for Neuro-Affective Development"; Konner, *The Evolution of Childhood*; Bogin, "Evolutionary Hypotheses for Human Childhood."

33. Bowlby, *Attachment and Loss*, 64.

34. We do not know precisely what conditions existed in our "environment of evolutionary adaptiveness," but it is presumed that social relationships in that environment would have much in common with those in the hunter-gatherer societies that remain today. (See Konner, *The Evolution of Childhood*; Lee and DeVore, "Problems in the Study of Hunters and Gatherers.")

35. Lamb et al., "Security of Infantile Attachment as Assessed in the 'Strange Situation,'" 143.

36. Hinde and Stevenson-Hinde, "Attachment."

37. Hinde, "Some Implications of Evolutionary Theory and Comparative Data for the Study of Human Prosocial and Aggressive Behavior," 25.

38. Konner, *The Evolution of Childhood*, 544.

39. Belsky, Steinberg, and Draper, "Childhood Experience, Interpersonal Development, and Reproductive Strategy."

40. Belsky, Fish, and Isabella, "Continuity and Discontinuity in Infant Negative and Positive Emotionality"; Belsky, "The Development of Human Reproductive Strategies."

41. Belsky, "The Development of Human Reproductive Strategies"; Ellis et al., "Fundamental Dimensions of Environmental Risk."

42. Belsky, Steinberg, Houts, Halpern-Felsher, and the NICHD Early Child Care Research Network, "The Development of Reproductive Strategy in Females."

43. Hinde and Stevenson-Hinde, "Attachment."

44. Charvet and Finlay, "Embracing Covariation in Brain Evolution."

45. Tottenham, "The Importance of Early Environments for Neuro-Affective Development."

46. While we have very limited understanding of all the forces that were at work during the course of early human evolution, one study found that it coincided with a period of rapid and repeated ecosystem restructuring caused by fluctuating changes in water availability. In such an environment, the ability to adapt to changes would be crucial for survival. (See Magill, Ashley, and Freeman, "Water, Plants and Early Human Habitats in Eastern Africa.")

47. Pascual-Leone et al., "The Plastic Human Brain Cortex," 379.

48. Lupien et al., "Effects of Stress throughout the Lifespan on the Brain, Behaviour and Cognition."

49. Konner, *The Evolution of Childhood*, 189.

50. Gee et al., "Early Developmental Emergence of Human Amygdala–Prefrontal Connectivity after Maternal Deprivation."

51. Tottenham, "The Importance of Early Environments for Neuro-Affective Development."

52. Gee et al., "Maternal Buffering of Human Amygdala Prefrontal Circuitry during Childhood but Not During Adolescence."

53. Gee et al., "Early Developmental Emergence of Human Amygdala–Prefrontal Connectivity after Maternal Deprivation."

REFERENCES

Ainsworth, Mary D. Salter, Mary C. Blehar, Everett Waters, and Sally N. Wall. *Patterns of Attachment: A Psychological Study of the Strange Situation*. New York: Wiley and Sons, 1978.

Belsky, Jay. "The Development of Human Reproductive Strategies: Progress and Prospects." *Current Directions in Psychological Science* 21, no. 5 (2012): 310–16.

Belsky, Jay, and R. M. Pasco Fearon. "Early Attachment Security, Subsequent Maternal Sensitivity, and Later Child Development: Does Continuity in Development Depend Upon Continuity of Caregiving?" *Attachment & Human Development* 4, no. 3 (2002): 361–87.

Belsky, Jay, Margaret Fish, and Russell A. Isabella. "Continuity and Discontinuity in Infant Negative and Positive Emotionality: Family Antecedents and Attachment Consequences." *Developmental Psychology* 27, no. 3 (1991): 421–31.

Belsky, Jay, Michael Rovine, and Dawn G. Taylor. "The Pennsylvania Infant and Family Development Project, III: The Origins of Individual Differences in Infant-Mother Attachment: Maternal and Infant Contributions." *Child Development* 55, no. 3 (1984): 718–28.

Belsky, Jay, Laurence Steinberg, and Patricia Draper. "Childhood Experience, Interpersonal Development, and Reproductive Strategy: An Evolutionary Theory of Socialization." *Child Development* 62, no. 4 (1991): 647–70.

Belsky, Jay, Laurence Steinberg, Renate M. Houts, Bonnie L. Halpern-Felsher, and the NICHD Early Child Care Research Network. "The Development of Reproductive Strategy in Females: Early Maternal Harshness→ Earlier Menarche→ Increased Sexual Risk Taking." *Developmental Psychology* 46, no. 1 (2010): 120.

Bogin, Barry. "Evolutionary Hypotheses for Human Childhood." *American Journal of Physical Anthropology* 104, no. 25 (1997): 63–89.

Bowlby, John. *Attachment and Loss: Vol. 1. Attachment.* New York: Basic Books, 1969/1982.

———. *A Secure Base: Clinical Applications of Attachment Theory.* New York: Basic Books, 1988.

———. *Separation, Anxiety, and Anger.* London: Hogarth Press, 1973.

Cassidy, Jude. "Emotion Regulation: Influences of Attachment Relationships." *Monographs of the Society for Research in Child Development* 59, no. 2–3 (1994): 228–49.

Center for the Developing Child; http://developingchild.harvard.edu/key_concepts/brain_architecture/.

Charvet, Christine J., and Barbara L. Finlay. "Embracing Covariation in Brain Evolution: Large Brains, Extended Development, and Flexible Primate Social Systems." *Progress in Brain Research* 195 (2012): 71–87.

Dodge, Kenneth A., and Judy Garber. "Domains of Emotion Regulation." In *The Development of Emotion Regulation and Dysregulation*, edited by Judy Garber and Kenneth A. Dodge, 3–11. Cambridge: Cambridge University Press, 1991.

Ellis, Bruce J., Aurelio José Figueredo, Barbara H. Brumbach, and Gabriel L. Schlomer. "Fundamental Dimensions of Environmental Risk." *Human Nature* 20, no. 2 (2009): 204–68.

Gee, Dylan G., Laurel J. Gabard-Durnam, Jessica Flannery, Bonnie Goff, Kathryn L. Humphreys, Eva H. Telzer, Todd A. Hare, Susan Y. Bookheimer, and Nim Tottenham. "Early Developmental Emergence of Human Amygdala–Prefrontal Connectivity after Maternal Deprivation." *Proceedings of the National Academy of Sciences* 110, no. 39 (2013): 15638–43.

Gee, Dylan G., Laurel Gabard-Durnam, Eva H. Telzer, Kathryn L. Humphreys, Bonnie Goff, Mor Shapiro, Jessica Flannery et al. "Maternal Buffering of Human Amygdala Prefrontal Circuitry during Childhood but Not During Adolescence." *Psychological Science* 25, no. 11 (2014): 2067–78.

Hinde, Robert A. "Some Implications of Evolutionary Theory and Comparative Data for the Study of Human Prosocial and Aggressive Behavior." In *Development of Anti-Social and Prosocial Behavior*, edited by Dan Olweus, Jack Block and Marian Radke-Yarrow, 13–32. Orlando, FL: Academic Press, 1986.

Hinde, Robert A., and Joan Stevenson-Hinde. "Attachment: Biological, Cultural and Individual Desiderata." *Human Development* 33, no. 1 (1990): 62–72.

Keltner, Dacher, and Paul Ekeman. "The Science of 'Inside Out.'" *The New York Times Sunday Review*, July 3, 2015, SR10; http://www.nytimes.com/2015/07/05/opinion/sunday/the-science-of-inside-out.html?_r=0 .

Konner, Melvin. *The Evolution of Childhood: Relationships, Emotion, Mind.* Cambridge, MA: Harvard University Press, 2010.

Lamb, Michael E., Ross A. Thompson, William P. Gardner, Eric L. Charnov, and David Estes. "Security of Infantile Attachment as Assessed in the 'Strange Situation': Its Study and Biological Interpretation." *Behavioral and Brain Sciences* 7, no. 01 (1984): 127–47.

Lee, Richard B., and Irven DeVore. "Problems in the Study of Hunters and Gatherers." In *Man the Hunter*, edited by Richard B. Lee and Irven DeVore. Chicago: Aldine-Atherton, 1968.

Leerkes, Esther M., A. Nayena Blankson, and Marion O'Brien. "Differential Effects of Maternal Sensitivity to Infant Distress and Nondistress on Social-Emotional Functioning." *Child Development* 80, no. 3 (2009): 762–75.

Lewis, Michael, Candice Feiring, and Saul Rosenthal. "Attachment over Time." *Child Development* 71, no. 3 (2000): 707–20.

Lupien, Sonia J., Bruce S. McEwen, Megan R. Gunnar, and Christine Heim. "Effects of Stress throughout the Lifespan on the Brain, Behaviour and Cognition." *Nature Reviews Neuroscience* 10, no. 6 (2009): 434–45.

Magill, Clayton R., Gail M. Ashley, and Katherine H. Freeman. "Water, Plants, and Early Human Habitats in Eastern Africa." *Proceedings of the National Academy of Sciences* 110, no. 4 (2013): 1175–80.

Main, Mary, Nancy Kaplan, and Jude Cassidy. "Security in Infancy, Childhood, and Adulthood: A Move to the Level of Representation." *Monographs of the Society for Research in Child Development* 50, no. 1/2 (1985): 66–104.

Main, Mary, and Donna R. Weston. "Avoidance of the Attachment Figure in Infancy: Descriptions and Interpretations." In *The Place of Attachment in Human Behavior*, edited by Colin M. Parkes and Joan Stevenson-Hinde, 203–17. New York: Basic Books, 1982.

Pascual-Leone, Alvaro, Amir Amedi, Felipe Fregni, and Lotfi B. Merabet. "The Plastic Human Brain Cortex." *Annual Review of Neuroscience* 28 (2005): 377–401.

Perroud, Nader, Karen Dieben, Rosetta Nicastro, Michel Muscionico, and Philippe Huguelet. "Functions and Timescale of Self-Cutting in Participants Suffering from Borderline Personality Disorder." *Journal of Personality Disorders* 26, no. 2 (2012): 267–79.

Schore, Allan N. "Attachment, Affect Regulation, and the Developing Right Brain: Linking Developmental Neuroscience to Pediatrics." *Pediatrics in Review* 26, no. 6 (2005): 204–17.

Schore, Allan N., and Daniella Sieff. "On the Same Wave-Length: How Our Emotional Brain Is Shaped by Human Relationships." In *Understanding and Healing Emotional Trauma: Conversations with Pioneering Clinicians and Researchers*, edited by Daniella F. Sieff, 11–136. London: Routledge, 2015.

Siegel, Daniel J. "Attachment and Self-Understanding: Parenting with the Brain in Mind." *Journal of Prenatal and Perinatal Psychology and Health*, 18, no. 4 (2004): 273–85.

———. *The Developing Mind, Second Edition: How Relationships and the Brain Interact to Shape Who We Are*. New York: Guilford Publications, 2012.

Spangler, Gottfried, and Klaus E. Grossmann. "Biobehavioral Organization in Securely and Insecurely Attached Infants." *Child Development* 64, no. 5 (1993): 1439–50.

Sroufe, L. Alan. "The Role of Infant-Caregiver Attachment in Development." In *Clinical Implications of Attachment*, edited by Jay Belsky and Teresa Nezworski, 18–38. Hillsdale, NJ: Erlbaum, 1988.

Thompson, Ross A. "The Legacy of Early Attachments." *Child Development* 71, no. 1 (2000): 145–52.

———. "Socialization of Emotion and Emotional Regulation in the Family." In *Handbook of Emotional Regulation*, edited by James J. Gross, 173–86. New York: The Guilford Press, 2014.

Tottenham, Nim. "The Importance of Early Environments for Neuro-Affective Development." *Current Topics in Behavioral Neurosciences Series* 16, (2014): 109–29.

Vandell, Deborah Lowe, Jay Belsky, Margaret Burchinal, Laurence Steinberg, and Nathan Vandergrift and the NICHD Early Child Care Research Network. "Do Effects of Early Child Care Extend to Age 15 Years? Results from the NICHD Study of Early Child Care and Youth Development." *Child Development* 81, no. 3 (2010): 737–56.

Waters, Everett, German Posada, Judith Crowell, and Keng-Ling Lay. "Is Attachment Theory Ready to Contribute to Our Understanding of Disruptive Behavior Problems?" *Development and Psychopathology* 5, no. 1–2 (1993): 215–24.

Zelenko, Marina, Helena Kraemer, Lynne Huffman, Miriam Gschwendt, Natalie Pageler, and Hans Steiner. "Heart Rate Correlates of Attachment Status in Young Mothers and Their

Infants." *Journal of the American Academy of Child & Adolescent Psychiatry* 44, no. 5
(2005): 470–6.

Chapter Four

Toddlers and Preschoolers

Bonds with Parents, Teachers, and Peers

To what extent do attachment patterns observed during the Strange Situation lay the groundwork for successful adaptation in a young child's next few years? As emphasized in the previous chapter, nothing is set in stone. As families experience successes and challenges, children's paths of development will be influenced, for better or for worse. But, for many children, particularly those in middle-class families who are not buffeted by economic woes or social stresses, there is considerable continuity in parenting and family life. In families where stability is the norm, what have we learned about the sequelae of secure and insecure attachments during infancy? How do attachment patterns prepare children for new stages and challenges?

We now have the benefit of a wealth of information mined from careful observations of Child Veterans of the Strange Situation Procedure, who have been followed by researchers until late adolescence or adulthood. Four major longitudinal studies began in the late 1970s or 1980s, one in Minnesota, one in Berkeley, California, a third in Germany, and a fourth in London.[1] In the London and German studies, children were observed with fathers as well as mothers in the Strange Situation, so researchers were able to see the ways in which fathers contributed to their children's development.[2] The Minnesota study continues to this day, with participants who are now in their forties. All told, hundreds of children were periodically interviewed and observed for two or more decades.

Children who participated in these longitudinal studies included some living in middle-class families (those in Germany, Berkeley, California, and London) and some living in poverty, who faced more stressors. While several cohorts of children were studied in Minnesota, including a middle-class group, the Minnesota study that will be referred to most frequently in this book was a very large and long-running study of families considered at risk for later caretaking problems. In this study that eventually continued over several decades, researchers gathered a group of pregnant mothers considered at risk due to factors such as poverty, low educational level (41 percent had not completed high school), lack of support, single parenthood, chaotic living conditions, and high life stress.[3] The researchers chose to study individuals who lived in "modest poverty"; the children and families were assumed to be at risk, but the risk was assumed to be less high compared to families who had lived in poverty for generations.

In the Minnesota "at risk" group, forty-four mothers were providing care that was sufficiently inadequate to be deemed "maltreatment" by the end of infancy. This was less than one-quarter of the original sample; over 267 mothers had been recruited before birth, and 212 remained in the sample when children were two years old.[4] Children whose care was deemed maltreatment had generally been referred to child protective services or had been assigned a social work caseworker.[5, 6, 7]

In addition to these major longitudinal studies, there have been many "short-term" longitudinal studies that have followed children over briefer periods of time, but have the benefit of showing how behavior at one age predicts adjustment at later ages.[8] These studies have looked at a variety of aspects of child and parent behavior, as well as at experiences children and families encounter, and in many ways have added to our understanding of children's emotional and social development.

So, we will begin to consider the life trajectories that children may take beyond their first year, drawing upon the comprehensive information that researchers in the United States and in Europe amassed in observations in psychological laboratories, homes, and schools. Different research teams, working on different continents, chose different points in time at which to observe children, and their observations were obtained in somewhat different ways. To create as comprehensive an understanding as possible, I will draw upon the work of a number of researchers who have studied how children relate to parents and to other significant figures in the toddler and preschool period.

Toddlers and Problem-Solving

One of the first studies to show the power of the Strange Situation to predict aspects of later adaptation was conducted in Minnesota by researchers who followed Strange Situation Child Veterans into their second year. In a Minnesota middle-class sample, two-year-olds and their mothers came back to the laboratory for a tool-using, problem-solving task.[9] When the task became too challenging, mothers were instructed to provide support for their toddlers, so researchers observed the quality of both mothers' supportive efforts and children's problem-solving behaviors. Children were rated on a number of variables, including compliance with mothers' suggestions, enthusiasm, and positive and negative affect.

The findings were striking. Children who had shown a secure attachment in the Strange Situation were more enthusiastic, more compliant with maternal requests, less inclined to ignore their mothers, spent less time away from the task, and exhibited less frustration. In contrast, children who had been insecure-avoidant (i.e., those who appeared to maintain a "stiff upper lip") showed more ignoring, more time away from the task, more aggression, and less enthusiasm and positive affect. As the researchers noted, these behaviors were quite different from those that had earned the insecure-avoidant children their label. In the Strange Situation, the insecure-avoidant children had spent a considerable time with toys, engaged the stranger, and tended to cry only when left entirely alone; they did not tantrum and were not petulant.

These findings have to be understood in context; mothers of children who had been securely attached in the Strange Situation generally continued to be rated higher on parenting variables related to supportiveness and quality of assistance. So, this study demonstrated that security in the Strange Situation predicts higher marks for *both* children and their mothers one year later in this stable middle-class sample. Thus, when parenting remained stable, attachment patterns were found to predict degree of success on a task designed to challenge the skills and persistence of the budding two-year-old problem-solver.

Preschoolers' Competence in the Classroom

Researchers in Minnesota and Germany had the opportunity to observe children's behavior in preschool. The Minnesota cohort studied was from the impoverished, longitudinal sample, while the German children were from middle-class backgrounds. In these two different groups, differing in socio-economic status as well as nationality, researchers sought to find out how well-adapted their Strange Situation Child Veterans had become.

Preschoolers in Minnesota

When children in the longitudinal Minnesota study of high-risk children were four or five years old, forty of them from the larger sample attended a university-affiliated preschool, providing the researchers with a unique window into their social and emotional lives.[10] Over the course of six weeks, a team of researchers observed the children carefully. In order to be able to study a large number of children with insecure histories, researchers disproportionately drew children with insecure attachments from their larger sample of almost 200 children. This allowed them to investigate how the children considered most at risk for behavioral and relationship difficulties were faring.

During the preschool day, members of the Minnesota team watched for signs of curiosity, self-confidence, self-reliance, self-esteem, empathy with others, social skills, and popularity. They also had extensive opportunity to observe behavior problems of children in the school setting. Perhaps not surprisingly, children with strength in one area typically were strong across the board. Children who were rated as having high self-esteem tended to also be highly curious, independent, able to cope with challenges flexibly, and to have good social skills. Further, they approached others in an open, positive manner and were empathic with other children.

Looking back at the histories of these preschoolers with their mothers, researchers found that indeed, children who had shown security with their mothers in the Strange Situation were as a group the most competent, socially skilled children, compared to those who had shown insecure attachment several years earlier. Certainly, there were exceptions, but for many children there was a clear pathway of capacity for positive social engagement in infancy leading to positive relationships in the preschool setting.[11]

In considering reasons why exceptions occurred, the Minnesota researchers were able to draw upon information about mothers and families obtained at three points in time between the Strange Situation Procedure and the preschool observations. Mothers had come into the laboratory with the children twice for problem-solving and teaching tasks, once when their children were two and later when they were three and a half. The mothers were also visited at home when children were two and a half years old.

With the information provided by these three observations of mothers, the Minnesota researchers were able to document that changes in children's quality of adjustment over time were predictable. Thus, as in the National Institute of Child Health and Human Development study discussed in the previous chapter,[12] children's changes in adjustment were lawfully associated with changes in maternal behavior. In the Minnesota study, when children who had been securely attached earlier showed problems in preschool, mothers had not seemed quite as sensitive and competent in the intervening visits, compared to mothers of still-thriving secure children. And, when children with histories of insecure attachments were doing better than expected, compared to those who still had problems, their mothers had appeared more involved and helpful in supporting them with frustrating tasks in the laboratory.

The Minnesota group's careful and frequent observations of mothers and children remind us that quality of caregiving continues to remain important as children grow and develop. But, it is important to recognize that the components of "good quality caregiving" may change, at least to some degree. In infancy, mothers who are sensitive to their infants' signals may or may not later be skilled at supporting autonomy in problem-solving with their toddler or preschooler. While connections between early behavior and later adjustment are intriguing, it is imperative that readers fully appreciate that development is an on-going process, with change possible at many points. I, along with many attachment theorists and researchers, believe that early quality of attachment is meaningful, but it is only the first chapter of many, in a life story that may take twists and turns.

Preschoolers in Germany

The thirty-nine children observed by the German researchers attended thirty-three different preschools and thirty-eight play groups.[13] Undaunted by the need to travel to so many different settings, the research team watched the children as they played, sometimes harmoniously and sometimes with conflict. In addition to observing the children, they involved them in a sort of "social perception" test that provided insight into their views of the social world.

These children had undergone the Strange Situation with mothers at twelve months and with fathers at eighteen months. About one-quarter of the group had been classified as having a secure attachment with both parents, and another quarter showed the insecure-avoidant pattern with both parents (i.e., they had appeared to maintain a "stiff upper lip"). The other half were secure with one parent and insecure-avoidant with the other. In this small sample only a handful of children had shown the insecure-resistant pattern as infants (i.e., they had appeared to resist consolation in the Strange Situation), and for one reason or another they did not attend preschool, so they could not be included in the study.

Like the Minnesota researchers, the German group found that children who had shown secure patterns of attachment in the Strange Situation were as a group more competent in preschool. The ratings of attachment security with mother more strongly predicted children's competency, but attachment security with father contributed as well. And, when security of attachment was the same with both parents, it seemed to have a cumulative affect; children with two secure attachment relationships in the first year of life were doing particularly well in preschool, and children with two insecure relationships were faring poorly by comparison.

Early Signs of Problems in the Minnesota and German Children

We have seen that in two different cultures, and in two groups differing in wealth and privilege, children with early histories of secure attachment stand out as a group as the more socially skilled of preschoolers. While there are exceptions, more often than not the securely attached children are having an easier time interacting with their preschool peers.

What specifically did researchers find when looking at children with insecure attachment histories? In both the German and the Minnesota samples, the insecure-avoidant children were beginning to look like a somewhat troubled group. When children started settling into the school year and as relationships started to form, the Minnesota researchers observed that these children had difficulty and often retreated from social activities, becoming increasingly isolated.[14] The insecure-resistant children did not isolate themselves as did the insecure-avoidant children. They were definitely interested in peers, often hovering near a group of children or attempting, with limited success, to engage in play with another child. These children had difficulty controlling their frustration and sometimes acted aggressively, for example, by flailing out in reaction to some provocation or perceived slight.

When children were asked to list three peers they liked and three they disliked, the insecure-avoidant children were more frequently named as being disliked. Common reasons given by their peers for disliking them were things like "She's mean" or "He hits." Indeed, these children were observed to be more aggressive than those from the other attachment groups.[15] In contrast, the children who had resisted consolation in the Strange Situation, those termed "insecure-resistant," did not act aggressive in an intentional way. While they did not tend to be named as being liked, they were not generally singled out for dislike, either.

Researchers were interested in any expressions of empathy children showed at these young ages.[16] They looked at all times when a child was injured or upset, and how children around the distressed child reacted. The most common reaction of those with secure histories was to be concerned and helpful, perhaps going to get a teacher. At these times, the insecure-resistant children tended to become very upset themselves, often going to a teacher for their own comforting. The researchers identified some troubling behavior among the insecure-avoidant children, who could be quite unempathetic. These children might do something to make the upset child feel worse, such as teasing a crying classmate or poking him in the stomach if he had complained of a stomachache.

Cartoon Interpretations as Windows into Children's View of the World

In an attempt to look at what might drive children to react in different ways in social situations, the German researchers used a clever "social perception" task. They asked children to respond to six cartoons showing typical kinds of social conflict preschool children experience. In two of the six cartoons, a problem arose from an accident; in one, a child's block construction fell over due to another child carelessly knocking into the table on which the structure was being built. In another two of the cartoons, it wasn't clear whether the problem was due to an accident or to an aggressive action. In the final two cartoons, the problem was clearly caused by a malicious act—for example, a child was depicted as punching another child in the face. The cartoon drawings are shown in Figure 4.1.[17]

The German researchers were interested in whether children with different attachment histories would interpret the cartoons differently. And, indeed, they did. Some children's responses were rated as "realistic or well meaning"—that is, they interpreted the cartoons accurately, or else gave the benefit of the doubt in ambiguous situations (or even when the cartoon showed clear-cut aggression). Other children's responses were labeled as "unrealistic or negative." In this group, there were two possibilities. Sometimes children saw aggressive intentions in ambiguous situations as well as in cases where the problem was clearly unintentional. Alternatively, children might see aggressive intentions only when the problem was ambiguous, or would give confusing responses, sometimes seeing aggression as accidental and accidents as intentional.

It probably comes as no surprise at this point that children with a secure attachment history were more likely to give "realistic or well meaning" responses. The "unrealistic or negative" responses came disproportionately from children with insecure attachment histories. As noted earlier, the German preschool study did not include children who had been insecure-resistant, so it was the children with an insecure-avoidant history who gave the more negative or less realistic descriptions of the cartoons.[18]

The German cartoon study showed that at this early age, children with different attachment histories were making sense of the world in different ways. The more frequent aggressive play during the school day observed in the insecure-avoidant children makes sense when we understand that these children actually see the world as a more hostile place. Often, in social interactions, it isn't entirely clear whether a peer or playmate has intended to do something hurtful, or whether a problem arose accidentally. If one expects that others are out to get you, why wouldn't one be ready to throw the first punch?

Preschool Bullying

The Minnesota study arranged for some play times where two children were paired, and found some very interesting results when they looked at fourteen pairs of children who had met with a play partner for at least seven play sessions.[19] Some children were paired with partners who had been judged as one-year-olds to have the same attachment pattern (secure, insecure-avoidant, or insecure-resistant), and other pairs combined children whose attachment status had been different. Over this period, pairs developed dis-

Figure 4.1. Pictorial stimuli used to illustrate aggression (negative consequences) toward objects (I–III) or persons (IV–VI), which is accidental (I, VI), intentional (III, V), or ambiguous (II, IV). *Source*: G.J. Suess, K. E. Grossmann, and L. Alan Sroufe, *International Journal of Behavioral Development*, volume 15, issue 1, p. 23. © 1992. Reprinted by permission of SAGE Publicatons, Ltd.

tinctively different ways of interacting together, depending upon their attachment histories.

The researchers were particularly intrigued by patterns of what they termed "victimization" that developed in some relationships. The play of two boys, whom I will here call "Sam" and "Ted," illustrates victimization well. In an early session, Sam begins calling Ted names and whispering "naughty" words: "bugger nose, bugger face, hey poop," and so forth. After four minutes of this, Sam suddenly becomes more hostile, alternating between ignoring Ted and provoking him by taking Ted's toys and either throwing them or saying they belong to him. Finally, Ted hesitantly calls Sam a liar. In response, Sam acts shocked saying, "Oh, you said a naughty word. I'm telling my momma. You said bad words. I'm telling the teacher. I'm gonna tell everyone!" while Ted becomes confused and upset.[20]

More victimization between these two boys is illustrated in another play session:

> Sam and Ted pretend they are at the doctor's office. Sam takes the role of doctor and Ted takes the role of patient. Sam wants to give Ted a shot with a play hypodermic needle. Ted does not want a shot but Sam reassures him, promising "it won't hurt." He then gradually presses harder and harder with the plastic needle until Ted is finally in pain and cries out "ouch!" Sam then smiles and says "It don't hurt!" gives Ted the needle, and walks away.[21]

Sadly, this basic pattern—with Sam being the aggressor and Ted the passive victim—was repeated over and over by these two boys. In fact, victims typically had an active role in sustaining a pattern of victimization, as illustrated in an interaction between two other boys:

> After a pattern of victimization between two boys (Robert victimizing Andrew) had been clearly established, Robert began a session by playing independently of Andrew. After less than one minute of this, Andrew went over to Robert and in a pleading voice said. "Why don't you tease me, Robert? I won't get mad."[22]

It seems that poor Robert, at this tender age, had figured out the way to get attention from Andrew.

Which children tended to develop victimization relationships? Strikingly, if one of the children in a pair had a secure attachment history, as was the case with eight dyads, there was no victimization. But, in five of the six instances where two children with insecure histories were paired, an aggressor-victim relationship developed. When one of the insecure children had been insecure-resistant, he or she inevitably became the victim, with the insecure-avoidant taking the aggressor role. Only in the one case where two insecure-resistant children were paired did no victimization take place. When two insecure-avoidant children were paired, a victimization relationship still developed; the weaker of the two usually moved into the victim role. In one such play dyad with two girls, the two girls alternated in and out of the victim role several times during the series of play sessions. [23]

When two children with different attachment histories were paired, a variety of outcomes were possible. If a secure child was paired with an insecure-avoidant child, either the two of them would engage in what researchers termed "counter-assertiveness" or else a mutual distance was maintained. Those with secure histories tended to form nurturing relationships with insecure-resistant children; they never victimized them. When two insecure-resistant children were paired, the play may have been very subdued, but victimization was not observed. [24]

Relationships with Teachers

In the Minnesota study, teachers were asked to write a phrase descriptive of each child, summarizing the most outstanding impression they had formed. Teachers' statements were classified by an independent coder. Children who had been insecure-avoidant in the Strange Situation fell into groups summarized as "hostile," "isolated," or "disconnected," while children in the insecure-resistant group were classified either as generally "impulsive" or "helpless." [25]

Children's behavior clearly tended to elicit responses from teachers that were consistent with their attachment histories. Securely attached children were able to meet their teachers' age-appropriate expectations, and were treated warmly. Teachers also had positive attitudes towards those with insecure-resistant histories, but tended to be overly nurturing, to the point of infantilizing them. With children who had insecure-avoidant histories, teachers showed low warmth, high controllingness, and low expectations for compliance. [26] As the researchers noted, "Whenever a child so infuriated a teacher that he or she wanted to isolate the child in another room or in the corner, it was inevitable that this child had a history of chronic unavailability or rejection [and had been an insecure-avoidant infant]." [27] It seemed that children elicited reactions from teachers that could perpetuate the non-optimal relationships they had had with their parents.

The Minnesota researchers also gathered information about the degree to which children were appropriately dependent on teachers, compared to being overly dependent. [28] Somewhat surprisingly, *both* groups of children judged as insecurely attached in the Strange Situation were considered overly dependent on their preschool teachers, compared to those who had been securely attached. Dependency in the insecure-resistant children does not seem surprising, given that in the Strange Situation these children had been preoccupied with mother and showed anger-tinged clinginess.

More surprising is the finding that children with an insecure-avoidant history (those children who had appeared to maintain a "stiff upper lip" in the Strange Situation) showed greater dependency on teachers in preschool. This finding provides further reason to believe that these children's tendency to ignore, turn away from, or move away from their mothers in the reunion episode of the Strange Situation was based on the expectation that mother would not provide comfort, rather than on the fact that they did not desire comfort.[29] Consistent with this, it is noteworthy that in their interactions with teachers, children with an insecure-avoidant history did not always show dependency. It was exactly when they were most in need of comfort, such as when they were injured or upset, that they tended to choose *not* to go to a teacher for help.

The insecure-avoidant children's greater dependence on teachers when they were not particularly distressed (for example, during story time, when they might choose to sit next to a teacher or in a teacher's lap)[30] shows they were not inherently independent children. In fact, as the researchers noted, "When a later opportunity arises for contact with a nurturing adult, available over a period of time, these children show their underlying dependency needs."[31]

COGNITIVE AND LANGUAGE DEVELOPMENT

Early studies looking at whether attachment patterns influenced cognitive abilities in preschoolers found little evidence for this notion. However, it turned out that there was a fairly significant relationship between attachment and language ability. Securely attached children were found to have richer language skills during the early years.[32]

Researchers using data from the National Institute of Child Health and Human Development Study of Early Child Care were able to take advantage of this large sample to look more closely at three-year-olds' language ability in different attachment groups.[33] Children with insecure-avoidant attachment histories turned out to be significantly weaker in language comprehension and in expressive and receptive language. Children who were securely attached appeared to be protected from the impact of risk when language skills were assessed. In contrast to the other categories, increasing social risks did not impact their language abilities. In the other insecure attachment groups, high levels of risk did impact their language skills.

Why should secure attachment lead to better language skills? This is largely a matter of conjecture. The fact that language is a cognitive ability that is fundamentally social may be a central reason. Perhaps securely attached children interact and communicate more with their parents, and thus are more motivated to explore using language. Alternatively, perhaps parents

of insecurely attached children less frequently respond to their children's
verbalizations, and thus do not encourage their children's use of language.[34]

OVERALL BEHAVIORAL ADJUSTMENT

Does security of attachment predict behavior problems during early childhood? The evidence is not clear-cut. Early studies of children from disadvantaged, high-risk samples found that insecurely attached children had higher
rates of behavior problems.[35] However, there was limited evidence for this in
middle-class samples.[36]

Why should this be? One suggestion put forth in an early study was that
children in more disadvantaged families may have fewer chances for com-
pensatory relationships, such as with a warm, supportive father.[37] To better
understand what factors might explain the finding of more behavior problems
in children from disadvantaged groups, researchers studied three-year-olds
from the large National Institute of Child Health and Human Development
Study of Early Child Care data set.[38] With this sample of close to 1,000
children, researchers were able to look more closely at how various kinds of
risks increased the likelihood of behavior problems in children with different
patterns of attachment security.

About 45 percent of children lived with no risk factors, but the rest had
one, two, or more risks. Looking at a total of nine possible risk factors,
researchers found that challenges such as maternal depression, parenting
stress, low social support, and low income had a cumulative impact on behavior problems. They also identified children with insecure-avoidant classifications as being the most sensitive to risk factors. Compared to the other
groups, children with insecure-avoidant histories in the Strange Situation
Procedure needed fewer risk factors to increase rates of behavior problems.
Thus, they appeared as a group to be more vulnerable to environmental
challenges.

The findings that (at least in the absence of significant risk factors) insecure attachments do not necessarily predict behavior problems is an important one. We must be careful not to assume that insecurity in attachment
means a child will be poorly adjusted overall. Children with insecure attachment histories *may* be at risk of behavioral difficulties, at least under some
circumstances, but we need to look at other risks which may contribute to
poorer outcomes. Protective factors need to be considered as well.[39]

CHILDREN WITH DISORGANIZED ATTACHMENT

As readers may recall from Chapter Two, disorganized attachment was not
identified until Mary Ainsworth's student Mary Main described this pattern

in the mid-1980s. Thus, the longitudinal studies that began in the 1970s did not code for disorganized attachment behaviors in the Strange Situation. Disorganized attachment, which is distinguished by odd, contradictory behaviors during the reunion episode, is found much more commonly in highly stressed, low-income families than in middle-class families, and there is evidence that it is associated with frightening or frightened parenting behaviors.

When disorganized attachment is identified, it is often, but not always, viewed as a sort of "add-on" to one of the three major categories.[40] For example, a child might generally appear insecure-avoidant, but at times during the reunion show behaviors that are disorganized. These children may be classified as both insecure-avoidant and disorganized. Interestingly, some children who show moments of disorganization may otherwise show a secure attachment; these children more often come from low-risk settings.[41]

How do children with disorganized attachment fare as preschoolers? In an important study of high-risk children where insecure-avoidant and disorganized attachment were looked at as distinct categories, disorganized attachment was the most likely attachment classification to predict deviant levels of hostility in preschool as rated by teachers. Children with avoidant classifications showed levels of hostility intermediate between disorganized and secure.[42] Preschoolers with highly hostile behavior were six times more likely to have been classified as disorganized in the Strange Situation than to have been classified as secure.[43] Clearly, this is a group of children that may be very much at risk for social and emotional problems.

THE POTENTIAL FOR CHANGE

As hostile, rejecting, and just plain nasty as a preschool child's behavior can be, it is critical to recognize that personality patterns are far from firmly established at this age. Without intervention, there is a risk that these characteristics will solidify into an antisocial personality pattern. However, experiences of sensitive caregiving beyond infancy can have a striking impact on a child's developmental course.

Interventions in School

The Minnesota study provides an example of how teachers can play a role in giving at-risk children a sense of themselves as valuable and of adults as protective and caring. The researchers described an intervention with a boy whom I will call "Tommy." Tommy was a four-year-old who was malicious and who took pleasure at others' distress, fearlessly contesting wills with teachers, and giving the impression of being beyond reach.

Tommy's sensitive teachers learned to see opportunities for closeness with him and to disconfirm his feelings of low self-worth by not rejecting him. His teachers worked hard to prevent him from engaging in hostile behavior, and when he had to be separated from other children, a teacher would stay with him. Tommy eventually formed a strong attachment to one teacher and made remarkable progress towards allowing himself to become close and to learn the rewards that relationships can provide.[44]

Interventions in Therapy

Years ago, I got a call at my private office from a young mother of a five-year-old girl whom I will call "Karen." In kindergarten, Karen's teacher said she was fresh, demanding, mean, lied, and, at one time or another during the school year, had made "pretty much everyone in the class cry."

When I met with Allison, Karen's mother, I learned that Allison had unintentionally become pregnant during her freshman year of college, and had dropped out of school in order to raise her child. The parents ended their relationship shortly after Karen was born, and Karen's father rarely visited with her.

Allison was a young woman who maintained a cool and unemotional veneer. She was not very comfortable in a therapist's office, but was motivated to help her daughter. I came to learn that before her pregnancy with Karen, Allison had been a talented student. However, even though she very much wanted to earn a Bachelor's degree, she turned down the offer of a relative to care for the child until she finished college. I was moved by Allison's motivation to directly care for her daughter.

When Karen had started kindergarten, her mother began to attend college part-time, in addition to her full-time job. When they came in together for therapy sessions, I could see that Allison was chronically exhausted. Beyond that, she seemed to have difficulty being responsive and emotionally open with her daughter. But, in family therapy, mom worked hard to try to understand her daughter's feelings, and also to provide some quality time at home. Karen was highly responsive to her mother's attention.

Six months later, Karen began first grade. After a month of school, I spoke with her teacher, who told me that Karen got along with all of her peers, and was beginning to develop a couple of friendships. Karen had clearly turned a corner, and I was hopeful that she would continue in this positive trajectory. For Karen, it seemed clear that positive attention from her mother, and her mother's effort to be more emotionally available, paid off handsomely.

The story of Karen and her mother provides yet another reminder that parental qualities of "insensitivity" and "unresponsiveness" reflect parents' own struggles. Some difficulties may come from current stressors, and others have their origins in parents' emotional histories. As noted earlier in this chapter, additional stressors exacerbate already existing relationship difficulties.

In the next chapter, we will move to exploring parents' emotions and characteristic ways of relating. Adults come to the job of parenting with their own histories of attachment, which have origins in their lives as infants and growing children. As it turns out, there are often patterns from one generation to the next that are remarkably similar.

NOTES

1. Sroufe et al., *The Development of the Person*; Main, Hesse, and Kaplan, "Predictability of Attachment Behavior and Representational Processes at 1, 6, and 19 Years of Age"; Grossman, Grossman, and Kindler, "Early Care and the Roots of Attachment and Partnership Representations"; Steele and Steele, "Understanding and Resolving Emotional Conflict."

2. Grossman et al., "German Children's Behavior towards Their Mothers at 12 Months and Their Fathers at 18 Months in Ainsworth's Strange Situation"; Steele, Steele, and Fonagy, "Associations among Attachment Classifications of Mothers, Fathers, and Their Infants."

3. Erickson, Sroufe, and Egeland, "The Relationship between Quality of Attachment and Behavior Problems in Preschool in a High-Risk Sample."

4. Sroufe et al., *The Development of the Person*, 52.

5. Ibid., 61.

6. There were four patterns of maltreatment identified: physical abuse (hitting, beating, burning, or hurting the child in some other way), physical neglect (failure to provide adequate care in terms of food, shelter, clothing, or supervision), psychological unavailability (a complete lack of emotional engagement or emotional responsibility for the child), and verbal abuse (chronic verbal expression of hostility or derision towards the child, or chronic yelling and verbal threats).

7. When it began, this program was called the "Minnesota Mother-Child Interaction Project." Eventually, it was renamed "The Minnesota Study of Risk and Adaptation from Birth to Adulthood."

8. E.g., Belsky, "Attachment Theory and Research in Ecological Perspective."

9. Matas, Arend, and Sroufe, "Continuity of Adaptation in the Second Year."

10. Sroufe et al., *The Development of the Person*.

11. Ibid.; Sroufe, "Infant-Caregiver Attachment and Patterns of Adaptation in Preschool."

12. Belsky and Fearon, "Early Attachment Security, Subsequent Maternal Sensitivity, and Later Child Development."

13. Suess, Grossmann, and Sroufe, "Effects of Infant Attachment to Mother and Father on Quality of Adaptation in Preschool."

14. Sroufe, "Infant-Caregiver Attachment and Patterns of Adaptation in Preschool."

15. Erickson, Sroufe, and Egeland, "The Relationship between Quality of Attachment and Behavior Problems in Preschool in a High-Risk Sample."

16. Sroufe, "Infant-Caregiver Attachment and Patterns of Adaptation in Preschool."

17. Suess, Grossmann, and Sroufe, "Effects of Infant Attachment to Mother and Father on Quality of Adaptation in Preschool," 49.

18. Ibid., 56.

19. Troy and Sroufe, "Victimization among Preschoolers," 167.

20. Ibid., 168–169.

21. Ibid., 168.

22. Ibid., 169.

23. Ibid., 169.

24. Sroufe et al., *The Development of the Person*.

25. Sroufe, "Infant-Caregiver Attachment and Patterns of Adaptation in Preschool."
26. Elicker, Englund, and Sroufe, "Predicting Peer Competence and Peer Relationships in Childhood from Early Parent-Child Relationships."
27. Sroufe, "Infant-Caregiver Attachment and Patterns of Adaptation in Preschool," 76.
28. Sroufe, Fox, and Pancake, "Attachment and Dependency in Developmental Perspective."
29. Ibid., 1625.
30. Sroufe, "Infant-Caregiver Attachment and Patterns of Adaptation in Preschool," 61.
31. Sroufe, Fox, and Pancake, "Attachment and Dependency in Developmental Perspective," 1625.
32. van IJzendoorn, Dijkstra, and Bus, "Attachment, Intelligence, and Language."
33. Belsky and Fearon, "Infant–Mother Attachment Security, Contextual Risk, and Early Development."
34. Ibid., 294.
35. Erickson, Sroufe, and Egeland, "The Relationship between Quality of Attachment and Behavior Problems in Preschool in a High-Risk Sample"; Shaw and Vondra, "Infant Attachment Security and Maternal Predictors of Early Behavior Problems."
36. Bates, Maslin, and Frankel, "Attachment Security, Mother-Child Interaction, and Temperament as Predictors of Behavior-Problem Ratings at Age Three Years"; Fagot and Kavanagh, "The Prediction of Antisocial Behavior from Avoidant Attachment Classifications."
37. Bates, Maslin, and Frankel, "Attachment Security, Mother-Child Interaction, and Temperament as Predictors of Behavior-Problem Ratings at Age Three Years."
38. Belsky and Fearon, "Infant–Mother Attachment Security, Contextual Risk, and Early Development."
39. Ibid.
40. Main and Solomon, "Procedures of Identifying Infants as Disorganized/Disoriented During the Ainsworth Strange Situation."
41. Lyons-Ruth, Alpern, and Repacholi, "Disorganized Infant Attachment Classification and Maternal Psychosocial Problems as Predictors of Hostile-Aggressive Behavior in the Preschool Classroom."
42. In studies of children from high-risk populations which assigned both disorganized and an alternate classification for children, insecure-avoidant was the most common alternative classification.
43. Lyons-Ruth, Alpern, and Repacholi, "Disorganized Infant Attachment Classification and Maternal Psychosocial Problems as Predictors of Hostile-Aggressive Behavior in the Preschool Classroom."
44. Sroufe, "Infant-Caregiver Attachment and Patterns of Adaptation in Preschool," 77.

REFERENCES

Bates, John E., Christine A. Maslin, and Karen A. Frankel. "Attachment Security, Mother-Child Interaction, and Temperament as Predictors of Behavior-Problem Ratings at Age Three Years." *Monographs of the Society for Research in Child Development* 1/2, no. 50 (1985): 167–93.

Belsky, Jay. "Attachment Theory and Research in Ecological Perspective: Insights from the Pennsylvania Infant and Family Development Project and the NICHD Study of Early Child Care." In *Attachment from Infancy to Adulthood: The Major Longitudinal Studies*, edited by Klaus. E. Grossmann, Karin Grossmann, and Everett Waters, 71–97. New York: Guilford, 2005.

Belsky, Jay, and R. M. Pasco Fearon. "Early Attachment Security, Subsequent Maternal Sensitivity, and Later Child Development: Does Continuity in Development Depend upon Continuity of Caregiving?" *Attachment & Human Development* 4, no. 3 (2002a): 361–87.

———. "Infant–Mother Attachment Security, Contextual Risk, and Early Development: A Moderational Analysis." *Development and Psychopathology* 14, no. 2 (2002b): 293–310.

Elicker, James, Michelle Englund, and L. Alan Sroufe. "Predicting Peer Competence and Peer Relationships in Childhood from Early Parent-Child Relationships." In *Family-Peer Relationships: Modes of Linkage*, edited by Ross W. Parke and Gary W. Ladd, 77–106. Hillsdale, NJ: Erlbaum, 1992.

Erickson, Martha Farrell, L. Alan Sroufe, and Byron Egeland. "The Relationship between Quality of Attachment and Behavior Problems in Preschool in a High-Risk Sample." *Monographs of the Society for Research in Child Development* 50, no. 1/2 (1985): 147–66.

Fagot, Beverly I., and Kate Kavanagh. "The Prediction of Antisocial Behavior from Avoidant Attachment Classifications." *Child Development* 61, no. 3 (1990): 864–73.

Grossmann, Klaus E., Karin Grossmann, Franz Huber, and Ulrike Wartner. "German Children's Behavior towards Their Mothers at 12 Months and Their Fathers at 18 Months in Ainsworth's Strange Situation." *International Journal of Behavioral Development* 4, no. 2 (1981): 157–81.

Grossmann, Karin, Klaus E. Grossmann, and Heinz Kindler. "Early Care and the Roots of Attachment and Partnership Representations: The Bielefeld and Regensburg Longitudinal Studies." In *Attachment from Infancy to Adulthood: The Major Longitudinal Studies*, edited by Klaus. E. Grossmann, Karin Grossmann, and Everett Waters, 98–136. New York: The Guilford Press, 2005.

Lyons-Ruth, Karlen, Lisbeth Alpern, and Betty Repacholi. "Disorganized Infant Attachment Classification and Maternal Psychosocial Problems as Predictors of Hostile-Aggressive Behavior in the Preschool Classroom." *Child Development* 64, no. 2 (1993): 572–85.

Main, Mary, Erik Hesse, and Nancy Kaplan. (2005). "Predictability of Attachment Behavior and Representational Processes at 1, 6, and 19 Years of Age: The Berkeley Longitudinal Study." In *Attachment from Infancy to Adulthood: The Major Longitudinal Studies*, edited by Klaus. E. Grossmann, Karin Grossmann, and Everett Waters, 245–304. New York: Guilford, 2005.

Main, Mary, and Judith Solomon. "Procedures of Identifying Infants as Disorganized/Disoriented During the Ainsworth Strange Situation." In *Attachment in the Preschool Years: Theory, Research, and Intervention*, edited by Mark T. Greenberg, Dante Ciccetti, and Mark E. Cummings, 121–60. Chicago: University of Chicago Press, 1990.

Matas, Leah, Richard A. Arend, and L. Alan Sroufe. "Continuity of Adaptation in the Second Year: The Relationship between Quality of Attachment and Later Competence." *Child Development* 49, no. 3 (1978): 547–56.

Shaw, Daniel S., and Joan I. Vondra. "Infant Attachment Security and Maternal Predictors of Early Behavior Problems: A Longitudinal Study of Low-Income Families." *Journal of Abnormal Child Psychology* 23, no. 3 (1995): 335–57.

Sroufe, L. Alan. "Infant-Caregiver Attachment and Patterns of Adaptation in Preschool: The Roots of Maladaptation and Competence." *Minnesota Symposium in Child Psychology* 16 (1983): 41–83.

Sroufe, L. Alan, Byron Egeland, Elizabeth A. Carlson, and W. Andrew Collins. *The Development of the Person: The Minnesota Study of Risk and Adaptation from Birth to Adulthood.* New York: The Guilford Press, 2005.

Sroufe, L. Alan, Nancy E. Fox, and Van R. Pancake. "Attachment and Dependency in Developmental Perspective." *Child Development* 54, no. 6 (1983): 1615–27.

Steele, Howard, and Miriam Steele. "Understanding and Resolving Emotional Conflict: The London Parent-Child Project." In *Attachment from Infancy to Adulthood: The Major Longitudinal Studies*, edited by Klaus. E. Grossmann, Karin Grossmann, and Everett Waters, 137–64. New York: Guilford, 2005.

Steele, Howard, Miriam Steele, and Peter Fonagy. "Associations among Attachment Classifications of Mothers, Fathers, and Their Infants." *Child Development* 67, no. 2 (1996): 541–55.

Suess, Gerhard J., Klaus E. Grossmann, and L. Alan Sroufe. "Effects of Infant Attachment to Mother and Father on Quality of Adaptation in Preschool: From Dyadic to Individual Organization of Self." *International Journal of Behavioral Development* 15, no. 1 (1992): 43–65.

Troy, Michael, and L. Alan Sroufe. "Victimization among Preschoolers: Role of Attachment Relationship History." *Journal of the American Academy of Child & Adolescent Psychiatry* 26, no. 2 (1987): 166–72.

van IJzendoorn, Marinus H., Jarissa Dijkstra, and Adriana G. Bus. "Attachment, Intelligence, and Language: A Meta-Analysis." *Social Development* 4, no. 2 (1995): 115–28.

Chapter Five

Mothers, Fathers, and Their Own Histories of Attachment

What have we learned about how parents' earlier experiences with their own caretakers influence interactions with their children? We now know quite a lot, as will be described in this chapter.

> Susan (William's mother) appears to be more interested in what 3-year-old William does than in who he is. When he cries in frustration because he can't make a toy work the way he wants it to, she says things like "You're smarter than that" and "Just keep trying—you'll get it"—and stays where she is seated across the room. To another adult on hand, she might add, "I was just like that when I was his age, and my mother made me keep at it till I got it right. It's how I've gotten where I am today."[1]

In this vignette, when William cries in frustration, Susan does not understand his distress as a signal that he needs assistance and comfort. Because of her own early experiences, it is hard for her to recognize that a little more help from her would likely allow her son to happily master the challenging toy. Susan is quite clearly well-intentioned, and truly feels that early lessons in self-reliance will prepare one for life success. That, as she tells us, is the lesson that her mother taught her. Yet, as we will see in later chapters, research does not support the view that withholding support is the best approach to encouraging competency and independence.

The glimpse we have of Susan's parenting—she tends not to respond to William's distress and to his cries for help—suggests William likely would have been found to be classified as an insecure-avoidant child if he participated in the Strange Situation Procedure with Susan when he was a one-year-old.[2] Might Susan herself have attempted to maintain a "stiff upper lip" and

been judged insecure-avoidant if she had been observed in this same laboratory procedure with her own mother when a young child? And, is there
something about her manner of thinking and feeling that suggests she might
be judged a grown-up variant of this attachment pattern? In thinking about
these question, issues to ponder include:

- How would we start to investigate attachment variations in an adult?
- Do parents and their children typically share similarities in their sense of
  attachment security, and hence tend to receive similar classifications?
- Does Susan have working models of attachment that influence the way she
  relates to others—not only her children, but also romantic partners and
  friends?

LEARNING ABOUT PARENTS' MINDS

John Bowlby's interest in human attachments was not limited to the bonds
between adults and young children. Bowlby asserted that "Evidence is accumulating that human beings of all ages are happiest and able to deploy their
talents to best advantage when they are confident that, standing behind them,
there are one or more trusted persons who will come to their aid should
difficulties arise."[3] Bowlby called these trusted persons "attachment figures"
and asserted that throughout life they provide an individual with a secure
base from which to explore.

Adults come to the job of parenting with the history of having had attachment relationships with parents or other caregivers. And, as parents, most
people rely for support on one or more individuals. In adulthood, attachment
figures may be partners, parents, friends, or, at some times in their lives,
psychotherapists.

Until the mid-1980s, researchers had no systematic methods to probe and
describe adults' working models of attachment. Then, researchers in two
different areas of psychology independently devised methods for assessing adult attachment. Both groups of researchers were inspired by John
Bowlby's theorizing and by Mary Ainsworth's identification of three distinct
patterns of attachment in infants.[4] Researchers in the two areas had different
objectives for working to describe and understand adult attachment status,
and the work of these researchers and those they inspired have contributed to
our understanding of attachment in quite different ways.

The first approach to assessing adults' attachment status was spearheaded
by Mary Ainsworth's student Mary Main. Main, like Ainsworth, was trained
in developmental psychology, and she is now carrying on Ainsworth's legacy as a professor of psychology at the University of California, Berkeley.
Mary Main and the graduate students and colleagues who worked with her

were interested in devising an adult assessment tool that would describe the minds of adults who were parents. Specifically, the goal was to characterize individual differences in the minds of parents who were raising children with different patterns of attachment.

The adult measure Main and her graduate students Carol George and Nancy Kaplan developed—simply titled "The Adult Attachment Interview" (AAI)[5]—has turned out to provide a remarkable window into the ways parents can be expected to interact with their young children. Like the Strange Situation Procedure, this interview has become a well-known and widely used measure; when a last accounting was made in 2009, over 10,000 AAI's had been conducted, transcribed, and analyzed.[6] Understanding the AAI helps us to appreciate the link between mothers' and fathers' personal histories and their approach to parenting.

Mary Ainsworth, Mary Main, and other developmental psychologists who continued Ainsworth's work were focused on child development and parenting. Understanding romantic relationships was not a priority in their research. But, this became a topic of considerable interest to two social/ personality psychologists, Cindy Hazan and Phillip Shaver. In a 1987 article entitled "Romantic Love Conceptualized as an Attachment Process," Hazan and Shaver proposed that Bowlby's theory, which primarily focused on parent-child attachment, might offer a great deal to help understand love, loneliness, and grief at other points in the life cycle.[7] They believed that Bowlby's notions about mental models of self and others likely explained continuity in relationship "style" (as they termed it) over time.

The social/personality psychologists shared an assumption with Mary Main and other developmental psychologists that one would find adult variants of the three major child attachment patterns identified by Mary Ainsworth: secure, insecure-avoidant, and insecure-resistant. And, despite using very different methods, researchers from the two different branches of psychology succeeded in finding adult groups that showed similarities to the three child attachment categories.

Different Methods Lead to Different Findings

As it (unexpectedly) turned out, the methods developed by the developmental and social/personality psychologists did not lead to solid agreement as to what was a "secure-like," an "avoidant-like," or a "resistant-like" adult. In other words, the two different frameworks resulted in classifying adults differently. Looking at a number of studies, the overlap in classifications using the two frameworks has been judged to be "trivial to small."[8]

Does this mean that one group of psychologists has gotten it right and the other wrong? Given the voluminous research produced in the two areas during the past thirty years or so, this would be a rash conclusion.[9] In part, since the two groups initially had different goals—one to understand adults-as-parents and the other to understand adults-as-partners—some unanticipated differences in classifications might be expected.

To provide a foundation for understanding what we have learned from the two psychology traditions, descriptions of the assessment approaches used by developmental and social/personality psychologists is helpful. As will become clear, the assessment measures developed by the two schools of psychology fundamentally differ as to how much weight they place on what individuals *report* about themselves (the social/personality psychological approach) and what is *inferred* from interviews (the developmental approach).[10] Ultimately, with a better understanding of the two measures, we can then look at what each approach has contributed to our understanding of attachment through the lifespan.

ADULT ATTACHMENT: THE DEVELOPMENTAL APPROACH

Mary Main and colleagues were interested in conceptualizing individual differences in attachment status in adults as reflecting differences in their working models of attachment relationships.[11] Yes, Mary Ainsworth had identified parenting *behaviors* that distinguished parents of children who were secure, insecure-avoidant (that is, those who appeared to maintain a "stiff upper lip"), and insecure-resistant (those who resisted consolation), but was it possible to identify the *mental processes* that lay behind and actually motivated these parenting behaviors?

The approach to adult attachment assessment devised by Mary Main together with Carol George and Nancy Kaplan—The Adult Attachment Interview (AAI)—was based on the notion that parents could reveal their working models about attachment through their language and thought processes if engaged in a reflective, open-ended interview about their early childhood experiences.[12] Bowlby's psychoanalytic framework continued to influence those who worked with Mary Ainsworth, and psychoanalytic concepts such as unconscious processes and defenses were employed in interpreting interview responses.

The goal of the AAI was to measure "the security of . . . attachment in its generality rather than in relation to any particular present or past relationship."[13] In the AAI, adults are not asked simply to explain their attitudes about relationships; the developers assumed that verbally expressed responses to interview queries might be very different than the internal working models of the speaker's own experiences which were generally operating. The scoring system that was developed for the AAI[14] took into account not only what adults said but also how they said it, and what omissions or distortions of their own parenting history could be inferred from the transcribed interview text. Contradictions and incoherent phrasings which the speaker did not recognize and correct were held to be as important as the views deliberately expressed. [15]

The attachment categories derived from the AAI are referred to as representing "states of mind with respect to attachment." This terminology is important, since it helps make a distinction with the social/personality psychologists' categories, which are referred to as "attachment styles." As noted earlier, individuals who have, say, a "dismissing state of mind with respect to attachment" do not necessarily get classified as having an avoidant or dismissing attachment style when they respond to brief self-report inventories.

The Adult Attachment Interview (AAI)

Compared to the measures developed by social/personality psychologists, the AAI is complex. To provide the reader with a firm basis for understanding the meaning of research findings in studies using the AAI, more time will be devoted to describing it. Understanding this measure will help the reader comprehend what it tells us about adults as parents, and in more recent research, as partners. Readers are cautioned that the content presented in this chapter is meant to simply give a taste of what the interview is like. The AAI requires a great deal of training in order to classify adults, and the entire interview needs to be considered carefully before a classification is given. [16] Yet, consideration of some sample AAI responses may give hints as to the significance of different individuals' ways of coping with emotional discussions as well as the meaning of different kinds of dialogue.

The AAI: Interview Content

The AAI, which typically lasts sixty to ninety minutes, is designed to bring out individual differences in deeply internalized strategies for regulating emotion and attention when interviewees are discussing attachment-related experiences. [17] It consists of a series of increasingly probing questions about an adult's early relationships and experiences with caretakers. Among the interview questions are inquiries about childhood experiences of being upset, ill, separated from caregivers, rejected, and of having suffered loss or abuse. Sample questions appear in Table 5.1.

The reader might want to pause and think about responses to these questions. The seemingly simple questions are not always so easy to answer. In responding, one must sort through a variety of memories, which may be linked with strong feelings. Was one's mother generous, caring, and thoughtful? Was one's father pre-occupied, punitive, teasing, or absent? The process

Table 5.1. Sample Adult Attachment Interview (AAI) Protocol Questions

1. Could you start by helping me get oriented to your early family situation, and where you lived and so on? If you could tell me where you were born, whether you moved around much, what your family did at various times for a living?

2. I'd like you to try to describe your relationship with your parents as a young child . . . if you could start from as far back as you can remember?

3. Now I'd like to ask you to choose five adjectives or words that reflect your relationships with your mother starting as far back as you can remember in early childhood—as early as you can go, but say, age 5 to 12 is fine. I know this may take a bit of time, so go ahead and think for a minute . . . then I'd like to ask you why you chose them. I'll write each one down as you give them to me.

4. Now, I wonder if you could tell me, to which parent did you feel closest, and why? Why isn't there this feeling with the other parent?

7. What is the first time you remember being separated from your parents?

11. Why do you think your parents behaved as they did during your childhood?

Note: The AAI cannot be conducted on the basis of these sample questions from the protocol. It is necessary to ask all twenty AAI questions as well as specific follow-up probes. The most recent AAI protocol (George, Kaplan, and Main, 1996) is available from Naomi Gribneau Bahm (ngbreliability@gmail.com). George, Kaplan, and Main, *Adult Attachment Interview Protocol (3rd edition)*. Copyright 1996 by the authors. Adapted by permission.

of reflecting about one's early experiences with parents may bring up warm, grateful feelings, or alternatively, feelings of sadness, regret, or anger.

Examples of AAI Responses

Three sample responses from adults who each described their mother as "loving" illustrate the kinds of responses given by adults in the three groups differing in their "state of mind with respect to attachment." Certainly, not every respondent used this adjective, but looking at those who did provides a way of contrasting the kinds of explanations that are given by individuals in the three "state of mind" categories. In the first case, a speaker who was eventually classified as secure-autonomous (based on the entire interview) justified use of the adjective "loving" as follows:

> *Speaker #1*: "(pause) I don't know if this is the sort of thing you're looking for, but one thing that comes to mind is the way she stuck up for me when I got in trouble at school. Boy, if I told her about some problem at school and she thought I was in the right, or if I told her someone or some teacher had treated me bad, she'd go out and investigate and she'd stick up for me to the teacher, or to the kid's parents, or . . . anybody, really. I could put it another way, too. I just knew where I stood with her, and that she'd be comforting if I was upset or crying or something."[18]

Speaker #1 provides a clear and coherent justification for the use of the term "loving." The speaker remembers that his mother was consistently aware of what was happening to him at school, would sort out the facts, and would intervene appropriately when needed. She also was comforting if the speaker was distressed as a child.

In a second case, a speaker who chose "loving" as one adjective for his mother and was eventually classified as "dismissing of attachment" said:

> *Speaker #2*: "I don't remember . . . (pause). Well, because she was caring and supportive."
> (Here the interviewer prompts for more information: "Well, this can be diffi-cult, because a lot of people haven't thought about these things for a long time, but take a minute and see if you can think of an incident or example.")
> "(pause) Well . . . (pause), I guess like, well, you know, she was really pretty, and she took a lot of care with her appearance. Whenever she drove me to school, I was always really proud of that when we pulled up at the play-ground."[19]

When Speaker #2 is pressed to give further detail about why he used the term "loving," the speaker gives the odd explanation that his comment was based on her appearance. This explanation does not provide convincing evidence that mother was indeed loving—if anything, we are left with the impression that she was rather self-focused. The speaker seems unable to provide any kind of solid evidence to support the descriptor "loving."

Finally, a third individual who described mother as "loving" and was later classified as "preoccupied with early attachments" said:

> *Speaker #3*: "Uh, yeah, sort of very loving at times, like people were in the old days—uh, my youth, lot of changes since then. I remember home, and home was good and that. And uh, loving, that's just like my wife is with [child]—taking him out to the movies tonight, dadadada, special thing he's been want-ing to see all week. Actually, it's more like a month, that turtle movie, don't like it too much myself. Saw it, though, now, when was it, um, maybe 6 months ago. Yeah, she's very loving with [child]."

When prompted for more information about why he described his mother as loving, the speaker said:

> "Really great things, felt really special, really grateful to her for that. My childhood, I remember just sitting on the porch, rocking, rocking back and forth watching my parents, or maybe having some lemonade—this, that, and the other. Really special sorts of things, just me and her, grateful for all she did for me. I wasn't easy, my temperament was hard on her, kind of hard. Me and my cousins . . . going down soon—really big birthday, she gonna be 80, gives my age away."[20]

Speaker #3 gives a rather disjointed and confusing account to justify the descriptor of "loving." This man jumps from the past to the present, gets caught up with describing a movie his wife is planning to attend with their child, and later describes himself as having a "hard" temperament. Aside from the fact that mother served him lemonade, we are not provided with any clear evidence of loving behavior, nor of how his mother lovingly addressed his self-described hard temperament.

Scoring and Interpreting the AAI

In reading about the interview content, the reader should remember that the AAI is interpreted based on a review of the entire audio-taped interview transcript. Raters make judgments about the interviewee's responses on two different types of scales, "Probable Experiences" and "State of Mind" scales.

The five scales estimating the interviewee's probable experiences are focused on judgements of the kinds of experiences the interviewee had had with each parent during childhood (e.g., how loving, rejecting, demanding, neglecting, or pressuring-to-achieve the parent was). It is important to emphasize that coders selecting scores on these Probable Experiences scales might assign a score far different than the speaker might have assigned. This would occur if an interviewee gave extremely positive adjectives to describe a parent but then provided examples which contradict the positive view.[21]

Eight scales are designed to assess the participant's "state of mind with respect to attachment." The State of Mind scales are used to rate interviewees' comfort with close relationships as well as the ways in which they manage the task of dealing with attachment-related emotions and childhood memories. Scales in the State of Mind category include "Coherence of transcript," "Idealization of the speaker's primary attachment figure(s)," "Insistence on lack of memory for childhood," and "Passivity or vagueness in discourse."[22] After all scales are rated, the interviewee is assigned to a single attachment category reflecting their overall "state of mind." In addition to the three main categories already described (secure, dismissing, and preoccupied), an additional category, "cannot classify," is assigned if the interview texts seem to indicate contradictory states of mind.

Careful research has shown that the most telling parts of the interview do not have to do with the exact nature of recalled early experiences, but something more subtle. After studying the responses of mothers in the initial group interviewed, Main and colleagues teased out three major state of mind classifications that paralleled children's Strange Situation attachment patterns. The developers of the AAI classification system—Mary Main, Ruth Goldwyn, and Erik Hesse—found that the degree of coherence in interviewees' descriptions of their childhood experiences was one of the most important factors in distinguishing the different state of mind classifications.

Parallels between the AAI and the Strange Situation Procedure

It was in fact no coincidence that the adult attachment state of mind classifications paralleled children's Strange Situation attachment patterns. In the sample in which the classification guidelines were developed, Mary Main and co-authors intentionally sought to find what aspects of adult interviews matched up with particular infant attachment patterns. The parents they initially studied had children who had participated in the Strange Situation Procedure five years earlier, when they were aged one. Beginning with a hunch as to what kind of interview responses would match with an infant pattern of attachment, they worked to develop a coding system for distinguishing the interviews of mothers of, say, children who had been sturdily unemotional and avoidant of their mothers during the Strange Situation Procedure.[23]

What Main and her colleagues essentially found was that there were striking similarities between how adults *approached* answering questions about significant attachment experiences, and how their children had *approached* the parent during reunions. Just as securely attached babies have no hesitation in going directly to a parent when he or she returns in the Strange Situation, their parents generally could straightforwardly and coherently describe their early experiences, a pattern of discourse which earned them the classification "secure-autonomous." Usually, but not always, they described at least one parent as having provided them with a secure base in childhood. More importantly, their communication style was clear and direct, and they seemed comfortable discussing attachment themes.

Parents of the insecure-avoidant children, who had appeared to maintain a "stiff upper lip" throughout the Strange Situation Procedure, tended to give interview responses that were described as "dismissing of attachment." These parents conveyed a sense that early attachment relationships were of minimal concern, and they seemed uncomfortable with the process of self-reflection that the interview required. Their interview texts appeared to indicate that they would just as soon avoid emotional discussions regarding the parenting they themselves had experienced, and saw themselves as strong and independent, paralleling the way their children avoided showing emotion and turning to parents for comfort during reunion in the Strange Situation.[24]

While adults with a "dismissing state of mind with respect to attachment" often described their parents in a positive, or even an idealized way, they seemed to have difficulty when they were asked to back up their positive views with descriptions of remembered interactions. Sometimes, however, these parents contradicted themselves later in the interview. For example, one respondent described his mother as "very loving," but later said that he once had hidden a broken arm because his mother often responded with anger when he had hurt himself.[25]

The third group of parents, whom Main described as "preoccupied by past relationships,"[26] became quite distressed at times, overwhelmed with emotions, and flooded with memories. Their attempted discussions of early experiences were often poorly organized and sometimes somewhat incoherent. Their memories of their childhoods were sometimes, but not always, unhappy memories. Just as their insecure-resistant children seemed to have confused and ambivalent emotions upon reunion in the Strange Situation, preoccupied adults' responses to attachment-related questions were infused with emotional wording and could sometimes be quite confusing.

A reasonable question is whether differences in verbal fluency or memory could explain the different kinds of responses given by adults in the AAI. For example, might dismissing adults offer fewer details about their childhood experiences because they have poorer verbal and/or memory abilities? One group of Israeli researchers working with Abraham Sagi cleverly studied people's ability to remember details of their childhoods by asking about details of TV and radio program titles that were popular when they were young. Adults classified as having a dismissing state of mind on the AAI were as good at remembering information about TV and radio shows as were those classified as secure; dismissing individuals could remember quite well on memory tests that did not require that they retrace attachment-related childhood experiences.[27] Overall, neither verbal fluency nor memory have been found to be weaker with dismissing adults compared to those in other groups.[28]

One More Category: The AAI and Unresolved Loss or Trauma

Early on, Main and colleagues noted that in her quite stable middle-class sample, parents of infants who were described as "disorganized/disoriented" in the Strange Situation often spoke in unusual ways about loss or trauma experiences during the AAI. Over time, it became clear that what these parents had in common was that during discussion of experiences of loss or trauma, they would show brief slips in their thinking or reasoning, i.e., lapses in their monitoring of what they were saying. This would result in odd statements or abrupt shifts in speech.[29]

A few years after the AAI was developed, Mary Main and her colleague Erik Hesse began to give separate classifications to parents who showed these lapses in reasoning and discourse, describing them as "unresolved/disorganized."[30] These parents could become unusually absorbed in traumatic memories, so that they were unable to express their thoughts in fully logical ways. One example is found in the following response: "It was almost better when she died, because then she could get on with being dead and I could get on with raising my family." This rather odd statement suggested that the speaker could not fully shake the feeling that the deceased person remained in some sense alive.[31]

A dramatic example of a lapse in reasoning is provided in the following quote from a woman whose AAI was judged insecure regarding loss; the loss was that of her after-school care provider when she was in grade school. When asked in the interview about loss of substitute parent figures, she responded in this way: "Yes, there was a little man," and she began to cry. She went on to say: "I don't remember his face—I remember his clothes, his smell, the essence of a person, I think. . . ." As it turned out, this man died of a brain hemorrhage when she was eight years old. One day shortly before his sudden death he had asked her whether she would marry him when she grew older, and she said, "No, you'd be dead." So when he died she felt she had killed him—"with one sentence," she added. She went on to say she believed in reincarnation in a way. "As long as you think of people, so you can carry them with you, there's no death; it's here!"—pointing to her heart and beginning to cry. "I've felt him in me for a long time."[32]

In this example, which was actually provided by Mary Ainsworth from a study conducted with colleague Carolyn Eichberg, we might not have expected the loss itself to be so terribly traumatic. However, her childhood belief—that she had killed someone who was important to her with a sentence or a thought—was very frightening and continued to cause her great pain. This unresolved sense of guilt prompted her to say in the AAI that she believed she had killed him with "one sentence."[33] This woman did not correct her statement by noting that this was obviously impossible, an omission important for this statement to be identified as an indication of a lapse in reasoning or discourse.

Interestingly, these lapses in reasoning and odd statements might only be made occasionally during an interview. Throughout much of the interview, at least some "unresolved" parents were able to speak coherently about less troubling memories. In the AAI, parents who at times show evidence of being unresolved or disorganized are now given two classifications, one classification from one of the main groups (secure/autonomous, dismissing, or preoccupied) and a second classification of unresolved/disorganized.

In Chapter Two, it was noted that parents of children classified as having disorganized attachment have been observed to act in frightened or frightening ways with children.[34] It has been hypothesized that the forces that lie behind the lapses in reasoning that some adults show may reflect feelings of fear; classic manifestations of fear include attack, flight, and freezing. If parents try to push feelings of fear out of consciousness, the submerged feelings may emerge in ways that unwittingly cause them to act in frightened or frightening ways with their children.[35] (See Appendix A of this chapter for more information about how unconscious processes and psychological defenses influence thinking and behavior.)

Daniel Siegel provides the following description of the behavior of one father who had an unresolved state of mind on the AAI:

> [With this man,] abrupt shifts into dramatically different states of mind would often occur when he initially felt rejected, either by his wife or by his daughter. He described the experience as if something would then happen that would activate a "crazy feeling"—as if "something was about to pop." He would sense a pressure in his head and a trembling in his arms. He would feel that he was going out of his mind, ready to explode, "receding from the world," and drawing away from people as if in a tunnel. At this moment he could no longer stop the process. He knew that his face looked enraged and tightly drawn, and that the muscles in his body were stiff. Sometimes he would hit his daughter. Sometimes he would squeeze her arm. Other times he would just yell at her, at the top of his lungs, filled with a rage he could not control.
>
> The father tried to deny his repeated and sudden shifts into a frightening rageful state. He felt so ashamed of these outbursts that he did not engage in any repair process with his daughter during or after such terrifying interactions.[36]

State of Mind Classifications:
How Common Are the Various Categories?

Parallel to secure attachments in infancy, secure-autonomous states of mind are the most common classifications found. A mid-1990s review of studies that included almost 500 individuals found that 55 percent of mothers without a clinical disorder were secure-autonomous. Thus, while the most common attachment status, the secure state only reflects a slim majority. Almost one-fifth of the nonclinical mothers were found to give evidence of unresolved loss or trauma.[37]

Researchers concluded that the distribution of adult attachment classifications is remarkably similar to the distributions of infant-mother attachment classifications, and that nonclinical mothers may be less universally "healthy" than one might expect. Slightly less than 50 percent of individuals studied in community samples, in which no clinical diagnoses are identified, receive one of the three insecure classifications (insecure-dismissing, insecure-preoccupied, or insecure-unresolved).

These findings would seem to raise questions about what should be considered "normal." When researchers have looked at groups of individuals who suffer from specific diagnosable mental health problems, they generally have found higher rates of insecure states of mind, compared to rates in the general population. For example, in a small study of twelve individuals diagnosed with "dysthymia," a form of chronic depression which is not severe but does result in considerable distress, they found that ten of these twelve individuals had insecure or unresolved states of mind on the AAI.[38]

However, we have no reason to presume that all, or even the majority of, individuals who are insecure or unresolved suffer from clinical disorders. We would certainly not think that fully 45 percent of the population is psychiatrically ill. A reasonable conclusion may be that a great many people—including some of our dear friends and relatives—lead their lives with a less than optimal sense of security, and that in situations of stress they may perhaps be more vulnerable to psychological distress. But, most of these people certainly manage to lead productive lives, raise families, and contribute to activities that benefit society.

And, an argument can be made that society functions better when there is some diversity in personality inclinations. John Bowlby once commented that "for society to function maybe you need certain individuals to be dismissing, certain ones to be preoccupied." He went on to suggest that it might be best for people in some professions (for example, stock brokers or brain surgeons) to be dismissing, and for people in other professions to be preoccupied.[39] This is an interesting notion that has not been investigated to date.

The AAI: Prediction of Child Attachment Patterns

Over the years, there have been a great many studies that have looked at the correlation between parental state of mind with respect to attachment and children's attachment security. In fact, Mary Ainsworth and her graduate student Carolyn Eichberg were the first to replicate such a study uncovering a very strong match between a mother's Adult Attachment Interview classification and her infant's Strange Situation behavior.[40] In an early (1995) article that reviewed findings from eighteen studies that examined the correlation between parental AAI classification and children's attachment security, it was concluded that there indeed was a very significant correlation between adult and child attachment measures. Marinus van IJzendoorn, a professor and prolific researcher located at Leiden University in the Netherlands, wrote: "The stable and large overlap between autonomy of the parent and security of the child is impressive because the measures are different: a semi-structured interview involving the coding of discourse characteristics versus a structured laboratory procedure involving the coding of infants' behavioral response to reunions with their attachment figure."[41]

More recently, another, even larger meta-analytic review of ninety-five studies that was conducted internationally and included over 4,800 individuals confirmed that there indeed is a significant relationship between parent and child attachment classifications.[42] In this 2016 article, the relationship between mothers' states of mind and their children's attachment security was found to be roughly the same as that between fathers' states of mind and child security. And, there was clear evidence that the correlation between parents' and children's degree of attachment security is not based simply on

genetic factors, but rather on something happening in the relationship between parent and child.[43]

Interestingly, this study found evidence that a smaller percentage of parents are classified as secure than are children, suggesting that some caregivers who themselves are not secure on the AAI do manage to build secure
attachment relationships with their children. The strength of the relationship
between parent and child classifications in this most recent study was not
quite as impressive as in the earlier study, a finding the authors suggest could
be attributable to a variety of explanations, including the fact that the second
review study included more individuals with greater risk factors.[44, 45]

Studies in which researchers had administered the AAI when mothers
were pregnant, over a year before their children were assessed in the Strange
Situation, have found roughly the same degree of correlation as have studies
conducted after the child is born, indicating that AAI responses cannot be
explained by anything about parents' relationship with the child over the first
year.[46] In the research world, scientists have found it quite remarkable that
a parent interview administered before a child's birth could predict children's behavior. In fact, a prominent researcher mentored by John Bowlby,
Miriam Steele, recalls early on telling Bowlby the results of her study using
the AAI with parents during pregnancy, where she found strong correlations
with children's Strange Situation classifications at one year. When she told
Bowlby of this finding, he found this result remarkable, noting how hard it
was simply to predict London weather.[47]

Research conducted in West European, Scandinavian, Asian, and Middle
Eastern cultures has continued to find significant correlations between child
attachment security and parents' "state of mind with respect to attachment."[48] And, two studies that looked at security of attachment in three
generations—in mother, her child, and in mother's own mother—also have
found at least moderate stability in states of mind with respect to attachment
across generations.[49]

Transmission of Security (or Insecurity) from Parents to Children

While studies have found significant correlations between adult attachment
and child attachment measures, the evidence as to how parents "transmit"
their attachment-related states of mind to children has been less clear-cut.
Meeting children's needs in a sensitive manner had been identified by Mary
Ainsworth as the most critical parenting quality for helping children develop
a secure attachment.[50]

But, years ago statistical analyses pointed to the conclusion that sensitivity was not the only important parental quality in determining child attachment security; unknown factor(s) were assumed to contribute to what was
termed a "transmission gap."[51] Indeed, in the ninety-five studies reviewed in

the 2016 meta-analytic article, parental sensitivity again explained only a part of the correlation between parents' security in their own attachment representations and their children's observed secure behavior.

What does a "transmission gap" mean? Simply put, there is some missing element—pertaining to the ways in which parents "transmit" to their children their own sense of how trustworthy attachment figures can be expected to be—that cannot be explained simply based on *behavioral observations* of mothers' sensitivity. In research parlance, it means that statistical analyses indicate that ratings of sensitivity don't entirely account for why some children are judged secure and others judged insecure. A gap had been identified in knowledge of what other factors might explain the "transmission" of security.

Conceptually, caregivers' ability to respond sensitively to their children's needs has been thought to reflect their own representations of attachment. Caregivers who themselves had experienced sensitivity as young children are believed to have internalized these experiences, and their internal working models allow them to naturally respond sensitively to their own children.[52, 53]

One factor that has been identified that helps solve the "transmission gap" puzzle comes from a concept termed "reflective functioning." Reflective functioning, which is assessed in AAI transcripts, refers to the ability of an individual to explore his or her own mind, and this promotes a similar enquiring stance towards the mental states of others.[54] Mothers who are secure and comfortable with their own thoughts, desires, and wishes are able to use their knowledge of their own minds to make sense of their children's minds, and adding a measure of mother's capacity for reflective functioning helps better explain the correlation between parental "state of mind with respect to attachment," as assessed by the AAI, and children's attachment security.[55]

Having the capacity for reflective functioning[56] may help transmit to children a strategy for expressing and regulating emotions. The secure Strange Situation pattern is based on observations that children can openly communicate fear, distress, or anger—all feelings that may be evoked by mother's brief separation in the Strange Situation—without concern that their mother will disapprove or push them away. Secure children's mothers are comfortable with a range of emotions and with the idea of asking others for support, and so are they.[57]

With mother-child pairs in which children are insecure-avoidant and parents have a dismissing state of mind with respect to attachment, children will have learned to show as little as possible about their experiences of negative emotions, which makes sense given that their mothers have been observed to be quite nonresponsive to negative affect.[58] Observations of children in the Strange Situation suggest they tend to act as if all is well even when they are quite distressed. In contrast, children who demonstrate an insecure-resistant attachment pattern, that is who resist consolation during reunion episodes, have learned it is okay to show intense negative emotions, but they haven't learned to expect that their needs will be met when they express anger or distress.[59] They convey a sense of acute emotional conflict and confusion as to from where, and from whom, a strategy to deal with their painful circumstances will come.[60]

Recently, yet another variable has been discovered that contributes to explaining the missing part of the "transmission gap" puzzle. This further variable was found once more in *behavioral observations*—this time, in measures of parental "autonomy support." Measures assessing autonomy support looked at parents' ability to support exploration in their children.[61] The authors proposed that their findings support the notion that in their interactions with caregivers, children not only learn an answer to the question "What do others do when I am upset?" but also "What happens when I venture to explore?"[62] Importantly, the researchers who discovered this finding also found that mothers with a secure attachment state of mind are more likely than insecure mothers *both* to be able to respond to children's needs for emotional security *and* to encourage greater competence in supporting their attempts to master challenges in the environment whenever their attachment needs are fulfilled.[63]

ADULT ATTACHMENT:
THE SOCIAL/PERSONALITY PSYCHOLOGY APPROACH

With the belief that "the search for connections between attachment in childhood and attachment in adulthood must begin somewhere," the two researchers who pioneered this tradition, Cindy Hazan and Phillip Shaver, developed three descriptions of relational styles which they believed paralleled Ainsworth's secure-autonomous, insecure-avoidant, and insecure-resistant patterns. Their first survey was conducted through a "love quiz" printed in a Colorado newspaper. Respondents were asked simply "Which of the following best describes your feelings?" and were presented with three alternatives:

[Secure] I find it relatively easy to get close to others and am comfortable depending on them and having them depend on me. I don't often worry about being abandoned or about someone getting too close to me.
[Avoidant] I am somewhat uncomfortable being close to others. I find it difficult to trust them completely, difficult to allow myself to depend on them. I am nervous when anyone gets too close, and often, love partners want me to be more intimate than I feel comfortable being.
[Anxious/Ambivalent][64] I find that others are reluctant to get as close as I would like. I often worry that my partner doesn't really love me or won't want to stay with me. I want to merge completely with another person, and this desire sometimes scares people away.[65]

In the hundreds of replies to the "love quiz," slightly over half (56 percent) of the respondents chose the "Secure" response, 25 percent chose the "Avoidant" description, and 19 percent chose the "Anxious" response, which was consistent with the insecure-resistant pattern. In a second sample in which respondents were all students in a social psychology class (and thus were not self-selected respondents), the proportions of students who classified themselves in the three groups was virtually identical to that in the newspaper sample. And, the breakdown of secure, insecure-avoidant, and insecure-resistant classifications in their adult samples were remarkably similar to the figures that Mary Ainsworth and others had obtained with infants in the Strange Situation.

In the social/personality psychological tradition, adults' attachment styles are referred to in exactly that way—"attachment styles." So, as you read this book as well as any other literature, it is important to distinguish between "states of mind with respect to attachment" and "attachment styles."

THE SELF-REPORT APPROACH: DEVELOPMENTS IN THE SOCIAL/PERSONALITY PSYCHOLOGY TRADITION

In the years following Hazan and Shaver's publication of the results of their "love quiz," a good many paper-and-pencil adult attachment self-report questionnaires were developed that attempted to provide a somewhat more sophisticated way to measure adult attachment styles. Later questionnaires included a variety of questions probing attitudes about relationships in more nuanced ways, but they continued with the tradition of asking adults to self-report about their relationships, without further probing by researchers.

With the development of many self-report questionnaires, researchers faced uncertainty as to which of the various questionnaires should be used. Phillip Shaver, one of the developers of the original "love quiz," eventually worked with two new co-authors, Kelly Brennan and Catherine Clark, to select items from the many questionnaires which would best identify different romantic attachment styles.[66] They concluded that a questionnaire with thirty-six items, eighteen of which reflected high or low levels of Avoidance, and eighteen which reflected high or low levels of Anxiety, seemed to best distinguish attachment styles in the group of over 1,000 undergraduate participants they studied.[67] The resulting scale, called the Experiences in Close Relationships (ECR) scale,[68] has become one of the most widely used self-reports of romantic attachment styles.[69] There are also other self-report scales that are used regularly, but for simplicity the ECR will be discussed in this book as an example of the kinds of measures used by social/personality psychologists.

Sample items from the ECR's Avoidance scale include the following: "I prefer not to show a partner how I feel deep down"; "I want to get close to my partner, but I keep pulling back"; and "I tell my partner just about everything" (reverse scored). Items from the Anxiety scale include: "I need a lot of reassurance that I am loved by my partner"; "I worry about being alone"; and "I resent it when my partner spends time away from me."

With the two basic scales of Avoidance and Anxiety, an individual could score low on both, high on both, or high on only one scale. Thus, with the Experiences in Close Relationships questionnaire, there are four possible clusters of individuals. Those falling in the "secure" cluster are low on both Avoidance and Anxiety. Those whose responses place them high on both scales are placed in a "fearful" cluster. Earlier research had distinguished a "fearful avoidant" style that was distinct from a "dismissing avoidant" style,[70] and the ECR fearful cluster was consistent with this grouping. Those high only on Avoidance were characterized as "dismissing" and those high only on Anxiety were described as "preoccupied."[71]

The Experiences in Close Relationships Scale has been revised slightly using psychometric techniques to improve the precision in which it measures attachment styles; the revised version is referred to as ECR-R.[72] Despite increased sophistication from the original "love quiz," the Experiences in Close Relationships scale as well as numerous other self-report scales that have been developed remain much simpler, easier tests to administer compared to the developmental psychologists' Adult Attachment Interview. In fact, the amount of training needed to accurately administer and score the AAI is a major reason that it is not used even more widely.

The developers of the ECR questionnaire were frank about the limitations of their approach. They noted that results clearly depend on respondents' honesty and self-insight, which the authors note "are probably limited in any case but especially so when fears and defenses are at issue."[73] However, they asserted that they hoped that the longer-than-usual scale might circumvent some of the temptation towards biased responding aroused by simple measures which require people to state directly whether or not they are secure.

ATTACHMENT IN ADULTHOOD: WHAT HAVE WE LEARNED?

As is clear, the two traditions—originating in the two sub-fields of psychology, developmental and social/personality—have approached the problem as to how to understand security in adult attachment in quite different ways. And, as noted at the outset, the developmental psychologists who devised the Adult Attachment Interview (AAI) were initially interested simply in how to understand the minds of parents who had children with different attachment patterns. However, over time, not only self-report scales but also the AAI have been used to investigate aspects of couples functioning, that is, adult-adult attachment.

As noted earlier in this chapter, the methods devised by the developmental and social/personality psychologists did not lead to solid agreement as to what was a "secure-like," an "avoidant-like," or a "resistant-like" adult. The overlap in classifications resulting from the two frameworks has consistently turned out to be non-existent or quite small.[74] (For more information about how to understand the differences between the two traditions, see Appendix B).

Given that the measures developed by the two psychology traditions often fail to reach agreement about adults' attachment classifications, it is critical to know the measure that was used to assess for adult attachment security. As stated by authors who studied the overlap between, and correlates of, the two types of measures, "results from the AAI and self-report literatures should not be cited and discussed in narrative reviews as if the measures were interchangeable."[75] Thus, for example, if a study classifies individuals as "avoidant" or "dismissive" through use of a self-report measure, these individuals cannot be assumed to behave or think in the same ways as those classified as having a "dismissing state of mind with respect to attachment" on the AAI. Put another way, individuals who are assigned a particular internal working model on the AAI may endorse a different working model with self-report measures.[76]

What Can We Learn from the Social/Personality Approach?

Research using self-report measures is abundant; the relative ease of administering self-report questionnaires makes it much easier to investigate various aspects of emotional relationships. Researchers have looked at many factors associated with different attachment styles—including patterns of expectations, needs, emotions, and social behavior—to understand how attachment styles influence both personal functioning and behavior in relationships.[77] In studying these aspects of functioning, researchers have sought to identify factors that account for the success and stability of some relationships and for the failure and dissolution of others.[78]

Individuals who self-report relatively secure attachment styles have been shown to be more likely than those who are insecure to report experiencing greater satisfaction, as well as to both demonstrate and report less conflict in their relationships.[79] Security in self-reported attachment style has been shown to be associated with whether individuals divorce and how happily married they report themselves to be. Interestingly, one study found that those with the most anxious attachments before marriage were *less* likely to divorce than those who reported greater security in attachment style. However, while those who rated themselves as most anxiously attached tended to still be married four years later, they were unhappy in their marriages, and they also reported higher levels of depression.[80]

There is a very large literature relating self-reported attachment styles to many aspects of personal thoughts, feelings, and behavior, as well as to individuals' functioning in relationships.[81] One area of research has focused on the relationship between self-reported attachment styles and likelihood of responding with anger, hostility, and aggression in response to frustrating events.[82]

Mario Mikulincer, one of the pioneers of work in the social/personality field, conducted an interesting study regarding anger responses in individuals of varying attachment styles.[83] The study was designed to test Bowlby's idea that "internal working models of attachment" play a critical role in the experience of anger. Bowlby believed that secure attachment experiences promote beliefs that others have good intentions, that others' negative behaviors are temporary and reversible, and that one has the capacity to successfully deal with these responses. Individuals who are securely attached are able to use anger constructively to discourage others' negative behavior in the future, to overcome relational obstacles, and to maintain strong attachment bonds.[84]

Mikulincer's study investigated how attachment styles influenced individuals' reactions to, and their perceptions of, imaginary scenarios of conflictual interaction between two partners. One hundred Israeli students, who averaged twenty-four years of age, were asked to respond to six scenarios, three that were intended to be anger eliciting and three others that elicited positive feelings. The anger scenes included one in which the partner's intent was hostile, one where it was ambiguous, and one nonhostile.[85] Subjects were then asked a variety of questions, including how angry they themselves would be, and also their imagined perception of the partner's responsibility, control, intentionality, and hostility.

While in general self-reported insecure persons were more prone to seeing the partner's behavior as reflecting hostile intent, this tendency was more accentuated among self-reported avoidant persons, who despite clear cues that a partner's intention was benign were more likely to attribute hostility. In the ambiguous scenario, both groups of insecure individuals attributed more hostile intent than did secure persons.

This study also found an odd pattern of anger arousal and hostility attribution among self-reported avoidant persons. These individuals, as a group, attributed hostile intent even in the nonhostile scene. However, they did not report feeling anger in any of the scenes, including the hostile scene. But, while not reporting feeling angry, avoidant individuals had increased heart rate, thus showing physiological arousal.

ADULT RELATIONSHIPS: COMPARING THE DEVELOPMENTAL AND SOCIAL/PERSONALITY MEASURES

As emphasized in this chapter, the methods developed by developmental and social/personality psychologists have not led to solid agreement as to what is a "secure-like," an "avoidant-like," or a "resistant-like" adult. Overall, the two different frameworks result in classifying adults quite differently. How do we understand this?

At this point I will provide a very brief overview of findings regarding differences between the two types of measures. For easy reference, Table 5.2 provides a comparison of basic differences between the two measures. Interested readers who want to understand more about variations in the kinds of information provided by the two measures are encouraged to turn to Appendix B of this chapter.

Briefly, the conclusion of those who have investigated the overlap between two approaches to studying attachment security in adulthood—the AAI interview versus self-reports—is that these approaches tap different aspects of an individual's attachment representations.

One important difference between the two measures is that the AAI focuses specifically on the parental domain, while the self-report looks at relationships with peers and romantic partners. Also, the AAI assesses general state of mind, while self-reports look at specific beliefs. And, the AAI taps less conscious aspects of experience, while self-reports assess aspects of which the individual is more aware. [86]

Evidence presented in Appendix B provides preliminary indication that the AAI sheds more light on what actually transpires between couples when they have to deal with conflict. As the attachment system is presumed to be activated during times of relationship distress, looking at conflict encounters between romantic partners has turned to be a good way to assess attachment processes. [87]

On the other hand, there is some evidence that we learn more about couples' sense of satisfaction with their relationships by directly asking them. Since the marital satisfaction questionnaire used in one study described in Appendix B has been shown to predict whether couples stayed together or separated over a two-and-a-half-year period, [88] these results appear potentially quite meaningful. However, it is important to consider whether couples' direct answers about their marital satisfaction are always honest, or whether at least some couples might be overly optimistic.

Table 5.2. Comparison of Measures: Developmental and Social/Personality Psychology

Field of psychology	Developmental psychology	Social/Personality psychology
Measure most commonly used	Adult Attachment Interview (AAI)	Experiences in Close Relationships (ECR or ECR-R)
Term for adult attachment	State of mind with respect to attachment	Attachment style
Original use for measure	Assessment of attachment status of parents of children undergoing Strange Situation Procedure	Assessment of attachment status of adults in romantic relationships
Other uses for measure	-Assessment of attachment security status of adolescent and adult veterans of SSP -Assessment of well-being in adult romantic relationships	Assessment of correlations between adult attachment status and measures of earlier caretaking experiences
Format	Semi-structured interview	Paper-and-pencil questionnaire
Aspects of thought and experience assessed	Interview responses are analyzed to assess conscious recollections as well as discrepancies in memories and beliefs which result from unconscious processes	Self-reports tap conscious thoughts and memories
Ease of use	Involves training for administration, and extensive training for scoring	Easy to administer and score

SUMMING UP

Over the last several decades, a great deal of work has been conducted in the fields of developmental and social/personality psychology that help us understand the beliefs, thoughts, and feelings of adults with different attachment classifications. While information from the two fields of psychology inform us about different aspects of adult attachment status, interesting information has emerged from both traditions.

In Chapter Seven, we will review the research that is accumulating about how adults with different attachment security classifications are faring in couple relationships. We will not only look at the romantic experiences of Child Veterans of the Strange Situation, but also consider the experiences of adults whose attachment security is identified later using the measures described in this chapter.

But, before discussing adults, in the next chapter we will turn back to childhood. Chapter Six reviews what we know about attachment security in middle childhood and adolescence. Indeed, in assessing adolescent security, the Adult Attachment Interview has become a useful tool for understanding adolescents' states of mind with respect to attachment. The information about the AAI as well as about self-report attachment measures that the reader has learned in this current chapter will soon have relevance to understanding continuity as well as discontinuity in attachment security status over time.

APPENDIX A

Defenses: The Key to Understanding Attachment States of Mind

Sigmund Freud is the best known of early proponents for the idea that many mental processes occur outside of our conscious awareness.[89, 90] Defense mechanisms can relegate anxiety-provoking or otherwise disturbing thoughts to our unconscious mind. We lack self-knowledge and self-understanding about ideas in our unconscious mind, and hence are unaware when and how we defend against becoming aware of unpleasant or unwanted thoughts.[91]

Sometimes defenses are largely beneficial, in that they protect people from feeling too much anxiety. Humor, for example, as seen in pointing out absurdities or making jokes, can be a healthy way to ease tension. Other defense mechanisms are less helpful, sometimes making one bury thoughts, or distorting reality in a way that prevents people from seeing situations and relationships accurately.

John Bowlby wrote at some length about the issue of "defensive exclusion," by which he meant the selective exclusion of certain information from further processing. Bowlby noted that work in neurophysiology and cognitive psychology supports the notion that much processing of information is done outside of awareness.[92] Bowlby was primarily focused on how information about attachment figures and attachment-related feelings could be defensively excluded at various points. What Bowlby termed "defensive exclusion" can occur if incoming information is perceptually blocked and never used in any way, and also if some information reaches short-term storage and then is discarded. Additionally, information already stored in long-term memory can be unavailable due to amnesia.

If we go back and review the ways that parents responded to the Adult Attachment Interview, we can see the manner in which varying degrees of defensive exclusion could have influenced responses. The parents who were judged to have a "secure-autonomous state of mind with respect to attachment" were able to answer questions about their family history and relationships in an open, direct way. Thoughts and feelings about their early emotional experiences with parents had not been defensively excluded to any great degree, so their recollections flowed smoothly.

In contrast, the parents classified as having a "dismissing state of mind with respect to attachment" answered questions in a guarded way. They seemed to push away emotional topics or to have largely buried memories from their childhoods. Defensive exclusion was quite apparent when these parents dealt with attachment-related emotional topics.

The third group of parents, described as "preoccupied," communicated intense emotions in a confused and sometimes incoherent manner. Defensive exclusion was evident, but these parents did not suppress thoughts and feelings as effectively as did dismissing parents. In general, throughout the AAI, we can infer that preoccupied parents' defenses do not seem to work very effectively in preventing them from feeling anxiety as they confront painful topics.

The notion that emotional effort is required to maintain defensive exclusion is supported by the findings of a group of London researchers who wondered whether mood played a part in the kind of answers that parents gave on the AAI.[93] While they found no differences in self-rated mood before the interview, they did find that the kind of responses given in the AAI did affect the person's mood *after* the interview. Adults who provided interviews judged "autonomous-secure" were more likely to be in a good mood following the interview. The researchers concluded that it feels satisfying to discuss openly and in an organized manner how one has managed and resolved emotional conflicts in one's history.

In contrast, adults with a "dismissing state of mind with respect to attachment" seemed to feel the strain of pushing away feelings. While they tended to feel in a poorer mood after the interview, they did not see their avoidance of emotional conflicts as the cause of their lowered mood. Those who were judged preoccupied on the AAI were also in a less positive mood after the interview.

APPENDIX B

Adult Attachments:
Comparing the Developmental and Social/Personality Measures

Very few studies have looked at the same people in the same type of situation and compared how they are classified on the two types of measures. To provide just a little understanding of what the two approaches to assessment tell us about couple relationship functioning, we will look at studies that have included measures from the two traditions.

In attempting to understand how the developmental psychology and social/personality psychology traditions differ, one informative study focused on the kinds of AAI responses given by individuals with a "dismissing state of mind with respect to attachment."[94] As individuals classified as dismissing on the AAI are distinguished by tending to describe their childhoods in an unrealistically idealistic manner and to have difficulty recalling much about their youth, one might wonder whether these individuals can be accurate self-reporters about attachment relationships.

To explore how a group of individuals classified as dismissing on the AAI responded on the two types of instruments—the AAI and a self-report measure—the researchers first looked at responses on both of these measures that summarized direct, conscious views about parents. As discussed earlier, the AAI includes two "Probable Experiences" subscales—Love and Rejection—that are coded based on judgments by the person coding the transcript of how the interviewee's parents behaved when the interviewee was young. When looking at interviewees' directly expressed views about their parents, there was a very significant correlation between views expressed on the AAI and the self-report measure.

However, on other AAI subscales that are particularly good at distinguishing avoidant-like characteristics—characteristics which are termed "dismissing states of mind" on the AAI—the results from the two types of measures diverged. Self-reported attachment styles showed no correlation with the AAI scales which are particularly key to identifying dismissing individuals; these scales are "Idealization" and "Lack of Recall."[95] A self-reporter classified as having an avoidant style was not more likely than others to score high on Idealization and Lack of Recall, as would be expected if an AAI "dismissing state of mind" was similar to a self-reported avoidant style.

The authors of this study concluded that when dismissing individuals are completing attachment questionnaires, their "mechanism of idealization" is activated. They cautioned that attachment self-reports may provide a falsely positive picture for dismissing individuals, and that therefore self-reports may be more valid for some individuals than others.

Relational Conflict and Marital Satisfaction

Two studies included both the AAI and self-report measures and looked at how couples handled discussing a problem in their relationship and trying to resolve it.[96] In these two studies, the couples' discussions were coded with the same observational measure.[97] Observers rated participants on a number of dimensions, including aspects of communication such as self-disclosure and assertiveness, support and validation of partner, withdrawal through avoidance or unresponsiveness to partner, displays of conflict such as hostility and negative affect, and problem-solving skills. Both nonverbal and verbal behaviors were noted.

In both studies, AAI state of mind classifications predicted at least some aspects of *observed* couple behavior during the discussions about an area of conflict. For example, in one study, spouses who had secure states of mind showed higher levels of support/validation behaviors towards their partner.[98] Men who were classified as having secure states of mind on the AAI also had higher levels of communication expressiveness and lower levels of with-drawal than men with insecure states of mind. In the second study, when both partners had secure states of mind, they showed higher levels of collabora-tion.[99] The authors concluded that being able to talk coherently about one's childhood experiences plus having a partner who is able to do so leads to more skilled negotiation of mild conflict in one's relationship.[100]

In contrast, the self-report measures used in the two studies did not pre-dict ratings of observed couple behavior. But, in one of the studies, partici-pants' self-reports did predict ratings on *another* self-report measure. When participants were asked to make ratings of the emotional tone in their rela-tionship,[101] those higher on self-reported avoidance reported more negativity in emotional tone.

Another research project that used both types of measures, interviews and self-reports, found self-reports more informative than the AAI. This study used a brief questionnaire on which couples were asked to rate their subjec-tive sense of marital satisfaction, with questions such as "In general, how often do you think that things between you and your partner are going well?" In this study, AAI interview classifications did not predict self-reported mari-tal satisfaction. With questionnaires, in contrast, when women self-reported lower attachment avoidance, both they and their partners self-reported great-er marital satisfaction.[102]

Self-Reports of Attachment Style and Earlier Life Experiences

The social/personality tradition of research offers relatively little information about relationships between early-childhood attachment-related experiences and adult attachment style.

There is good reason for this; the social/personality approach was devel-oped specifically to look at adults' attachments to other adults, and not to search for childhood antecedents of adult attachment styles. Recently, how-ever, a few studies in this tradition have looked at correlations between some measures of early experiences and later attachment styles. While studies have not focused on correlations between Strange Situation Procedure classifica-tions and adult attachment styles, they have looked at correlates of measures of early parent-child interactions.

One study drew upon data from the National Institute of Child Health and Human Development (NICHD) to gain information about mothers' sensitiv-ity in interactions with children at various points in infancy and childhood (mothers were observed when children were 6, 15, 24, 36, and 54 months, and when children were in grades one, three, and five). When youngsters from this study were eighteen years old, over 700 of them completed a self-report attachment-style measure. Individuals who experienced high levels of maternal sensitivity early in life tended to self-report less avoidance at age eighteen. Additionally, individuals who experienced increases in maternal sensitivity over time (relative to other study participants) also tended to acknowledge less avoidance at eighteen years. [103]

Another study used data from the Minnesota Longitudinal Study of Risk and Adaptation, and specifically looked at mothers' interactions with their children at age two. Researchers correlated ratings of mother-child interaction when children were toddlers with self-reported level of romantic relationship commitment when individuals had reached the ages of twenty and twenty-one. This study found that when participants had had mothers who were more consistently supportive, enthusiastic, and patient in assisting them as toddlers with problem-solving tasks, they were more likely as adults to self-report greater commitment to their current partner and to be observed to show lower hostility during a videotaped conflict-resolution task. [104]

In a third study, mothers were observed playing with children when they were eighteen months, and observers rated mothers as to their sensitivity, controlling behavior, and unresponsiveness. When the children grew up and reached twenty-two years of age, they completed a self-report attachment-style inventory. Both greater maternal sensitivity and lower controlling caregiving at eighteen months predicted lower avoidance to friends in adulthood. For those individuals involved in a romantic relationship, greater maternal sensitivity and lower maternal control predicted less avoidance and less anxiety with partners. [105]

Thus, there is a limited but growing body of research providing evidence that early experiences of sensitive caregiving are correlated with greater degrees of security in self-reported adult attachment style. So, even though self-reported attachment styles and inferred states of mind with respect to attachment are minimally correlated, there is reason to believe that both tell us something about children's early caretaking experiences, and, presumably, their early attachment security.

What are we to conclude about the usefulness of the different types of measures for studying adult attachment? There is not yet enough research comparing the two measures with the same group of individuals to give us a firm sense of what the measures tell us about adult romantic functioning. The measures, coming from two different psychological traditions, both may give us useful information, but it does not appear to be the same information. Hopefully, future research will provide greater clarification regarding the meaning of findings from the developmental and social/personality psychology traditions.

NOTES

1. Powell et al., *The Circle of Security Intervention*, 98.
2. The Strange Situation Procedure as developed by Mary Ainsworth is appropriate for children twelve to eighteen months of age. Other assessment methods, such as Main and Cassidy's separation-reunion procedure for six-year-olds and their parents can be used to assess security of attachment in somewhat older children. (See Main and Cassidy, "Categories of Response to Reunion with the Parent at Age Six.")
3. Bowlby, *The Making and Breaking of Affectional Bonds*, 124–55.
4. As discussed in Chapter Two, a fourth category was eventually identified by Mary Main and Judith Solomon to describe children who lacked any organized pattern of attachment; see Main and Solomon, "Discovery of a New, Insecure-Disorganized/Disoriented Attachment Pattern."
5. George, Kaplan, and Main, "The Adult Attachment Interview Protocol"; George, Kaplan, and Main, "The Adult Attachment Interview Protocol (Third Edition)."
6. Bakermans-Kranenburg and van IJzendoorn. "The First 10,000 Adult Attachment Interviews."
7. Hazan and Shaver, "Romantic Love Conceptualized as an Attachment Process."
8. Roisman et al., "The Adult Attachment Interview and Self-Reports of Attachment Style."
9. Crowell, Fraley, and Shaver, "Measurement of Individual Differences in Adolescent and Adult Attachment."
10. Bernier and Matte-Gagné, "More Bridges."
11. Main, Kaplan, and Cassidy, "Security in Infancy, Childhood, and Adulthood."
12. George, Kaplan, and Main, *Adult Attachment Interview Protocol*.
13. Main, Kaplan, and Cassidy, "Security in Infancy, Childhood, and Adulthood," 78.
14. Main and Goldwyn, *Adult Attachment Scoring and Classification System;* Main, Goldwyn, and Hesse, *Adult Attachment Scoring and Classification System*.
15. Main, Kaplan, and Cassidy, "Security in Infancy, Childhood, and Adulthood."
16. Psychologists, researchers, and others seeking to learn the Adult Attachment Interview must attend two-week training institutes, and pass a thirty-case reliability check in order to be qualified as "AAI coders." Information about available training can be found at www.attachment-training.com.
17. Hesse, "The Adult Attachment Interview: Protocol, Method of Analysis, and Selected Empirical Studies."
18. Ibid., 558.
19. Ibid., 558.
20. Ibid., 559.
21. Ibid., 562.
22. Ibid., 564–66.
23. After they developed classification guidelines, the researchers used these guidelines to classify another group of parents where they did not know children's attachment classification, and found that they indeed could successfully predict children's Strange Situation classifications with this new group. (See Hesse, "The Adult Attachment Interview: Historical and Current Perspectives," 400; Main, "Recent Studies in Attachment.")
24. Main, "The Organized Categories of Infant, Child, and Adult Attachment."
25. Main, Hesse, and Kaplan, "Predictability of Attachment Behavior and Representational Processes at 1, 6, and 19 Years of Age," 276.
26. Main, "Recent Studies in Attachment," 438.
27. Sagi et al., "Stability and Discriminant Validity of the Adult Attachment Interview."
28. Bakermans-Kranenburg and van IJzendoorn, "A Psychometric Study of the Adult Attachment Interview"; van IJzendoorn, "Adult Attachment Representations, Parental Responsiveness, and Infant Attachment."
29. Hesse and Main, "Second-Generation Effects of Unresolved Trauma in Nonmaltreating Parents."; Hesse and Main, "Disorganized Infant, Child, and Adult Attachment."

30. Main and Hesse, "Parents' Unresolved Traumatic Experiences are Related to Infant Disorganized Attachment Status."

31. Hesse, "The Adult Attachment Interview: Protocol, Method of Analysis, and Selected Empirical Studies," 570; Hesse and Main, "Disorganized Infant, Child, and Adult Attachment."

32. Ainsworth and Eichberg, "Effects on Infant-Mother Attachment of Mother's Unresolved Loss of an Attachment Figure, or Other Traumatic Experience," 175–76.

33. Hesse and Main, "Disorganized Infant, Child, and Adult Attachment," 1112.

34. Hesse and Main, "Second-Generation Effects of Unresolved Trauma in Nonmaltreating Parents"; Hesse and Main, "Frightened, Threatening, and Dissociative Parental Behavior in Low-Risk Samples."

35. Hesse, "The Adult Attachment Interview: Historical and Current Perspectives," 417.

36. Siegel, *The Developing Mind*, 139.

37. van IJzendoorn and Bakermans-Kranenburg, "Attachment Representations in Mothers, Fathers, Adolescents, and Clinical Groups."

38. van IJzendoorn and Bakermans-Kranenburg, "The Distribution of Adult Attachment Representations in Clinical Groups."

39. Personal communication, Miriam Steele, August 2016.

40. Ainsworth and Eichberg, "Effects on Infant-Mother Attachment of Mother's Unresolved Loss of an Attachment Figure, or Other Traumatic Experience." Of note is the fact that Ainsworth had attended two AAI institutes taught by Main and Hesse and had become a "certified" AAI coder, and—being "blind" to which videotaped Strange Situation was associated with which mother—was able to assist in the Strange Situation coding for this study. Ainsworth's attendance at two AAI institutes is documented in an unpublished document distributed to all AAI institute attendees through January 2005.

41. van IJzendoorn, "Adult Attachment Representations, Parental Responsiveness, and Infant Attachment:"

42. Verhage et al., "Narrowing the Transmission Gap."

43. Bernier et al., "Taking Stock of Two Decades of Attachment Transmission Gap"; Verhage et al., "Narrowing the Transmission Gap," 337.

44. A greater percentage of the studies surveyed in the more recent article were conducted with higher risk groups, and groups with higher risk generally show less concordance between parent and child security. Additionally, the researchers suggested that problems with coding could reduce the strength of relationships.

45. Verhage et al., "Narrowing the Transmission Gap," 357.

46. Benoit and Parker, "Stability and Transmission of Attachment across Three Generations"; Fonagy, Steele, and Steele, "Maternal Representations of Attachment during Pregnancy Predict the Organization of Infant-Mother Attachment at One Year of Age."

47. Miriam Steele, personal communication, 2015.

48. Bernier et al., "Taking Stock of Two Decades of Attachment Transmission Gap."

49. Hautamäki et al., "Transmission of Attachment across Three Generations"; Benoit and Parker, "Stability and Transmission of Attachment across Three Generations."

50. Ainsworth et al., *Patterns of Attachment*.

51. van IJzendoorn, "Adult Attachment Representations, Parental Responsiveness, and Infant Attachment," 398.

52. Verhage et al., "Narrowing the Transmission Gap."

53. Recent research has uncovered some of the neural mechanisms related to these differences in mothers' ways of responding to their children. Studies have discovered that individuals with different attachment representations show different patterns in the activation of brain structures involved in the processing of emotions, threat recognition, and reward processing. These structures are part of a complex neural circuit that is thought to drive sensitive parenting. (See Verhage et al., "Narrowing the Transmission Gap," 338; Lenzi et al., "Attachment Models Affect Brain Responses in Areas Related to Emotions and Empathy in Nulliparous Women"; Riem et al., "Attachment in the Brain"; Strathearn et al., "Adult Attachment Predicts Maternal Brain and Oxytocin Response to Infant Cues"; Swain, "The Human Parental Brain."

54. Fonagy and Target, "Bridging the Transmission Gap."

55. Slade et al., "Maternal Reflective Functioning, Attachment, and the Transmission Gap."

56. A similar concept is metacognitive monitoring, see Main, "Metacognitive Knowledge, Metacognitive Monitoring, and Singular (Coherent) vs. Multiple (Incoherent) Models of Attachment."

57. Steele and Steele, "Understanding and Resolving Emotional Conflict," 142–43.

58. Grossmann, Grossmann, and Schwan, "Capturing the Wider View of Attachment."

59. Cassidy and Berlin, "The Insecure/Ambivalent Pattern of Attachment."

60. Steele and Steele, "Understanding and Resolving Emotional Conflict."

61. Bernier et al., "Taking Stock of Two Decades of Attachment Transmission Gap."

62. Thompson, "Early Attachment and Later Development," 282.

63. Bernier et al., "Taking Stock of Two Decades of Attachment Transmission Gap," 1861.

64. This term provides a parallel to Ainsworth's insecure-resistant, or overtly anxious and angry infants.

65. Hazan and Shaver, "Romantic Love Conceptualized as an Attachment Process."

66. Brennan, Clark, and Shaver, "Self-Report Measurement of Adult Attachment."

67. Social/personality psychologists often use the term "anxiety" to describe what developmental psychologists describe as resistant or ambivalent in infants and as preoccupied in adults.

68. Brennan, Clark, and Shaver, "Self-Report Measurement of Adult Attachment."

69. Bernier and Matte-Gagné, "More Bridges."

70. Bartholomew, "Avoidance of Intimacy."

71. Brennan, Clark, and Shaver, "Self-Report Measurement of Adult Attachment."

72. Fraley, Waller, and Brennan, "An Item Response Theory Analysis of Self-Report Measures of Adult Attachment."

73. Brennan, Clark, and Shaver, "Self-Report Measurement of Adult Attachment," 68.

74. Cohn et al., "Working Models of Childhood Attachment and Couple Relationships"; Roisman et al., "The Adult Attachment Interview and Self-Reports of Attachment Style."

75. Roisman et al., "The Adult Attachment Interview and Self-Reports of Attachment Style," 694.

76. Bouthillier et al., "Predictive Validity of Adult Attachment Measures in Relation to Emotion Regulation Behaviors in Marital Interactions."

77. Mikulincer and Shaver, *Attachment in Adulthood: Structure, Dynamics, and Change, Second Edition.*

78. Frei and Shaver, "Respect in Close Relationships."

79. Frei and Shaver, "Respect in Close Relationships"; Campbell et al., "Perceptions of Conflict and Support in Romantic Relationships"; Simpson, Rholes, and Phillips, "Conflict in Close Relationships."

80. Davila and Bradbury, "Attachment Insecurity and the Distinction between Unhappy Spouses Who Do and Do Not Divorce."

81. Mikulincer and Shaver, *Attachment in Adulthood: Structure, Dynamics, and Change, Second Edition.*

82. Mikulincer and Shaver, *Attachment in Adulthood: Structure, Dynamics, and Change, Second Edition*; Consedine, Fiori, and Magai, "Regulating Emotion Expression and Regulating Emotion Experience"; Fossati et al., "Alexithymia and Attachment Insecurities in Impulsive Aggression"; Mikulincer, "Adult Attachment Style and Individual Differences in Functional Versus Dysfunctional Experiences of Anger."

83. Mikulincer, "Adult Attachment Style and Individual Differences in Functional Versus Dysfunctional Experiences of Anger."

84. Bowlby, *A Secure Base.*

85. In the ambiguous scenario, two statements emphasized the partner's hostile intent, while the two other statements dismissed him or her from such an intent.

86. Mayseless and Scharf, "Adolescents' Attachment Representations and Their Capacity for Intimacy in Close Relationships."

87. Creasey and Ladd, "Generalized and Specific Attachment Representations."

88. Sabourin, Valois, and Lussier, "Development and Validation of a Brief Version of the Dyadic Adjustment Scale with a Nonparametric Item Analysis Model."

89. Pierre Janet actually coined the term "unconscious," and some of his writings about the unconscious mind preceded those of Freud. However, he never achieved the recognition that Sigmund Freud received. (See Ellenberg, *The Discovery of the Unconscious*, 406–9.)
90. Ellenberger, *The Discovery of the Unconscious*, 454–57.
91. Eagle, *From Classical to Contemporary Psychoanalysis*.
92. Bowlby, *Attachment and Loss, Vol. 3*, 44–55.
93. Steele and Steele, "Understanding and Resolving Emotional Conflict."
94. Bernier, Larose, and Boivin, "Individual Differences in Adult Attachment."
95. Main and Goldwyn, unpublished, cited by Bernier, Larose, and Boivin, "Individual Differences in Adult Attachment."
96. Bouthillier et al., "Predictive Validity of Adult Attachment Measures in Relation to Emotion Regulation Behaviors in Marital Interactions"; Roisman et al., "The Adult Attachment Interview and Self-Reports of Attachment Style."
97. Interactional Dimensions Coding System (IDSC); Julien, Markman, and Lindhal, "A Comparison of a Global and a Microanalytic Coding System."
98. Bouthillier et al., "Predictive Validity of Adult Attachment Measures in Relation to Emotion Regulation Behaviors in Marital Interactions."
99. Roisman et al., "The Adult Attachment Interview and Self-Reports of Attachment Style."
100. Ibid.
101. Ibid.
102. Bernier and Matte-Gagné, "More Bridges."
103. Fraley et al., "Interpersonal and Genetic Origins of Adult Attachment Styles."
104. Oriña et al., "Developmental and Dyadic Perspectives on Commitment in Adult Romantic Relationships."
105. Zayas et al., "Roots of Adult Attachment."

REFERENCES

Ainsworth, Mary D. Salter, Mary C. Blehar, Everett Waters, and Sally N. Wall. *Patterns of Attachment: A Psychological Study of the Strange Situation*. New York and London: Psychology Press, 1978/2015.
Ainsworth, Mary D. Salter, and Carolyn Eichberg. "Effects on Infant-Mother Attachment of Mother's Unresolved Loss of an Attachment Figure, or Other Traumatic Experience." *Attachment across the Life Cycle* 3 (1991): 160–83.
Bakermans-Kranenburg, Marian J., and Marinus H. van IJzendoorn. "A Psychometric Study of the Adult Attachment Interview: Reliability and Discriminant Validity." *Developmental Psychology* 29, no. 5 (1993): 870–79.
———. "The First 10,000 Adult Attachment Interviews: Distributions of Adult Attachment Representations in Clinical and Non-Clinical Groups." *Attachment & Human Development* 11, no. 3 (2009): 223–63.
Bartholomew, Kim. "Avoidance of Intimacy: An Attachment Perspective." *Journal of Social and Personal Relationships* 7, no. 2 (1990): 147–78.
Benoit, Diane, and Kevin CH Parker. "Stability and Transmission of Attachment across Three Generations." *Child Development* 65, no. 5 (1994): 1444–56.
Bernier, Annie, Simon Larose, and Michel Boivin. "Individual Differences in Adult Attachment: Disentangling Two Assessment Traditions." *European Journal of Developmental Psychology* 4, no. 2 (2007): 220–28.
Bernier, Annie, and Célia Matte-Gagné. "More Bridges: Investigating the Relevance of Self-Report and Interview Measures of Adult Attachment for Marital and Caregiving Relationships." *International Journal of Behavioral Development* 35, no. 4 (2011): 307–16.
Bernier, Annie, Célia Matte-Gagné, Marie-Ève Bélanger, and Natasha Whipple. "Taking Stock of Two Decades of Attachment Transmission Gap: Broadening the Assessment of Maternal Behavior." *Child Development* 85, no. 5 (2014): 1852–65.

Bouthillier, Donald, Danielle Julien, Monique Dubé, Isabelle Bélanger, and Manon Hamelin. "Predictive Validity of Adult Attachment Measures in Relation to Emotion Regulation Behaviors in Marital Interactions." *Journal of Adult Development* 9, no. 4 (2002): 291–305.

Bowlby, John. "The Growth of Independence in the Young Child." *Royal Society of Health Journal* 76 (1956): 587–91.

———. *The Making and Breaking of Affectional Bonds*. London: Tavistock, 1979/2005.

———. *Attachment and Loss, Vol. 3, Loss: Sadness and Depression*. New York: Basic Books, 1980.

———. *A Secure Base: Clinical Applications of Attachment Theory*. New York: Basic Books, 1988.

Brennan, Kelly A., Catherine L. Clark, and Phillip R. Shaver. "Self-Report Measurement of Adult Attachment: An Integrative Overview." In *Attachment Theory and Close Relationships*, edited by Jeffry A. Simpson and W. Steven Rhodes, 46–76. New York: The Guilford Press, 1998.

Campbell, Lorne, Jeffry A. Simpson, Jennifer Boldry, and Deborah A. Kashy. "Perceptions of Conflict and Support in Romantic Relationships: The Role of Attachment Anxiety." *Journal of Personality and Social Psychology* 88, no. 3 (2005): 510–31.

Cassidy, Jude, and Lisa J. Berlin. "The Insecure/Ambivalent Pattern of Attachment: Theory and Research." *Child Development* 65, no. 4 (1994): 971–91.

Cohn, Deborah A., Daniel H. Silver, Carolyn P. Cowan, Philip A. Cowan, and Jane Pearson. "Working Models of Childhood Attachment and Couple Relationships." *Journal of Family Issues* 13, no. 4 (1992): 432–49.

Consedine, Nathan S., Katherine L. Fiori, and Carol Magai. "Regulating Emotion Expression and Regulating Emotion Experience: Divergent Associations with Dimensions of Attachment among Older Women." *Attachment & Human Development* 14, no. 5 (2012): 477–500.

Creasey, Gary, and Aimee Ladd. "Generalized and Specific Attachment Representations: Unique and Interactive Roles in Predicting Conflict Behaviors in Close Relationships." *Personality and Social Psychology Bulletin* 31, no. 8 (2005): 1026–38.

Crowell, Judith A., R. Chris Fraley, and Phillip R. Shaver. "Measurement of Individual Differences in Adult Attachment." In *Handbook of Attachment: Theory, Research, and Clinical Applications, Third Edition*, edited by Jude Cassidy and Phillip R. Shaver, 598–635. New York: The Guilford Press, 2016.

Davila, Joanne, and Thomas N. Bradbury. "Attachment Insecurity and the Distinction between Unhappy Spouses Who Do and Do Not Divorce." *Journal of Family Psychology* 15, no. 3 (2001): 371–93.

Eagle, Morris N. *From Classical to Contemporary Psychoanalysis: A Critique and Integration*. Vol. 70. New York/London: Routledge, 2011.

Ellenberger, Henri F. *The Discovery of the Unconscious: The History and Evolution of Dynamic Psychiatry*. New York: Basic Books, 1970.

Fonagy, Peter, Howard Steele, and Miriam Steele. "Maternal Representations of Attachment during Pregnancy Predict the Organization of Infant-Mother Attachment at One Year of Age." *Child Development* 62, no. 5 (1991): 891–905.

Fonagy, Peter, and Mary Target. "Bridging the Transmission Gap: An End to an Important Mystery of Attachment Research?" *Attachment & Human Development* 7, no. 3 (2005): 333–43.

Fossati, Andrea, Elena Acquarini, Judith A. Feeney, Serena Borroni, Federica Grazioli, Laura E. Giarolli, Gianluca Franciosi, and Cesare Maffei. "Alexithymia and Attachment Insecurities in Impulsive Aggression." *Attachment & Human Development* 11, no. 2 (2009): 165–82.

Fraley, R. Chris, Glenn I. Roisman, Cathryn Booth-LaForce, Margaret Tresch Owen, and Ashley S. Holland. "Interpersonal and Genetic Origins of Adult Attachment Styles: A Longitudinal Study from Infancy to Early Adulthood." *Journal of Personality and Social Psychology* 104, no. 5 (2013): 817–38.

Fraley, R. Chris, Niels G. Waller, and Kelly A. Brennan. "An Item Response Theory Analysis of Self-Report Measures of Adult Attachment." *Journal of Personality and Social Psychology* 78, no. 2 (2000): 350–65.

Frei, Jennifer R., and Phillip R. Shaver. "Respect in Close Relationships: Prototype Definition, Self-Report Assessment, and Initial Correlates." *Personal Relationships* 9, no. 2 (2002): 121–39.

George, Carol, Nancy Kaplan, and Mary Main. "Adult Attachment Interview Protocol." Unpublished Manuscript, University of California, Berkeley, 1984.

———. "Adult Attachment Interview Protocol" (Third Edition). Unpublished Manuscript, University of California, Berkeley, 1996.

Grossmann, Karin, Klaus E. Grossmann, Heinz Kindler, and Peter Zimmermann. "A Wider View of Attachment and Exploration: The Influence of Mothers and Fathers on the Development of Psychological Security from Infancy to Young Adulthood." In *Handbook of Attachment: Theory, Research, and Clinical Applications, Second Edition*, edited by Jude Cassidy and Phillip R. Shaver, 857–79. New York: The Guilford Press, 2008.

Grossmann, Klaus E., Karin Grossmann, and Anna Schwan. "Capturing the Wider View of Attachment: A Reanalysis of Ainsworth's Strange Situation." In *Measuring Emotion in Infants and Children (Vol. 2)*, edited by Carol Ellis Izard and Peter B. Read, 124–76. New York: Cambridge University Press, 1986.

Hautamäki, Airi, Laura Hautamäki, Leena Neuvonen, and Sinikka Maliniemi-Piispanen. "Transmission of Attachment across Three Generations." *European Journal of Developmental Psychology* 7, no. 5 (2010): 618–34.

Hazan, Cindy, and Phillip Shaver. "Romantic Love Conceptualized as an Attachment Process." *Journal of Personality and Social Psychology* 52, no. 3 (1987): 511–25.

Hesse, Erik. "The Adult Attachment Interview: Historical and Current Perspectives." In *Handbook of Attachment: Theory, Research, and Clinical Applications*, edited by Jude Cassidy and Phillip R. Shaver, 395–433. New York: The Guilford Press, 1999.

———. "The Adult Attachment Interview: Protocol, Method of Analysis, and Empirical Studies." In *Handbook of Attachment: Theory, Research, and Clinical Applications, Second Edition*, edited by Jude Cassidy and Phillip R. Shaver, 552–98. New York: The Guilford Press, 2008.

Hesse, Erik. "The Adult Attachment Interview: Protocol, Method of Analysis, and Selected Empirical Studies: 1985–2015." In *Handbook of Attachment: Theory, Research, and Clinical Applications, Third Edition*, edited by Jude Cassidy and Phillip R. Shaver, 553–97. New York: The Guilford Press, 2016.

Hesse, Erik, and Mary Main. "Second-Generation Effects of Unresolved Trauma in Nonmaltreating Parents: Dissociated, Frightened, and Threatening Parental Behavior." *Psychoanalytic Inquiry* 19, no. 4 (1999): 481–540.

———. "Disorganized Infant, Child, and Adult Attachment: Collapse in Behavioral and Attentional Strategies." *Journal of the American Psychoanalytic Association* 48, no. 4 (2000): 1097–127.

———. "Frightened, Threatening, and Dissociative Parental Behavior in Low-Risk Samples: Description, Discussion, and Interpretations." *Development and Psychopathology* 18, no. 2 (2006): 309–43.

Julien, Danielle, Howard J. Markman, and Kristin M. Lindahl. "A Comparison of a Global and a Microanalytic Coding System: Implications for Future Trends in Studying Interactions." *Behavioral Assessment* 11, no. 1 (1989): 81–100.

Lenzi, Delia, Cristina Trentini, Patrizia Pantano, Emiliano Macaluso, Gian Luigi Lenzi, and Massimo Ammaniti. "Attachment Models Affect Brain Responses in Areas Related to Emotions and Empathy in Nulliparous Women." *Human Brain Mapping* 34, no. 6 (2013): 1399–414.

Main, Mary. "Metacognitive Knowledge, Metacognitive Monitoring, and Singular (Coherent) vs. Multiple (Incoherent) Models of Attachment: Findings and Directions for Future Research." In *Attachment across the Life Cycle*, edited by Colin M. Parkes, Joan Stevenson-Hinde and Peter Marris, 127–59. London: Routledge, 1991.

———. "Recent Studies in Attachment: Overview, with Selected Implications for Clinical Work." In *Attachment Theory: Social, Developmental, and Clinical Perspectives*, edited by Susan Goldberg, Roy Muir, and John Kerr, 407–74. Hillsdale, NJ: The Analytic Press, 1995.

―――. "The Organized Categories of Infant, Child, and Adult Attachment: Flexible vs. Inflexible Attention under Attachment-Related Stress." *Journal of the American Psychoanalytic Association* 48, no. 4 (2000): 1055–96.

Main, Mary, and Jude Cassidy. "Categories of Response to Reunion with the Parent at Age Six: Predicted from Attachment Classifications and Stable over a One-month Period." *Developmental Psychology* 24, no. 3 (1988): 415–26.

Main, Mary, and Ruth Goldwyn. *Adult Attachment Scoring and Classification System*. Unpublished Manuscript, University of California at Berkeley, 1984.

―――. *Adult Attachment Classification System, Draft 6.2.* Unpublished Manuscript, University of California at Berkeley, 1998, cited by Bernier et al., 2007.

Main, Mary, Ruth Goldwyn, and Erik Hesse, *Adult Attachment Scoring and Classification System*. Unpublished Manuscript, University of California at Berkeley, 2003.

Main, Mary, and Erik Hesse. "Parents' Unresolved Traumatic Experiences Are Related to Infant Disorganized Attachment Status: Is Frightened and/or Frightening Parental Behavior the Linking Mechanism?" In *Attachment in the Preschool Years: Theory, Research, and Intervention*, edited by Mark T. Greenberg, Dante Cicchetti, and E. Mark Cummings, 161–82. Chicago: University of Chicago Press, 1990.

Main, Mary, Erik Hesse, and Nancy Kaplan. "Predictability of Attachment Behavior and Representational Processes at 1, 6, and 19 Years of Age: The Berkeley Longitudinal Study." In *Attachment from Infancy to Adulthood: The Major Longitudinal Studies*, edited by Klaus. E. Grossmann, Karin Grossmann, and Everett Waters, 245–304. New York: The Guilford Press, 2005.

Main, Mary, Nancy Kaplan, and Jude Cassidy. "Security in Infancy, Childhood, and Adulthood: A Move to the Level of Representation." *Monographs of the Society for Research in Child Development* 50, no. 1/2 (1985): 66–104.

Main, Mary, and Judith Solomon. "Discovery of a New, Insecure-Disorganized/Disoriented Attachment Pattern." In *Affective Development in Infancy*, edited by T. Berry Brazelton and Michael W. Yogman, 95–124. Westport, CT: Ablex Publishing, 1986.

Mayseless, Ofra, and Miri Scharf. "Adolescents' Attachment Representations and Their Capacity for Intimacy in Close Relationships." *Journal of Research on Adolescence* 17, no. 1 (2007): 23–50.

Mikulincer, Mario. "Adult Attachment Style and Individual Differences in Functional Versus Dysfunctional Experiences of Anger." *Journal of Personality and Social Psychology* 74, no. 2 (1998): 511–24.

Mikulincer, Mario, and Phillip R. Shaver. *Attachment in Adulthood: Structure, Dynamics, and Change, Second Edition*. New York: The Guilford Press, 2016.

Oriña, M. Minda, W. Andrew Collins, Jeffry A. Simpson, Jessica E. Salvatore, Katherine C. Haydon, and John S. Kim. "Developmental and Dyadic Perspectives on Commitment in Adult Romantic Relationships." *Psychological Science* 22, no. 7 (2011): 908–15.

Powell, Burt, Glen Cooper, Kent Hoffman, and Bob Marvin. *The Circle of Security Intervention: Enhancing Attachment in Early Parent-Child Relationships*. New York: The Guilford Press, 2013.

Riem, Madelon M. E., Marian J. Bakermans-Kranenburg, Marinus H. van IJzendoorn, Dorothée Out, and Serge A. R. B. Rombouts. "Attachment in the Brain: Adult Attachment Representations Predict Amygdala and Behavioral Responses to Infant Crying." *Attachment & Human Development* 14, no. 6 (2012): 533–51.

Roisman, Glenn I., Ashley Holland, Keren Fortuna, R. Chris Fraley, Eric Clausell, and Alexis Clarke. "The Adult Attachment Interview and Self-Reports of Attachment Style: An Empirical Rapprochement." *Journal of Personality and Social Psychology* 92, no. 4 (2007): 678–97.

Sabourin, Stephane, Pierre Valois, and Yvan Lussier. "Development and Validation of a Brief Version of the Dyadic Adjustment Scale with a Nonparametric Item Analysis Model." *Psychological Assessment* 17, no. 1 (2005): 15–27.

Sagi, Abraham, Marinus H. van IJzendoorn, Miri Scharf, Nina Koren-Karie, Tirtsa Joels, and Ofra Mayseless. "Stability and Discriminant Validity of the Adult Attachment Interview: A

Psychometric Study in Young Israeli Adults." *Developmental Psychology* 30, no. 5 (1994): 771–77.

Siegel, Daniel J. *The Developing Mind, Second Edition: How Relationships and the Brain Interact to Shape Who We Are.* New York: Guilford Publications, 2012.

Simpson, Jeffry A., W. Steven Rholes, and Dede Phillips. "Conflict in Close Relationships: An Attachment Perspective." *Journal of Personality and Social Psychology* 71, no. 5 (1996): 899–914.

Slade, Arietta, John Grienenberger, Elizabeth Bernbach, Dahlia Levy, and Alison Locker. "Maternal Reflective Functioning, Attachment, and the Transmission Gap: A Preliminary Study." *Attachment & Human Development* 7, no. 3 (2005): 283–98.

Steele, Howard, and Miriam Steele. "Understanding and Resolving Emotional Conflict: The London Parent-Child Project." In *Attachment from Infancy to Adulthood: The Major Longitudinal Studies*, edited by Klaus. E. Grossmann, Karin Grossmann, and Everett Waters, 137–64. New York: The Guilford Press, 2005.

Steele, Howard, Miriam Steele, and Peter Fonagy. "Associations among Attachment Classifications of Mothers, Fathers, and Their Infants." *Child Development* (1996): 541–55.

Strathearn, Lane, Peter Fonagy, Janet Amico, and P. Read Montague. "Adult Attachment Predicts Maternal Brain and Oxytocin Response to Infant Cues." *Neuropsychopharmacology* 34, no. 13 (2009): 2655–66.

Swain, James E. "The Human Parental Brain: *In Vivo* Neuroimaging." *Progress in Neuro-Psychopharmacology and Biological Psychiatry* 35, no. 5 (2011): 1242–54.

Thompson, Ross A. "Early Attachment and Later Development." In *Handbook of Attachment: Theory, Research, and Clinical Applications*, edited by Jude Cassidy and Phillip R. Shaver, 265–86. New York: The Guilford Press, 1999.

van IJzendoorn, Marinus H. "Adult Attachment Representations, Parental Responsiveness, and Infant Attachment: A Meta-Analysis on the Predictive Validity of the Adult Attachment Interview." *Psychological Bulletin* 117, no. 3 (1995): 387–403.

van IJzendoorn, Marinus H., and Marian J. Bakermans-Kranenburg. "Attachment Representations in Mothers, Fathers, Adolescents, and Clinical Groups: A Meta-Analytic Search for Normative Data." *Journal of Consulting and Clinical Psychology* 64, no. 1 (1996): 8–21.

———. "The Distribution of Adult Attachment Representations in Clinical Groups: A Meta-Analytic Search for Patterns of Attachment in 105 AAI Studies." In *Clinical Applications of the Adult Attachment Interview*, edited by Howard Steele and Miriam Steele, 69–96. New York: The Guilford Press, 2008.

Verhage, Marije L., Carlo Schuengel, Sheri Madigan, R. M. Fearon, Mirjam Oosterman, Rosalinda Cassibba, Marian J. Bakermans-Kranenburg, and Marinus H. van IJzendoorn. "Narrowing the Transmission Gap: A Synthesis of Three Decades of Research on Intergenerational Transmission of Attachment." *Psychological Bulletin* 143, no. 4 (2015): 337–66.

Zayas, Vivian, Walter Mischel, Yuichi Shoda, and J. Lawrence Aber. "Roots of Adult Attachment: Maternal Caregiving at 18 Months Predicts Adult Peer and Partner Attachment." *Social Psychological and Personality Science* 2, no. 3 (2011): 289–97.

Chapter Six

Links to Adaptation in Middle Childhood and Adolescence

As we return to considering attachment security in growing children, we come to a field of inquiry that has attracted less attention from researchers. As noted in a paper published in the year 2000:

> Traditionally, attachment theory has been a theory of infancy and of adult relationships, with a great deal of what lies in between left to the imagination. Completing this picture is essential to understanding the effects of early experience, the mechanisms underlying stability and change, and the relevance of ordinary socialization process in attachment development.[1]

The four longitudinal studies introduced in Chapter Four have now followed children from infancy to late adolescence or adulthood. A fifth longitudinal study begun in 1991, the National Institute of Child Health and Human Development Study of Early Child Care and Youth Development, has followed youngsters in the United States to mid-adolescence.[2]

The studies varied in a number of ways—e.g., the ages when children and parents were observed, aspects of youngsters' development that were studied, and ways of assessing youth. In this chapter we will look at what researchers have learned from the longitudinal studies about the strength of the correlation between early attachment security and behavioral, social, emotional, and cognitive development through childhood and adolescence.

While the major long-term studies provide some of the most important information we have about the influence of attachment security on children's adjustment, a great deal of other research has contributed to what we now know. With the development of new attachment measures appropriate for older children, other researchers have been able to initiate study of children when they are beyond infancy. The new measures also help to assess continuity of attachment security over time.

FOLLOWING CHILDREN AS THEY GROW

In considering the question "What does a securely attached child look like at later ages?" we have to think about what we are asking. Are we saying, "What does a child who is securely attached at one year look like when he or she is six, ten, or sixteen?" This question assumes there is continuity in security of attachment. As was discussed in Chapter Three, continuity in security of attachment depends upon stability in quality of parenting over time. Certainly, not every child in a sample experiences continuity in parenting, but do enough children experience on-going stability that we can find a statistical relationship between early security and later behavior, and also perhaps in underlying thoughts and feelings?

Even if expecting on-going stability as the norm, we certainly shouldn't expect all secure infants to develop in the same way, and to necessarily be well adjusted in later years. Even when parenting and family experiences don't change, parents who had skills in providing attachment security may be less adept in later parenting tasks, such as facilitating peer relationships, guiding problem solving, or setting limits. And, relationships with siblings, peers, and teachers influence children as well.

A second way of thinking about the question "What does a securely attached child look like at later ages?" is that one is inquiring about the current-day characteristics of a child when there is new, updated information about security in his or her attachment relationships. This question relies on having the newer assessment measures appropriate for children of older ages. In middle childhood and adolescence, attachment security cannot be easily identified by observing separation and reunion episodes, because separation is normally less stressful and does not trigger attachment behaviors.[3] Instead, researchers have developed techniques for helping children show their sense of attachment security, i.e., the representations they have abstracted and constructed out of their earlier experiences.[4]

One approach to probe representations of attachment experiences and expectations is to ask children to make up stories in response to attachment-related pictures. Alternately, children are given "story stems," i.e., they are asked to complete stories begun by the experimenter. Children's unique stories convey information about how children view attachment figures and about what kinds of responses they expect from them. Stories may also convey information about children's sense of their own self-worth, and with these techniques, researchers can see how comfortable children are discussing separation-related themes.

ASSESSMENT OF ATTACHMENT SECURITY
IN OLDER CHILDREN

As an example, one assessment measure that was developed to probe attachment security for children who are approximately four to seven years old is the Separation Anxiety Test (SAT).[5] Children are shown six photographs or drawings of children undergoing either brief, mild separations such as parents going out for the evening or simply tucking the child in bed and leaving the room, or more severe and longer separations. More stressful separations include the parent going away for the weekend while the child stays with a relative, or the child parting from the parent on the first day of school.

With the SAT, children's responses are rated as to their emotional openness as well as the degree to which they offer constructive responses as to what children would do. The validity of the SAT was demonstrated in a stable middle-class sample, where six-year-old children's security as measured by the SAT was very consistent with the degree of security they had earlier shown in the Strange Situation with mothers.[6]

Sample Responses to the SAT

The SAT is introduced to children in this way: *"Parents worry sometimes about what children think when they have to go away for a little while. So we thought we would ask you to tell us what you think a child your age would feel and what a child your age would do when parents go away for a little while."* Following this introduction, each of the six pictures is presented.

On the SAT emotional openness scale, children who receive high scores for security are able to imagine the pictured child as lonely, sad, fearful, or angry during many of the separations and to offer reasons for these emotions. High-scoring children show minimal resistance, withdrawal, or stress in responding.

In contrast, children who receive the lowest ratings are not able to spontaneously express open-ended feelings, and typically respond in a passive way. Some children are silent and appear depressed, and some make irrational responses or become disorganized. For example, one child insisted that the child in the picture would "feel good" or "feel *nothing*." This child became increasingly hysterical and started to hit a stuffed animal, saying, "Bad lion! Bad lion!" In infancy, this child had been classified as insecure-disorganized.[7]

Overall Behavioral Adjustment

In beginning to understand developing children with differing degrees of attachment security, we'll first consider readily apparent behaviors. These are the behaviors that an observer might comment on; e.g., "Emily tends to be a bit aggressive and disobedient," or "Christopher acts quite shy and anxious in new situations." In Chapter Four, we reviewed evidence about behavioral adjustment in preschoolers. The early studies conducted with this age group suggested that in disadvantaged, high-risk samples, insecurely attached children had higher rates of behavior problems, but there was limited evidence for this in middle-class samples.

In looking at a larger number of studies that have accumulated over several decades which have assessed the behavioral adjustment of children up to twelve years old, a somewhat different picture emerges. Many studies distinguished between problems that were of the "externalizing" versus the "internalizing" variety. Externalizing problems include aggression, oppositional behavior, conduct difficulties, or hostility; these problems typically affect interactions with others. Internalizing problems include symptoms such as anxiety, depression, social withdrawal, and somatic complaints, which reflect more internal suffering.

"Externalizing" Behavior Problems

To examine the issue of externalizing problems in a consistent way, researchers searched for and reviewed all studies that used observational methods for determining attachment security, such as the Strange Situation Procedure. In these studies, parents, teachers, caregivers, clinicians, or trained observers completed checklists of problem behaviors. In this meta-analysis, researchers identified more than sixty studies—involving almost 6,000 children—that looked at the relationship between externalizing problems and attachment patterns.[8]

This massive database indicated that early attachment insecurity is indeed correlated with subsequent higher rates of externalizing behaviors. Information about the behaviors of children with disorganized attachments was less clear; many studies did not specifically distinguish children with disorganized attachments from those with all forms of insecure attachment. In the studies that did, disorganized children were at slightly greater risk for externalizing problems than were other insecurely attached children.

Compared with the early preschool studies, this meta-analysis, which included older as well as younger children found that socio-economic status didn't distinguish insecurely attached children who had externalizing problems from those who did not. Thus, living in a "low-risk" family, at least low risk by economic standards, didn't protect children with attachment insecurity from developing higher levels of behavior problems.

"Internalizing" Problems

Turning to the relationship between attachment insecurity and internalizing problems, researchers again gathered a large database, drawing upon the results of forty-two studies. Compared with externalizing problems, researchers found a smaller, but still significant. correlation between attachment security and degree of internalizing problems. However, only the children who as infants had had insecure-avoidant attachments (i.e., those infants who had appeared to maintain a "stiff upper lip" when reunited with parents in the Strange Situation) were observed to have higher rates of internalizing problems; children with insecure-resistant or disorganized attachments were not rated higher in these areas.[9]

In considering the discovery that attachment insecurity was more strongly associated with externalizing than internalizing problems, researchers speculated what might explain this finding.[10] They noted that children's classifications as insecure or disorganized are based on a perceived inability to use attachment figures to relieve intense negative emotions. Lacking the ability to effectively manage these intense negative emotions might result in children developing impulsive regulation strategies. Children's impulsiveness may prevent them from inhibiting expressions of anger and aggression.[11]

This review of studies of behavior problems in insecurely attached children only begins to tell us a little bit about the path that children may take beyond the early years. And it is important to remember that these studies are correlational; significant findings only mean that, on average, children with different attachment histories differ during the childhood years in the way they act and are observed to feel.

The Social World: Predictions from Attachment Histories

To what extent do children's attachment experiences—their interactions with their mothers and fathers during infancy—lay a foundation that contributes to their ability to navigate the social world in later years? The results of two of the longitudinal studies are particularly helpful in addressing this question. Researchers with the National Institute of Child Health and Human Development provide careful quantitative analysis of children's social competence through age fifteen. In addition, the Minnesota longitudinal study provides rich data from careful observations of peer relationships during middle childhood and adolescence.

The National Institute of Child Health and Human Development (NICHD) Study

The NICHD study was very large and diverse in scope, following over 1,000 children from infancy to age fifteen. Researchers analyzing the data collected in this study were able to draw on a good number of direct observations as well as questionnaire measures of social skills. Observers rated mother's sensitivity interacting with her child at four points in time in the first three years, and then again at several times during elementary school and at age fifteen. The NICHD researchers also collected reports of children's social competence from parents and teachers throughout elementary school, and from parents when youngsters were fifteen.

Researchers found that the early ratings of maternal sensitivity had an ongoing and consistent level of influence on children's social competence through the years. They concluded that an "enduring effects" model fit the data better than a "revisionist" model, in which early experience would expect to have a declining effect on later adjustment. As researchers had observations of maternal sensitivity at later ages, they were able to statistically test whether the consistency might be explained by ongoing stability in the environment rather than by early experiences with mothers. Adding in later observations of mothers' sensitivity did not eliminate the significant influence of early maternal sensitivity.[12]

This very large study provides support for the validity of findings from the Minnesota study, which gathered qualitative observations as well as standardized measures. The observations made in Minnesota of youngsters in a variety of settings during childhood and adolescence will help make the NICHD study's findings more meaningful.

The Minnesota Longitudinal Study

The Minnesota researchers found that even in their high-risk sample, where lack of continuity of adaptation was more frequently observed than in middle-class families, the very early measure of a child's attachment security captured by the Strange Situation did continue to predict, at least to some degree, children's functioning for many years. The Minnesota researchers were able to get an in-depth look at the social relationships of some of the children in their sample by carefully observing a group of about four dozen children in a camp program when they were about ten years old, and then again at a camp reunion at fifteen years of age.

Summer Camp in Minnesota

The majority of the children who attended their camps had also participated in the pre-school programs described in Chapter Four. Just as they had arranged for some children in their sample to attend special pre-school programs, the Minnesota researchers offered the ten-year-olds the opportunity to participate in a four-week camp program. As these children engaged in sports, arts and crafts, circle times, and more relaxed activities, they formed friendships and maneuvered their way through a novel social setting. At the reunion, forty-one of forty-eight campers returned and were seen in large and small group activities, at meals, free time, and at a party. [13]

In the camp program for ten-year-olds, Strange Situation attachment security was significantly related to the broadest measures of competence at camp, such as the counselor ratings and rankings of social competence, self-confidence, and emotional health and self-esteem. Overall, camp counselors saw those who had secure attachment histories as being more self-confident, emotionally healthy, and competent. These children were as a group more peer focused. They spent more time with peers and less time alone with adults, and they were almost twice as likely to form friendships as those with insecure histories. In addition, they seemed more comfortable in larger social groups; those with secure attachment histories were more often in groups of three or more children. [14]

Certainly, there were many exceptions. The Minnesota researchers tested their ability to predict the importance of early attachment security by choosing pairs of children who looked similarly competent in middle-school camp, and then looking back at their attachment histories. While many of these pairs of similarly functioning children did indeed share a history of either secure or insecure adjustment, there were some notable exceptions. For example, of twelve children who were insecure-avoidant in the Strange Situation, only two resembled other insecure-avoidant children, and seven resembled children who had been secure as infants. So, particularly in the insecure-avoidant group, there was considerable flux in social adjustment in the first decade of life. [15]

In making predictions from early attachment history to later social and emotional competence, researchers found that combining information about social skills in the preschool years with attachment history from the Strange Situation Procedure contributed to a more accurate prediction of later adjustment. In other words, knowing a child's attachment classification *and* knowing how they functioned in preschool was more informative than only knowing their attachment history. Clearly, if early security contributes to a trajectory toward good social and emotional adjustment, continued solid parenting and healthy social experiences support that positive trajectory as children move toward the middle-childhood years. [16]

Parents and Teens at Thirteen Years

Between the time of the camp program and the later camp reunion, parents and their thirteen-year-old children were seen together. Researchers gave the parent-teen dyads various tasks, such as planning an anti-smoking campaign, having children direct their blindfolded parent in constructing an object, and engaging in discussions. Observations were coded on scales reflecting spontaneity and security, support and scaffolding, and ease and efficiency of

working together. These were summarized as "balance scales" which reflected the overall quality of the relationship.

The "balance scales," particularly the ratings regarding security and spontaneity in the parent-teen dyads, were quite strongly related to measures of
how competent children had appeared at camp three years earlier, when they
were ten years old. Looking at correlations over a slightly longer time frame,
there was a significant, but less strong, relationship between the observations
at age thirteen and ratings of early parental care and quality of home support
and stimulation at age six.[17]

Camp Reunion at Fifteen Years

Fourteen years after participating in the Strange Situation Procedure (SSP),
ratings of teens' social competence as given by camp counselors were significantly correlated with the campers' attachment history in the SSP. In fact,
surprisingly, the relationship between attachment history and adolescent social competence was as strong or stronger than it had been for preschoolers
and campers in middle childhood. Researchers looked at a number of qualities, including teens' willingness to be emotionally vulnerable and their
ability to negotiate the complexities of their peer group. Attachment history
was particularly correlated with the capacity for vulnerability, and teens who
were securely attached as one-year-olds were better able to negotiate the peer
group challenges.

While attachment history emerged as important, teen functioning could
best be explained by putting together much of the information researchers
had gathered at the various points in time when parents' behavior had been
observed. Attachment history in the SSP by itself could not fully explain
strengths and weaknesses in the teens. The ratings of relationship quality
between thirteen-year-olds and their parents were significantly correlated
with social competence in the reunion study, and these ratings sometimes
contributed an important dimension not captured by ratings of early care.

The Minnesota researchers found evidence to support the idea that much
of the basis for social competence in the mid-teen years had been established
by the end of the preschool period. In fact, after taking account of attachment
and preschool data, ratings of middle-childhood camp behavior did not stand
out as significant in predicting fifteen-year-old's behavior.[18]

Gender Boundary Issues

In the camp setting, the Minnesota researchers had an opportunity to look at
one aspect of typical middle-childhood behavior: adherence to same-gender
friendships and avoidance of associations with members of the other gender.
At age ten, most children have developed a strong sense that boys are sup-
posed to associate only with boys, and girls with girls. As the Minnesota

researchers noted: "At no other age do boys and girls behave as though one may be contaminated by mere interaction or proximity with members of the other gender. Claimed fear of 'cooties' and 'boy germs' conveys in a playful way the seriousness of the issues involved."[19]

Careful observations based on videotape clips made during camp activities showed that children in the camp program maintained gender boundaries to varying degrees.

The key question for researchers was whether maintenance of gender boundaries, or failure to do so, was related to attachment history. With an average of 300 observations for each child, the researchers were able to calculate "cross-gender" scores based on the proportion of times a child was engaged only with members of the opposite gender. The cross-gender interactions were coded as to whether they were casual and not truly violating boundaries, or whether children actively violated boundaries by behaviors such as hovering, joining, or engaging in behaviors with some sexual meaning.

There indeed was an association with attachment history. Those with secure histories maintained gender boundaries significantly more often and violated boundaries less often. One other rating from early observations stood out as significant: at twenty-four months, some mothers behaved "seductively" with children during a laboratory clean-up period, and their children were more likely later to engage in boundary violations. The small number of mothers who used techniques described as "seductive" showed behaviors such as bribes for affection, flirting or teasing which had a sensual quality, or sensual physical contact. In addition to seeming inappropriate to the situation, these behaviors were distinguished from purely affectionate behaviors by the fact that mothers showed these behaviors virtually exclusively with boys; mothers' behaviors had been judged inappropriate to the context.

At camp, seven children had mothers who had behaved seductively, and five of these children were among the ten children who most often engaged in boundary violations. The Minnesota researchers proposed that maintaining gender boundaries is likely useful in promoting the acquisition of skills for group functioning. It may also prevent premature heterosexual intimacy. By maintaining boundaries, intimacy and skill in functioning in groups can be mastered in the less complicated, same-gender peer group.[20]

Intimate Friendships

By the time children reach pre-adolescence, establishing a close friendship requires considerably more skill than at the preschool level. It is one thing to associate with peers, but more intimate friendships require more openness, trust, and the coordination of time and activities. The ability to provide mutual emotional support, to manage conflict, and to trust a friend with confidences leads to a satisfying relationship. However, intimate relationships pose risks of feeling hurt or betrayed, and take work to maintain.[21]

Perhaps unsurprisingly, children with secure attachment histories were more likely to form close friendships. And, these children were more likely to form friendships with *other* children with secure attachment histories. Two secure children were more likely to become friends than were other combinations of children (secure/insecure, insecure/insecure). However, there were many exceptions to secure/secure combinations; some secure/insecure friendship pairs certainly were formed.[22]

Coping with Conflict

The Minnesota researchers had noted that close peer relationships required some ability to handle the conflict that at times arises among intimate friends. A research group in London, which in the late 1980s initiated a longitudinal study called the London Parent-Child Project, were particularly interested in how early experiences might prepare children for understanding and resolving emotional conflict.

Why were the London researchers interested in conflict resolution? The lead researchers, Howard and Miriam Steele, noted that Bowlby had referred to the inevitable conflict between feelings of love and hate. Drawing from Bowlby's writings, they asserted that it is not the existence of these opposing emotions, often directed at the same person, but rather the ability to control, regulate, and resolve them that distinguishes healthy from unhealthy individuals. Bowlby felt that if parents can put up with outbursts of hostility and convey a belief that anger can be contained and controlled, children would be able to develop self-control.[23]

The London group actually began their research program before children were born, by administering the Adult Attachment Interview (AAI; described in Chapter Five) to pregnant mothers and their partners. As it turned out, children's later functioning could be predicted *both* by parents' classifications (i.e., parents' "states of mind with respect to attachment") on the Adult Attachment Interview as well as by children's Strange Situation attachment security. Parents who have secure states of mind are able to process and communicate feelings in an open, coherent way.

When these children were eleven years old, the London researchers engaged them in interviews about their most favorite and least favorite aspects of themselves, and their relationships to mother, father, sibling(s), and best friends. This "Friends and Family Interview" was introduced by the statement, "Something we have learned from studying children and families over time is that some of the strongest feelings we have, good and bad ones, arise in the context of our family relationships." The interviewers went on to say,

"There are ways in which we like things the way they are, and ways in which we would like things to change," adding, "We will be asking you about these things as we talk about yourself, your family and your best friend." Children were asked about how disagreements were negotiated, and also to support their responses with examples from daily life. To be sure that the quality of the children's responses was not influenced by their verbal ability, tests of verbal intelligence were also given, and the researchers were able to rule out verbal skills as the basis for qualitative differences in responses. [24]

Just as with adults taking the AAI, coherence of responses (i.e., children's ability to provide coherent and credible accounts of their attachment experiences and of their sense of themselves and of peer relationships) turned out to be a telling aspect of their interview responses. In predicting how coherently a child was able to talk about relationships with family and friends, researchers found that his or her parents' own understanding and communication of emotions as assessed by the earlier AAIs emerged as a central factor. [25] Children who told the most convincing and "truthful" accounts of their view of the positive and negative aspects of self and others were likely to have had mothers who were coherent, convincing, and truthful on the AAI when it was administered during pregnancy. Indeed, truthfulness has been highlighted as a core aspect of attachment security across the lifespan. [26]

RELATIONSHIPS WITH DADS

As much of attachment research has focused on the role of mothers in children's development, the London researchers were particularly interested in how the unique information they had obtained—the security of fathers on the AAI during pregnancy—might be linked to their children's social and emotional development. They found that fathers' security was related to children's behavioral adjustment at eleven years. A standard mental health screening tool that the children completed showed that some were experiencing strain in the domains of peer relations, conduct problems, and hyperactivity. When fathers had provided AAIs many years earlier that were classified insecure, their children showed evidence of more problem behaviors. [27]

A second research group, based in Germany, also looked carefully at the importance of father for children's adjustment in middle childhood. [28] In the German study, the lead researchers Klaus and Karin Grossmann, together with colleagues, were interested, among other things, in the relative importance of two distinct variables—quality of attachment (which is linked to general caregiving sensitivity) and sensitivity specifically in the area of play—in predicting children's later security of attachment.

In Chapter Two, we learned that the German researchers had found that fathers of children who were securely attached to them in the Strange Situation Procedure were not distinguished for being more sensitive during routine caregiving interactions, but were instead more sensitive during play interactions when the children were toddlers.[29] While intriguing, this finding must be understood in the social context in which the study was conducted. The German study began in the 1970s, and parents in this sample assumed traditional male and female roles, with mothers being primarily responsible for home and children, and fathers being the sole financial providers for the family.[30]

The researchers looked at what kinds of early parent-child interaction would predict attachment security at six and ten years of age. At age six, children were given the Separation Anxiety Test (SAT) (described at the beginning of this chapter); attachment security in the Strange Situation with both mothers and fathers predicted security on the SAT. However, at age ten, it was fathers' play sensitivity that predicted security of attachment in a measure of middle-childhood attachment.[31]

Security in adolescents was assessed with the Adult Attachment Interview. By adolescence, only *fathers'* early behavior—their play sensitivity—predicted security on the AAI at sixteen years. Neither the quality of infant-mother attachment nor mothers' play sensitivity were predictive of this adolescent measure. This finding underscores the importance of the (sadly, often-undervalued) role of father in early development.

Overall, the German researchers concluded that the mothers and fathers in their sample supported their children's attachment development in unique ways. Their research showed that children need both protection and sensitivity to their emotional needs in order to develop attachment security, and that they also need support for exploring the larger world. For toddlers, this support may occur during play; for older children, it may arise in a variety of arenas.[32] At least when mothers and fathers assume traditional roles in parenting, such as in the German study conducted during the 1970s and 1980s, fathers provide more of the support for exploration and mothers more of the sensitive nurturing.

DISORGANIZED ATTACHMENT: FOLLOW-UP IN MIDDLE CHILDHOOD AND ADOLESCENCE

In Chapter Two, the term "disorganized attachment" was introduced to describe children who behaved quite oddly during reunions in the Strange Situation Procedure. These children exhibited bouts of behavior that appeared to lack a clear goal, intention, or explanation. The early literature did not include much information about the later development of children with disorganized attachment in the Strange Situation. There is a good reason for this: disorganized behavior was identified a decade or so after the introduction of the three main categories (secure, insecure-avoidant, insecure-resistant), and the Minnesota and German longitudinal studies began before this category was described.[33]

In very high risk samples and those where children are known to have been maltreated, the majority of children show disorganized attachment.[34] However, in more affluent families, about 15 percent of children show disorganized attachment. In middle-class samples, parents of disorganized children often have a history of personal loss or trauma, and researchers have observed instances of these parents interacting with children in frightened or frightening ways.[35]

What happens to these children as they grow? Studies have shown that children with disorganized attachments have the most serious psychological problems during development, so it is important to spend some time discussing them. Valuable information comes from the Berkeley Longitudinal Study, a study of middle-class families that was initiated in the late 1970s by Mary Main. As Main was one of the primary individuals who identified disorganized attachment behaviors in the Strange Situation, she had particular interest in following these children as they grew.[36]

Disorganized Children at Age Six

The Berkeley study began with close to 200 participants. When these children were six years old, researchers created a smaller group that included a disproportionally large number of children who had been disorganized at one year. In this way, they were able to assemble a sample with a large enough number of this relatively rare category to allow comparison with two other groups: those who had been secure at age one, and those who had been insecure-avoidant at the same age. Each group contained about thirteen children.

An unanticipated behavioral transformation had occurred when these children came back to the lab five years after their Strange Situation visit. Many children with disorganized histories had developed very distinct but quite organized responses following a one-hour separation from their parents.[37] Further research has indicated that this shift occurs primarily between three and five years of age.[38] At six, the majority of children who were disorganized as infants exhibited behavior that was highly controlling, in either a punitive or caregiving manner.

In the punitive category, children act to humiliate, embarrass, or reject the parent. For example, just as the parent was returning, the child might say, "Don't bother me!" or might order the parent to leave. Or they might say: "Sit down and shut up, and keep your eyes closed! I said, keep them closed!" With the controlling-caregiving style, the child acted as if the parent was dependent on the child for guidance. "Want to play with me, mommy, in the sandbox? . . . It's *fun*, isn't it, Mommy?" Or: "Are you tired, Mommy? Would you like to sit down and I'll bring you some [pretend] tea?"[39]

Why would a child behave this way? Studies have found that mothers of disorganized children have higher levels of depression, dysfunctional marital relationships, parenting stress, and difficulties managing the parenting role.[40] One explanation might be that a need to control develops following interactions with a parent who has a disorganized approach to caregiving. This results in the child feeling a need to care for or control the parent.[41] Over time, the child may discover he or she can feel less helpless and gain more attention by organizing, comforting, or attending to the parent.[42]

A Third Pattern at Age Six: Behavioral Disorganization

As research proceeds, more complexities are discovered. In addition to the two controlling patterns, it was discovered that some children who are disorganized in infancy develop what has been termed an "insecure-other" or "behaviorally disorganized" pattern. These children display disordered, incomplete movements, confusion, and apprehension in the presence of the attachment figure and show no coherent strategy for seeking proximity. Their behavior is thus similar to that of disorganized infants.[43] An example of disorganized behavior at age five is provided:

> A 5-year-old boy is playing independently while his mother tries to draw his attention toward her. At one point, she asks the child to sing a song for her. He refuses, insisting that he wants to play on his own. The mother persists, saying it will make her happy and that he is a good singer. The child continues to refuse to sing a song. As the tension escalates between them, the child breaks down, saying "I will get beat up if I sing." The mother, surprised by his answer, asks him to explain himself. The child answers, "I'm ugly like my father." The mother seems quite shocked and says, "You're not ugly and neither is Dad!" The child then seems very surprised as if he did not remember his previous statement and asks, "What are you talking about?" Strikingly, during the whole interaction, the child's nonverbal behavior and posture remain neutral, and he keeps playing with his toys.[44]

In a large study (composed of a sample with a wide variety of income groups) that followed children for two years, from preschool to early school age, researchers found that approximately two-thirds of children classified at preschool age as disorganized had become controlling at the follow-up, while one-third were behaviorally disorganized.[45]

Learning from Children's Fantasies: Doll Play of Controlling Children

Two studies that included six-year-olds judged as "insecure-controlling" (a new term for disorganized children beyond infancy) observed them in a doll-play assessment. In the first study, children participated in a projective assessment in which they were given the beginning of stories dealing with potential emotionally charged interactions between child and mother and asked to complete the story, enacting it with doll families. For example, in one story, the child does not like what is served for dinner, and in another, the child has to do the one thing he or she most hates doing. The stories of children who were "insecure-controlling" often involved violent, hostile, negative, or bizarre behavior.[46]

The second study that used doll play to look at six-year-old children's underlying feelings distinguished between the play of controlling-punitive and controlling-caregiving children. The play of controlling-punitive children typically included themes of violence, punishment, and destruction, while the play of controlling-caregiving children was quite inhibited. This second group of children was extremely uncomfortable with the task and did not want to enact stories. The researchers theorized that the controlling-caregiving child views the parent as fragile and tries to protect the parent from his or her angry or fearful feelings. In this study, further information about controlling children came from teachers' ratings of school behavior; controlling children were rated as having more problems overall in the classroom, compared to children who were not controlling.[47]

Difficulties of Disorganized/Controlling Children in Later Years

Young children who show the disorganized pattern are at risk of developing serious psychological and behavioral problems as they grow. The Minnesota Mother-Child Project (which was composed of low-income families considered potentially at risk) yielded comprehensive information about disorganized children's emotional development through middle school and adolescence. In addition to higher rates of anxiety and depression in these children (indicated by their teachers' reports on behavior checklists), the researchers found high levels of dissociation.

What exactly is dissociation, and why are children who early on show the disorganized pattern at risk of dissociative symptoms? Daniel Siegel offers one way to think about dissociation. He states that in dissociation "normally associated cognitive processes, such as consciousness, emotion, and memory, become dissociated or fragmented."[48] The phenomenon of dissociation in the face of trauma has been described by K. Chase Stovall-McClough and Mary Dozier in the *Handbook of Attachment (Third Edition)* as follows:

> Dissociation involves turning away, presumably not volitionally, from some aspect of the environment. Dissociation in the face of trauma clearly has an adaptive function, in that it allows a person to avoid being overwhelmed with the experience. Evolution has predisposed infants and children to experience dissociative states readily when threatened.[49]

As discussed in Chapter Two, a good many of the children who show disorganized patterns of attachment in infancy have either experienced maltreatment, or their parents have been observed to act in frightened or frightening ways with them. If dissociation relieves some of the anxiety children feel when threatened, it is understandable that they may enter dissociative states, and perhaps do so more readily over time.[50]

In elementary school, dissociative symptoms were identified by teachers endorsing items such as "confused, seems to be in a fog" and "gets hurt a lot, accident prone." In high school, the items endorsed included "confused, seems to be in a fog," "strange behavior," and "deliberately harms self or attempts suicide." At age seventeen, adolescents also completed an interview[51] in which those who had been classified as disorganized in infancy self-reported symptoms of psychopathology and dissociation.[52]

Another group of researchers interested in the sequelae of early disorganized behavior conducted a study, also of low-income families, in which they investigated whether the three patterns of behavior seen in six-year-olds with disorganized histories—punitive, caregiving, and disorganized (in this study, termed "disoriented")—could be found much later in life, at age eighteen to twenty-three. These three patterns were, in fact, observed during interactions between these young adults and their parents. The three patterns were largely distinct from one another, but they could also occur in combination.[53]

However, only the pattern termed "disorientation" was significantly associated with classification as disorganized in infancy. Disorientation in adolescent-parent interactions closely resembled the classic description of disorganization in infancy. In this study, parents and adolescents were observed engaging in a discussion about sources of disagreement in their relationship. The adolescent behaviors that were coded as "disoriented/distractible" captured the extent to which the young person showed distracted, disoriented, or inwardly absorbed behavior. For example, the adolescent might suddenly stop in midsentence and freeze with hand in mid-air. Also related to disorganization in infancy were behaviors coded as "out-of-context." These behaviors included odd or contradictory behaviors, which could seem disjointed, startling, or inexplicable to an observer. Examples included using a forced, high-pitched, or childlike tone of voice or shifting into unusual, fantasy-based topics.

Disorganization and Cognitive Functioning

In addition to showing emotional and behavioral problems, there is evidence that disorganized children have some difficulties with cognitive functioning. The German study found that disorganized infants were the lowest-scoring group on the Bayley Test of Mental Development, and that during testing they showed low frustration tolerance, more agitation, and poor concentration.[54]

To investigate cognitive functioning at later ages, a group of researchers identified disorganized styles of attachment in seven-year-olds, using a test similar to the Separation Anxiety Test. Then, children were tested at ages seven, nine, twelve, and fifteen with a battery of Piagetian tasks to assess overall cognitive functioning. On these cognitive tasks administered over the years, the disorganized children consistently scored significantly lower than children with secure attachment. However, it should be noted that children with *insecure-avoidant* attachment styles also scored significantly lower than secure children.[55]

Another team of researchers that had identified children's attachment security at age six using a separation-reunion procedure looked at children's mastery motivation and academic performance at age eight. Mastery motivation was measured through a self-report questionnaire, where children reported how much they agreed with statements such as "I enjoy learning new things" and "It's important to keep trying even though you make mistakes." Children with disorganized/controlling attachment were at greatest risk for school underachievement, while insecure-avoidant and insecure-resistant children were lowest on mastery motivation.[56]

COMING FULL CIRCLE: STRANGE SITUATION VETERANS TAKE THE ADULT ATTACHMENT INTERVIEW

The Adult Attachment Interview was initially developed to be used with parents, to predict children's behavior in the Strange Situation Procedure. However, when Strange Situation Veterans reached adolescence and early adulthood, researchers often chose this interview as a way to assess current attachment security. Thus, researchers were able to examine how often children who were secure in infancy grew up to have a "secure-autonomous state of mind with respect to attachment" on the AAI. Or, alternatively, they examined how often insecure-avoidant children grew up to have a "dismissive state of mind," and insecure-resistant children to have a "preoccupied state of mind."

Finding a significant relationship between a measure given in infancy and one given many years later, in adolescence or early adulthood, would be remarkable. The major longitudinal studies produced somewhat mixed findings. The Berkeley Longitudinal Study, composed of a stable middle-class sample, did indeed find that children who were secure in the Strange Situation were significantly more likely to earn a "secure-autonomous state of mind" classification on the AAI at age nineteen. Looking a little more closely at the individuals in the study, they found that those who had experienced some kind of major trauma, such as a long, potentially fatal illness or the death of a parent or close family member, were far more likely to change from secure to insecure.[57]

The German study was also a very stable one; 75 percent of both parents remained in the family until children became young adults. Despite this stability, and thus perhaps surprisingly, there was no significant relationship between infant attachment security and classifications on the AAI at twenty-two years.[58] However, the German study did find that sensitive and supportive experiences with both parents during childhood (as assessed when children were between five and ten years old) predicted secure-autonomous states of mind on the AAI when individuals reached the age of twenty-two. The joint contribution of mother and father was more important in predicting secure-autonomous states than the individual sensitivity behaviors of either mother or father. And life events, particularly divorce and life-threatening illness of parents, had a powerful influence on children's representation of parental support at ten years.[59]

The Minnesota Mother-Child Project was focused on a high risk group of families. Remarkably, when Strange Situation Veterans were interviewed at age twenty-six, there was a significant relationship between their SSP classification as infants and their twenty-six-year-old classification on the Adult Attachment Interview.[60]

The Minnesota study had also administered the AAI to participants when they were nineteen, and with this group they sought to identify some factors that helped explain why originally secure children might have become insecure, and insecure children might have moved to secure. The considerable information gathered about children and parents over the years allowed researchers to look at life experiences that might explain changes in security. One important variable was maltreatment; none of the children who were originally insecure but became secure had been maltreated, while over 40 percent of the children who remained insecure had been maltreated. Depression in mothers was another important factor. Researchers found that when mothers were more often found to be depressed at the regular assessments, children were more likely to move from secure to insecure. Additionally, when children were thirteen, researchers got a glimpse of family functioning by observing adolescents interacting with parents. Children who were originally insecure but became secure showed better family functioning in the thirteen-year-old observation.[61]

CONCLUDING THOUGHTS

Studies that explore the factors that contribute to continuity as well as discontinuity—like the Minnesota and Berkeley research projects—are helpful to our understanding of attachment security over time. Once again, we see that experiences in infancy do not determine the life course of children. Major life events clearly can change the life trajectory.

Despite these changes, is there still some contribution from early experiences? We cannot answer this question with certainty. The relatively strong correlation between fifteen-year-olds' capacity to be vulnerable and their early attachment status perhaps provides some evidence that the early bond to some extent shapes one's emotional capacities. Research studies have to deal with a diverse array of families and life experiences, and capturing subtle factors is difficult. However, the ongoing experiences a child has while growing up clearly accumulate and appear to have the dominant influence on the person the child will become.

In Chapter Seven, our Child Veterans of the Strange Situation will have reached adulthood, and we will be able to consider whether children's attachment security as infants has an influence on adult functioning. We will also review studies that began following individuals in late adolescence or adulthood, and look at whether attachment security can inform us about happiness in mature romantic relationships.

NOTES

1. Waters and Cummings, "A Secure Base from which to Explore Close Relationships," 166.
2. Fraley, Roisman, and Haltigan, "The Legacy of Early Experiences in Development."
3. Main and Cassidy, "Categories of Response to Reunion with the Parent at Age 6"; Granot and Mayseless, "Attachment Security and Adjustment to School in Middle Childhood."
4. Main, Kaplan, and Cassidy, "Security in Infancy, Childhood, and Adulthood."
5. Klagsbrun and Bowlby, "Responses to Separation from Parents"; Main, Kaplan, and Cassidy, "Security in Infancy, Childhood, and Adulthood."
6. Main, Hesse, and Kaplan "Predictability of Attachment Behavior," 265.
7. Ibid., 87–88.
8. Fearon et al., "The Significance of Insecure Attachment and Disorganization in the Development of Children's Externalizing Behavior."
9. Groh et al., "The Significance of Insecure and Disorganized Attachment for Children's Internalizing Symptoms."
10. Ibid.
11. Ibid.; Eisenberg et al., "The Relations of Regulation and Emotionality to Children's Externalizing and Internalizing Problem Behavior."
12. Fraley, Roisman, and Haltigan, "The Legacy of Early Experiences in Development."
13. Sroufe et al., *The Development of the Person.*
14. Sroufe, Egeland, and Carlson, "One Social World."
15. Urban et al., "Patterns of Individual Adaptation across Childhood."
16. Sroufe et al., *The Development of the Person.*
17. Ibid.
18. Ibid.
19. Sroufe et al., "The Significance of Gender Boundaries in Preadolescence."
20. Ibid.
21. Shulman, Elicker, and Sroufe, "Stages of Friendship Growth in Preadolescence as Related to Attachment History."

22. Elicker, Englund, and Sroufe, "Predicting Peer Competence and Peer Relationships in Childhood from Early Parent-Child Relationships."

23. Bowlby, "Lecture 1"; Steele and Steele, "Understanding and Resolving Emotional Conflict."

24. Steele and Steele, "Understanding and Resolving Emotional Conflict."

25. Steele and Steele, "The Construct of Coherence as an Indicator of Attachment Security in Middle Childhood."

26. Cassidy, "Truth, Lies, and Intimacy."

27. Steele and Steele, "Understanding and Resolving Emotional Conflict."

28. Both the London and German studies were headed by married couples; Howard and Miriam Steele oversaw the London study and Karin and Klaus Grossmann were at the helm in the German study.

29. van IJzendoorn and de Wolff, "In Search of the Absent Father."

30. Grossmann, Grossmann, and Kindler, "Early Care and the Roots of Attachment and Partnership Representations."

31. The German research team used the Attachment and Current Relationship Interview when children were ten. This interview asks about the children's daily experiences and their thoughts about the emotional availability of their parents and close others. The interviews were rated for children's reported attachment behavior strategies in emotionally distressing situations; children were classified as secure if they were able to openly express distress to parents or other attachment figures. See Grossmann et al., "The Uniqueness of the Child–Father Attachment Relationship."

32. Grossmann et al., "The Uniqueness of the Child–Father Attachment Relationship."

33. Previously, these children had been placed, with some difficulty, into one of the two insecure groups, and occasionally in the secure group. So, earlier longitudinal studies did not provide information about how these children were doing in later years. Both the Minnesota and German researchers went back and reviewed videotapes to look for disorganized behavior. However, not all of the follow-up studies have described the functioning of children in the disorganized category.

34. Cyr et al., "Attachment Security and Disorganization in Maltreating and High-Risk Families."

35. Hesse and Main, "Frightened, Threatening, and Dissociative Parental Behavior in Low-Risk Samples."

36. Main, Hesse, and Kaplan, "Predictability of Attachment Behavior and Representational Processes at 1, 6, and 19 Years of Age."

37. Ibid.

38. Moss et al., "Understanding Disorganized Attachment at Preschool and School Age."

39. Main and Cassidy, "Categories of Response to Reunion with the Parent at Age 6"; Main, Hesse, and Kaplan, "Predictability of Attachment Behavior and Representational Processes at 1, 6, and 19 Years of Age."

40. Moss, Cyr, and Dubois-Comtois, "Attachment at Early School Age and Developmental Risk."

41. Main and Hesse, "Parents' Unresolved Traumatic Experiences Are Related to Infant Disorganized Attachment Status."

42. Macfie, Brumariu, and Lyons-Ruth, "Parent–Child Role-Confusion."

43. Moss, Cyr, and Dubois-Comtois, "Attachment at Early School Age and Developmental Risk."

44. Moss et al., "Understanding Disorganized Attachment at Preschool and School Age," 53.

45. Moss, Cyr, and Dubois-Comtois, "Attachment at Early School Age and Developmental Risk."

46. Cassidy, "Child-Mother Attachment and the Self in Six-Year-Olds."

47. Solomon, George, and De Jong, "Children Classified as Controlling at Age Six."

48. Siegel, "Attachment and Self-Understanding," 278.

49. Stovall-McClough and Dozier, "Attachment States of Mind and Psychopathology in Adulthood," 722.

50. Ibid, 722.

51. Adolescents completed the Kiddie Schedule for Affective Disorders and Schizophrenia Rating (epidemiological version, KSADS-E); Orvaschel et al., "Retrospective Assessment of Prepubertal Major Depression with the Kiddie-SADS-E."

52. Carlson, "A Prospective Longitudinal Study of Attachment Disorganization/Disorientation."

53. Obsuth et al., "Disorganized Behavior in Adolescent–Parent Interaction."

54. Jacobsen, Edelstein, and Hofmann, "A Longitudinal Study of the Relation between Representations of Attachment in Childhood and Cognitive Functioning in Childhood and Adolescence."

55. Ibid.

56. Moss and St-Laurent, "Attachment at School Age and Academic Performance."

57. Main, Hesse, and Kaplan, "Predictability of Attachment Behavior and Representational Processes at 1, 6, and 19 Years of Age."

58. Grossmann, Grossmann, and Kindler, "Early Care and the Roots of Attachment and Partnership Representations."

59. van IJzendoorn, "Commentary."

60. Hesse, "The Adult Attachment Interview."

61. Weinfield, Sroufe, and Egeland, "Attachment from Infancy to Early Adulthood in a High-Risk Sample."

REFERENCES

Bowlby, John. "Lecture 1: Psychoanalysis and Child Care." In *The Making and Breaking of Affectional Bonds*, 7–33. New York and London: Routledge, 1979/2012.

Carlson, Elizabeth A. "A Prospective Longitudinal Study of Attachment Disorganization/Disorientation." *Child Development* 69, no. 4 (1998): 1107–28.

Cassidy, Jude. "Child-Mother Attachment and the Self in Six-Year-Olds." *Child Development* 59, no. 1 (1988): 121–34.

———. "Truth, Lies, and Intimacy: An Attachment Perspective." *Attachment & Human Development* 3, no. 2 (2001): 121–55.

Cyr, Chantal, Eveline M. Euser, Marian J. Bakermans-Kranenburg, and Marinus H. van IJzendoorn. "Attachment Security and Disorganization in Maltreating and High-Risk Families: A Series of Meta-Analyses." *Development and Psychopathology* 22, no. 1 (2010): 87–108.

De Bellis, Michael D. "Developmental Traumatology: The Psychobiological Development of Maltreated Children and Its Implications for Research, Treatment, and Policy." *Development and Psychopathology* 13, no. 3 (2001): 539–64.

Eisenberg, Nancy, Amanda Cumberland, Tracy L. Spinrad, Richard A. Fabes, Stephanie A. Shepard, Mark Reiser, Bridget C. Murphy, Sandra H. Losoya, and Ivanna K. Guthrie. "The Relations of Regulation and Emotionality to Children's Externalizing and Internalizing Problem Behavior." *Child Development* 72, no. 4 (2001): 1112–34.

Elicker, James, Michelle Englund, and L. Alan Sroufe. "Predicting Peer Competence and Peer Relationships in Childhood from Early Parent-Child Relationships." In *Family-Peer Relationships: Modes of Linkage*, edited by Ross W. Parke and Gary W. Ladd, 77–106. Hillsdale, NJ: Erlbaum, 1992.

Fearon, R. Pasco, Marian J. Bakermans-Kranenburg, Marinus H. van IJzendoorn, Anne-Marie Lapsley, and Glenn I. Roisman. "The Significance of Insecure Attachment and Disorganization in the Development of Children's Externalizing Behavior: A Meta-Analytic Study." *Child Development* 81, no. 2 (2010): 435–56.

Fraley, R. Chris, Glenn I. Roisman, and John D. Haltigan. "The Legacy of Early Experiences in Development: Formalizing Alternative Models of How Early Experiences Are Carried forward over Time." *Developmental Psychology* 49, no. 1 (2013): 109–26.

Granot, David, and Ofra Mayseless. "Attachment Security and Adjustment to School in Middle Childhood." *International Journal of Behavioral Development* 25, no. 6 (2001): 530–41.

Chapter 6

Groh, Ashley M., Glenn I. Roisman, Marinus H. van IJzendoorn, Marian J. Bakermans-Kranenburg, and R. Pasco Fearon. "The Significance of Insecure and Disorganized Attachment for Children's Internalizing Symptoms: A Meta-Analytic Study." *Child Development* 83, no. 2 (2012): 591–610.

Grossmann, Karin, Klaus E. Grossmann, Elisabeth Fremmer-Bombik, Heinz Kindler, and Hermann Scheuerer-Englisch. "The Uniqueness of the Child–Father Attachment Relationship: Fathers' Sensitive and Challenging Play as a Pivotal Variable in a 16-Year Longitudinal Study." *Social Development* 11, no. 3 (2002): 301–37.

Grossmann, Karin, Klaus E. Grossmann, and Heinz Kindler. "Early Care and the Roots of Attachment and Partnership Representations: The Bielefeld and Regensburg Longitudinal Studies." In *Attachment from Infancy to Adulthood: The Major Longitudinal Studies*, edited by Klaus. E. Grossmann, Karin Grossmann, and Everett Waters, 98–136. New York: Guilford, 2005.

Hesse, Erik. "The Adult Attachment Interview: Protocol Method of Analysis, and Selected Empirical Studies: 1985–2015." In *Handbook of Attachment: Theory, Research, and Clinical Applications, Third Edition*, edited by Jude Cassidy and Phillip R. Shaver, 553–97. New York: The Guilford Press, 2016.

Hesse, Erik, and Mary Main. "Frightened, Threatening, and Dissociative Parental Behavior in Low-Risk Samples: Description, Discussion, and Interpretations." *Development and Psychopathology* 18, no. 2 (2006): 309–43.

Jacobsen, Teresa, Wolfgang Edelstein, and Volker Hofmann. "A Longitudinal Study of the Relation between Representations of Attachment in Childhood and Cognitive Functioning in Childhood and Adolescence." *Developmental Psychology* 30, no. 1 (1994): 112–24.

Klagsbrun, Micheline, and John Bowlby. "Responses to Separation from Parents: A Clinical Test for Young Children." *British Journal of Projective Psychology & Personality Study* 21 (1976): 7–21.

Macfie, Jenny, Laura E. Brumariu, and Karlen Lyons-Ruth. "Parent–Child Role-Confusion: A Critical Review of an Emerging Concept." *Developmental Review* 36 (2015): 34–57.

Main, Mary, and Jude Cassidy. "Categories of Response to Reunion with the Parent at Age 6: Predictable from Infant Attachment Classifications and Stable over a 1-Month Period." *Developmental Psychology* 24, no. 3 (1988): 415–26.

Main, Mary, and Erik Hesse. "Parents' Unresolved Traumatic Experiences are Related to Infant Disorganized Attachment Status: Is Frightened and/or Frightening Parental Behavior the Linking Mechanism?" In *Attachment in the Preschool Years: Theory, Research, and Intervention*, edited by Mark T. Greenberg, Dante Ciccetti, and Mark E. Cummings, 161–82. Chicago: University of Chicago Press, 1990.

Main, Mary, Erik Hesse, and Nancy Kaplan. "Predictability of Attachment Behavior and Representational Processes at 1, 6, and 19 Years of Age: The Berkeley Longitudinal Study." In *Attachment from Infancy to Adulthood: The Major Longitudinal Studies*, edited by Klaus. E. Grossmann, Karin Grossmann, and Everett Waters, 245–304. New York: The Guilford Press, 2005.

Main, Mary, Nancy Kaplan, and Jude Cassidy. "Security in Infancy, Childhood, and Adulthood: A Move to the Level of Representation." *Monographs of the Society for Research in Child Development* 50, no. 1/2 (1985): 66–104.

Moss, Ellen, Jean-François Bureau, Diane St-Laurent, and George M. Tarabulsy. "Understanding Disorganized Attachment at Preschool and School Age: Examining Divergent Pathways of Disorganized and Controlling Children." In *Disorganized Attachment and Caregiving*, edited by Judith Solomon and Carol George, 52–79. New York: The Guilford Press, 2011.

Moss, Ellen, Chantal Cyr, and Karine Dubois-Comtois. "Attachment at Early School Age and Developmental Risk: Examining Family Contexts and Behavior Problems of Controlling-Caregiving, Controlling-Punitive, and Behaviorally Disorganized Children." *Developmental Psychology* 40, no. 4 (2004): 519–32.

Moss, Ellen, and Diane St-Laurent. "Attachment at School Age and Academic Performance." *Developmental Psychology* 37, no. 6 (2001): 863–74.

Obsuth, Ingrid, Katherine Hennighausen, Laura E. Brumariu, and Karlen Lyons-Ruth. "Disorganized Behavior in Adolescent–Parent Interaction: Relations to Attachment State of Mind, Partner Abuse, and Psychopathology." *Child Development* 85, no. 1 (2014): 370–87.

Orvaschel, Helen, Joaquim Puig-Antich, William Chambers, Mary Ann Tabrizi, and Robert Johnson. "Retrospective Assessment of Prepubertal Major Depression with the Kiddie-SADS-E." *Journal of the American Academy of Child Psychiatry* 21, no. 4 (1982): 392–97.

Shulman, Shmuel, James Elicker, and L. Alan Sroufe. "Stages of Friendship Growth in Preadolescence as Related to Attachment History." *Journal of Social and Personal Relationships* 11, no. 3 (1994): 341–61.

Siegel, Daniel. J. Attachment and Self-Understanding: Parenting with the Brain in Mind. *Journal of Prenatal and Perinatal Psychology and Health* 18, no. 4 (2004): 273– 85.

Solomon, Judith, Carol George, and Annemieke De Jong. "Children Classified as Controlling at Age Six: Evidence of Disorganized Representational Strategies and Aggression at Home and at School." *Development and Psychopathology* 7, no. 3 (1995): 447–63.

Sroufe, L. Alan, Christopher Bennett, Michelle Englund, Joan Urban, and Shmuel Shulman. "The Significance of Gender Boundaries in Preadolescence: Contemporary Correlates and Antecedents of Boundary Violation and Maintenance." *Child Development* 64, no. 2 (1993): 455–66.

Sroufe, L. Alan, Byron Egeland, and Elizabeth A. Carlson. "One Social World: The Integrated Development of Parent-Child and Peer Relationships." *The Minnesota Symposia on Child Psychology* 30 (1999): 241–61.

Sroufe, L. Alan, Byron Egeland, Elizabeth A. Carlson, and W. Andrew Collins. *The Development of the Person: The Minnesota Study of Risk and Adaptation from Birth to Adulthood.* New York: Guilford Press, 2005.

Sroufe, L. Alan, and Mary J. Ward. "Seductive Behavior of Mothers of Toddlers: Occurrence, Correlates, and Family Origins." *Child Development* 51, no. 4 (1980): 1222–29.

Steele, Howard, and Miriam Steele. "The Construct of Coherence as an Indicator of Attachment Security in Middle Childhood: The Friends and Family Interview." In *Attachment in Middle Childhood*, edited by Kathryn A. Kerns and Rhonda A. Richardson, 137–60. New York: The Guilford Press, 2005.

———. "Understanding and Resolving Emotional Conflict: The London Parent-Child Project." In *Attachment from Infancy to Adulthood: The Major Longitudinal Studies*, edited by Klaus. E. Grossmann, Karin Grossmann, and Everett Waters, 137–64. New York: The Guilford Press, 2005.

Stovall-McClough, K. Chase, and Mary Dozier, "Attachment States of Mind and Psychopathology in Adulthood." In *Handbook of Attachment: Theory, Research, and Clinical Applications, Third Edition*, edited by Jude Cassidy and Phillip R. Shaver, 715–38. New York: The Guilford Press, 2016.

Urban, Joan, Elizabeth Carlson, Byron Egeland, and L. Alan Sroufe. "Patterns of Individual Adaptation across Childhood." *Development and Psychopathology* 3, no. 4 (1991): 445–60.

van IJzendoorn, Marinus H. "Commentary." *Human Development*, 39 (1996): 224–31.

van IJzendoorn, Marinus H., and Marianne S. Wolff. "In Search of the Absent Father—Meta-Analyses of Infant-Father Attachment: A Rejoinder to Our Discussants." *Child Development* 68, no. 4 (1997): 604–9.

Waters, Everett, and E. Mark Cummings. "A Secure Base from which to Explore Close Relationships." *Child Development* 71, no. 1 (2000): 164–72.

Weinfield, Nancy S., L. Alan Sroufe, and Byron Egeland. "Attachment from Infancy to Early Adulthood in a High-Risk Sample: Continuity, Discontinuity, and Their Correlates." *Child Development* 71, no. 3 (2000): 695–702.

Chapter Seven

Bonds in Adulthood

Relationships with Lovers and Friends

*While writing this book, I had a conversation with a highly educated, profes-
sional woman in her mid-thirties whom I will call Laurie. When I mentioned
the anecdote found in the first chapter, about Bowlby suffering when he lost
his beloved full-time nanny at the age of four, Laurie paused, and offered the
fact that she had had a series of nannies who came and went during her
childhood. Like Bowlby's parents, her mother and father were busy and
remote. It seemed that it was a novel thought to her that these experiences
might still have effects. Laurie went on to discuss her wish to marry and have
children, but said that her current professional position, which required
much traveling, neither gave her much opportunity to establish a relationship nor allowed her to become engaged in psychotherapy. I was left concerned that Laurie was fearful of allowing herself to be vulnerable in a
committed long-term relationship, and that her desire to bear children might
not be fulfilled.*

While John Bowlby's focus was largely on the role of attachment in the
lives of children, he did make a point of emphasizing the importance of close
relationships during the entire lifespan. Bowlby asserted that "Throughout
adult life the availability of a responsive attachment figure remains the
source of a person's feeling secure. All of us, from the cradle to the grave, are
happiest when life is organized as a series of excursions, long or short, from
the secure base provided by our attachment figure(s)."[1]

Come adulthood, most young people are nearing completion of the process of transferring their desire for companionship, safety, and security from
family to close friends and romantic partners. Adult intimate relationships
have the potential to bring joy and passion, as well as companionship and

emotional support. How successfully young adults will navigate dating relationships, succeed in making good choices of partners, and handle the stresses and strains that are part of long-term relationships has been a topic of great interest to attachment researchers.

Bowlby's claim that early attachment experiences lay a foundation for the course and quality of future love relationships[2] is viewed as one of the boldest assertions of attachment theory.[3] Simply put, Bowlby believed that a secure relationship with mother in infancy begins to shape the child's expectations of what to expect from others. The child will have a fundamental sense of being valued by mother, and his or her resulting self-confidence and openness to the world will encourage others to treat the child well. Unless unusual experiences occur that derail their development, secure children will grow to adulthood and find partners who provide the kind of security and sensitivity they experienced with their mothers.

As discussed in Chapter Three, Bowlby theorized that this continuity in relationships would occur because of the development of what he called "internal working models" in the brain, which include unconscious elements. While Bowlby recognized that experiences beyond early childhood could modify working models, he emphasized their role in shaping how children interpret later experiences. Bowlby's theory that cognitive models begin to shape the child's view of the world has been termed the "prototype hypothesis."

The prototype hypothesis has served as a lightning rod of controversy in developmental research.[4] The basic dispute: Does early experience really have an important role in shaping the kind of person the child will become? While some researchers have put forth evidence to support the prototype hypothesis,[5] it remains unproven. As researchers who continue to follow the Minnesota cohort have asserted, "We still do not know whether early social experiences occurring at specific time points (e.g., during the first few years of life) are uniquely and independently linked to specific types of adult relationship outcomes."[6] Indeed, given the complexity of relationship experiences individuals have between infancy and adulthood, it would be surprising if a simple trajectory were discovered.

ADULT BONDS AS ATTACHMENT RELATIONSHIPS

Fundamentally, attachment relationships reflect the use of another person as a "secure base." With adult partners, the roles of "secure base provider" and "secure base user" alternate, depending on the needs of each individual. As two important adult attachment researchers working at the State University of New York at Stony Brook, Judith Crowell and Dominique Treboux, note: "In providing secure base support, the other partner is interested and open to detecting signals, recognizes that the partner has a need or is in distress, correctly interprets the need and gives an appropriate response in a timely fashion."[7]

It is not hard to imagine how varying expectations about having one's attachment needs met might manifest themselves in relationships. In observing friends and relatives, we see that some people have the confidence to be relaxed and open as they date and form partnerships. Other individuals very quickly become enamored of partners, wanting their full attention and needing frequent reassurance that they are loved. Their high degree of emotionality in relationships may cause conflict and stress. Yet others may frustrate their partners by being distant and emotionally unavailable, having difficulty committing themselves to relationships.

The major longitudinal studies have sought to understand what individuals' early attachment experiences predict about their functioning in subsequent relationships. Other researchers have looked at how adults' present-day sense of attachment security, whether stemming from childhood or cultivated by later positive experiences, influences their functioning in romantic relationships. Indeed, some researchers have emphasized that a healthy, solid romantic relationship actually has the potential to create a new caregiving environment. If the partner is more sensitive and responsive than parents had earlier been, the new relationship may challenge older conceptions of attachment.[8]

BEYOND THEORY: WHAT RESEARCH STUDIES TELL US

In studies of adult attachment with romantic partners, researchers have posed a variety of questions. Beyond investigating the validity of the prototype hypothesis, researchers have explored questions such as:

1. How does security of attachment influence individuals' ability to handle "bumps in the road," i.e., the inevitable occurrences of difference and conflict?
2. Do secure individuals partner with other secure individuals?
3. In what ways might the attachment-related behaviors of one member of the dyad influence the other member?
4. What factors predict marital break-up?

Some answers have come from the major longitudinal studies, and some from studies that began looking at individuals when they were adolescents or young adults.

Dual Methods for Determining Adult Attachment Security

Before beginning to answer these important questions, I want to remind the reader about the two traditions, the developmental psychology approach and the social/personality psychology tradition, that have spawned prolific research regarding the study of adult relationships. Unfortunately, these two traditions complicate our understanding of adult attachment security. As was discussed in Chapter Five, security-of-attachment designations derived from the social/personality tradition and the developmental tradition result in very little overlap.[9] However, each tradition has proven useful in understanding aspects of the capacity for intimate and close relationships with friends and romantic partners.

Now, it is generally accepted that the two facets of attachment representations—"state of mind with respect to attachment" (derived from developmentalists' interview measures) and "attachment styles" (derived from social/personality self-report measures)[10]—relate to different aspects of an individual's beliefs and behaviors regarding attachment.[11] In understanding which tradition has been used in different studies, the reader should attend to the labels "attachment styles" and "states of mind."

FROM INFANCY TO ADULTHOOD

In Chapter Six, we saw that when researchers with the major longitudinal investigations looked at the degree to which early childhood Strange Situation classifications are associated years later with adolescent or young adult Adult Attachment Interview (AAI) states of mind with respect to attachment, some research found correlations while others did not. However, even when there is a significant correlation between SSP classifications and AAI states of mind, does this mean that early experience predicts *actual* quality of adult romantic relationships? Not necessarily. State of mind on the AAI is distinct from behavior and experiences in actual adult relationships, and researchers have sought ways to assess quality of interactions between partners.

Romantic Relationships in the Minnesota Study Cohort

The most in-depth longitudinal study, and the one that has continued for the longest period, has been the Minnesota study. It provides a great deal of information about the trajectory from infancy to adulthood for a relatively large group of participants. As discussed in previous chapters, what was originally called the "Minnesota Mother-Child Interaction Project" began in the mid-1970s and enrolled over 200 pregnant women.[12]

Over time, the project's name was changed to the Minnesota Study on Risk and Adaptation from Birth to Adulthood. At regular intervals, researchers interviewed and observed parents and children; the study continues today, and the original infant participants are now in their forties. In this chapter, we will review findings from when members of this cohort were assessed in their early twenties, and again when they had reached their thirties.

When young people in the Minnesota cohort reached the ages of twenty to twenty-one, those who could be located, and were involved in romantic relationships that had lasted at least four months, were interviewed, asked to fill out questionnaires, and observed with their partners. Approximately seventy-five individuals, along with their partners, took part in the study. Researchers were able to draw on considerable historical information, including participants' Strange Situation security classification as well as observations of the children when they were two and four, as well as later in elementary school and during adolescence.[13]

A central part of the early twenties assessment was an effort to observe couples dealing with conflict-inducing topics. In the lab, each couple first spent ten minutes discussing a problem they had identified as causing the most conflict in their relationship and tried to resolve it. Then, they "cooled down" for four minutes by discussing the areas in which they most agreed. Trained raters judged the videotaped interactions—both during the conflict discussion and during the "cool-down" period—on scales that assessed the quality of the couple relationship.[14] In addition to the videotaped observation, participants filled out a series of questionnaires, the results of which were summarized into two categories, which reflected self-reported closeness and positive perceptions of the romantic relationship.

Minnesota Adults: Key Findings

The Minnesota cohort of seventy-five couples offered researchers a precious opportunity to test the prototype hypothesis. If the prototype hypothesis is correct, working models formed in infancy would be carried forward and would be influential in individuals' choices of partners and in the resulting quality of the adult romantic relationships. While working models themselves were not assessed, children's classification in the Strange Situation were assumed to be based on then-operating working models, and models guiding adult behavior were inferred from observations of partner interactions.

Researchers indeed found significant correlations between Strange Situation classifications and adult interactions. Adults who as children had been more secure in the Strange Situation were observed to have higher romantic relationship quality, that is, they showed less anger and hostility and greater ability to resolve conflict and to share positive affect during the videotaped lab activities in their early twenties.[15] Adults who had been secure in infancy also reported greater positive perceptions of their romantic relationships.[16] The correlation between childhood security, adult romantic quality, and positive perceptions certainly did not hold for all participants, but it definitely occurred more often than would be expected by chance.

Data gathered from this study also contribute to answering the first question posed in the beginning of the chapter: "How does security of attachment influence individuals' ability to handle "bumps in the road," i.e., the inevitable occurrences of differences and conflict?" When the Minnesota Child Veterans of the Strange Situation visited the lab with their romantic partners in their early twenties, researchers examined their ability to recover from the conflict that arose during the discussion task. How well could they disengage from conflict and transition to a "cool-down" task? Individuals earned low scores on the cool-down task if they perseverated on the conflict discussion, brought up new problems which sabotaged the cool-down interaction, disputed suggestions made by their partner about topics on which they agreed, or simply refused to talk. High scores were assigned when individuals facilitated the cool-down process by bringing up positive aspects of the relationship or by building on positive aspects mentioned by their partner.[17]

Individuals who were more secure in infancy showed better conflict recovery in their early twenties with their romantic partners. Researchers wanted to be sure that the better conflict recovery wasn't due simply to higher relationship quality, as observed in the lab. Perhaps it would be easier to recover from conflict if discussions had been less heated. To avoid confounding these two factors, the researchers controlled statistically for relationship quality. Even with these controls, greater attachment security as an infant predicted better conflict recovery.[18]

As attachment security has been linked to the development of good self-regulation skills, this finding is consistent with theory and data regarding an association between attachment and affect regulation.[19] As noted in Chapter Three, attachment relationships are thought to help young children regulate emotional arousal, particularly when their emotions are disturbing or overwhelming.

Assessing Physiological Responses

As electrodermal reactivity indicates activity in the behavioral inhibition system and has been shown to be involved in the effortful inhibition of behavior, it offers an easy way to assess individuals' physiological states when engaged in various activities.[20] Researchers only need to ask individuals to allow sensors to be attached to their skin, and then physiological activity can be recorded as study participants engage in a variety of activities.[21] When members of the Minnesota cohort were in their thirties, researchers incorporated physiological measures to assess emotional responses to conflict.

As background for understanding findings with the Minnesota participants, it is helpful to present findings from studies that have shown that adults with different states of mind with respect to attachment show different patterns of physiological responses during conflict discussions. Secure adults (that is, those with a "secure-autonomous state of mind" on the AAI) show low levels of physiological change during conflict discussions, indicating that emotions do not interfere with their being able to freely share their thoughts and opinions with their partners.

In contrast, adults who are judged to have insecure states of mind on the Adult Attachment Interview show quite different patterns of electrodermal reactivity during conflict discussions with romantic partners. Adults with a dismissing state of mind show heightened electrodermal reactivity, indicating they are inhibiting emotions. This finding has been interpreted as indicating that they are motivated to avoid their spouses when called to resolve problems in their relationship. Conversely, adults with a preoccupied state of mind show increases in heart rate, indicating higher rates of arousal. This is not surprising, as preoccupied individuals are seen as emotionally overinvolved with their partners.[22]

Physiological Responses of Participants in the Minnesota Study

When members of the Minnesota cohort were in their thirties, those who had partners at the time of this follow-up assessment once again engaged in conflict-arousing discussions, and this time their electrodermal reactivity responses were measured. To investigate the influence of childhood maternal sensitivity in later years, researchers used a measure of childhood maternal sensitivity that combined ratings from observations of sensitivity at seven different ages; observations of mother-child interactions were gathered at seven points between three months and thirteen years of age. The measure derived from these combined ratings distinguished those who experienced more continuous sensitivity over time from those in whom sensitivity was lacking or less consistently observed. Results showed that with the Minnesota participants, greater maternal sensitivity across the childhood years was associated with significantly lower electrodermal reactivity during the conflict discussion.[23]

Perhaps surprisingly, electrodermal reactivity during conflict-arousing discussions predicted earlier maternal sensitivity *even when* researchers statistically ruled out reactivity being due to the quality of the current relationship, either as directly observed or self-reported. In fact, in this study, associations between electrodermal reactivity and current romantic quality were not significant. The researchers concluded that early parent-child relationships may provide a unique contribution to shaping autonomic responses during partner interactions, and that any contribution is largely outside conscious control.

Attachment Security and Physical Health

The finding that adults with different attachment classifications—either as assessed concurrently with the Adult Attachment Interview or as found in the Strange Situation Procedure many years earlier—show different autonomic response patterns in situations that involve interpersonal conflict raises questions about the impact of attachment security on physical health. Given that studies have shown that psychosocial stress in the early years of life is correlated with elevated rates of morbidity and mortality from chronic diseases of aging,[24] researchers following the Minnesota cohort looked for correlations between infant attachment security and adult health outcomes.

In one important study involving individuals from the original Minnesota cohort that looked at the correlation between child attachment security and adult health, adults who had been judged insecure-resistant at eighteen months were found to be three times more likely to report physical illnesses at age thirty-two, and also seven and a half times more likely to report inflammation-related illness (such as heart disease, asthma, diabetes, high blood pressure, or stroke) compared to those who had been securely attached at eighteen months. Thirty-two-year-olds who had been judged insecure-avoidant at eighteen months were three times more likely to report inflammation-related illnesses, again compared to those who were securely attached. These findings were obtained even when researchers controlled for factors that are correlated with reports of inflammation or non-specific symptoms, such as Body Mass Index (BMI), life stress, current negative emotional style, and gender.[25]

The degree of correlation between infant attachment security and adult health outcomes was remarkably strong. In some way, it appears that the experience of care that is less than optimally sensitive and responsive leads to heightened stress reactivity especially to interpersonal stress, and in the process initiates biological and/or behavioral pathways towards poor health.

We do not yet know enough to distinguish the relative importance of possible biological factors versus behavioral influences leading to poor health. Since it has been shown that infant attachment plays a role in the development of the biological processes that underlie stress regulation, it may be that insecure attachment results in children experiencing higher levels of stress.[26] Over time, the body's stress system could be modified by these experiences. Alternatively, early attachment security could conceivably set the stage for higher-quality interpersonal relationships and a greater tendency to adhere to medical treatment recommendations and to maintain health-promoting behaviors. Clearly, further research is needed to understand these important findings.

ASSESSING DYADS RATHER THAN INDIVIDUALS

With the increasing focus on the importance of an individual's attachment security for success in romantic relationships, attachment theory received criticism for its failure to describe how individual differences in personal histories "affect the development of a marriage once two people with different relationship needs come together."[27] During the last couple of decades, there has been more work focusing on this issue, and we have a growing understanding of how individuals with different attachment stances impact each other in romantic relationships.

Both developmental and social/personality psychologists have contributed to research on factors related to dyadic functioning. Developmental psychologists have moved from a quest for evidence of correlations with early childhood working models to the investigation of how states of mind with respect to attachment relate to functioning in romantic and other close adult relationships, without concern for historical roots. Social/personality psychologists have continued to investigate the correlates and consequence of self-reported attachment styles, and their findings will be discussed in a later section.

Current Adult Relationships:
New Methods in Developmental Psychology

In order to be able to look at dyadic functioning, developmental researchers have created new interview measures that are similar to the Adult Attachment Interview, but are focused on current adult relationships rather than on adults' memories of their childhood relationships with parents. One of the new measures that has been used fairly widely, the Current Relationship Interview (CRI), was designed to parallel the structure and context of the AAI. Participants are asked to explore their thoughts and feelings about memories related to their current romantic relationship. The interview covers the person's dating history, the nature of the present relationship and characteristics of the partner, and routine behaviors, especially those related to seeking and providing support. Like the AAI, the CRI emphasizes the coherence and verbal organization of responses.[28]

With the CRI, *secure* individuals are able to discuss their feelings in an open, contained, and, most importantly, coherent manner. *Dismissing* classifications are given when individuals avoid attachment concerns by either denying or minimizing the limitations of a rather unloving partner, or by emphasizing other aspects of life instead of the relationship. *Preoccupied* individuals appear confused or angry about the relationship or the partner's behavior, and may be anxious about the partner's ability to fulfill their needs for support and closeness.

How much correspondence is there between classifications on the AAI (which assesses feelings about earlier experiences with parents) and the CRI (which assesses current feelings about one's partner)? While one study found a significant correlation between the two measures, the correlation was far from perfect. In this study, 64 percent of individuals who were secure on the AAI were also secure on the CRI, which left 36 percent with differing classifications, indicating differences in security of representations between parents and partners. Researchers concluded that individuals have multiple, yet related, working models of close relationships. This result was interpreted as providing evidence for only a "weak" version of the prototype hypothesis.[29]

In the following section, I present some interesting but somewhat complicated findings about the effect of security or insecurity on the AAI and on the CRI. To help the reader to remember the meaning of different terms, I will use informal but meaningful labels to describe different groups. Table 7.1 summarizes the technical terms, their formal interpretation, and the informal labels.

Relationships during the First Six Years of Marriage

One large and important study, conducted at the State University of New York at Stony Brook, followed engaged couples from shortly before marriage to six years post-marriage. This study interviewed participants approximately three months prior to their wedding dates and twice more, after they had been married for eighteen months[30] and again after six years. As the majority of divorces occur early in marriage,[31] this study was able to look at predictors of early-marriage divorces.[32]

At the outset of the study, researchers gathered information about both members of the dyad, including their "states of mind with respect to attachment" as assessed via the Adult Attachment Interview (AAI) as well as via the Current Relationship Interview (CRI). Participants also completed a number of questionnaires assessing their degree of conflict, commitment, and positive feelings.

This study provides an answer to the second question posed at the start of this chapter: "Do secure individuals partner with other secure individuals?" The answer is yes, but only to a degree. The Stony Brook researchers found a small but significant correspondence in security on the AAI for partner pairs. In 60 percent of couples, both members had the same security classification (i.e., both "secure re parents" or both "insecure re parents"). That left a large number—40 percent—of couples composed of one individual with a secure classification and one classified as insecure.[33]

Table 7.1. Summary of Terms Used in Studies Including Both the AAI and the CRI

Technical Term	Meaning	Informal Descriptor
"AAI—Secure"	Secure state of mind on the Adult Attachment Interview (AAI), which focuses on memories of, and feelings about, parents	"Secure re parents"
"AAI—Insecure"	Insecure state of mind on the Adult Attachment Interview (AAI)	"Insecure re parents"
"CRI—Secure"	Secure state of mind on the Current Relationship Interview (CRI), which focuses on thoughts and feelings about current partner	"Secure re partner"
"CRI—Insecure"	Insecure state of mind on the Current Relationship Interview (CRI)	"Insecure re partner"

Note: This table is included to guide readers in understanding findings from studies using both the Adult Attachment Interview and Current Relationship Interview.

Researchers looked at whether the transition to marriage changed individuals' general sense of security and correspondingly had an effect on their AAI security status. It was found that virtually all of the "secure re parents" individuals remained secure when interviewed again eighteen months into their marriages. However, there was more fluidity among individuals who were initially "insecure re parents," with almost 60 percent of those who changed classifications becoming "secure re parents" and about a third changing from one insecure classification to another. Those who became "secure re parents" earned their new AAI classification because they expanded their reports of the past and drew more consistent and coherent inferences from their memories during the Adult Attachment Interview.

The potential for some people to shift from an insecure status to a secure one during the transition to marriage is remarkable. Perhaps more remarkably, when the researchers analyzed transcripts of these participants' interviews, they discovered that those who transitioned from insecure to secure did not appear to be especially aware of having done so. In just eighteen months of marriage, their feelings about their relationships with their parents had undergone a shift that was as unconscious as it was impressive. In examining transcripts, researchers found no evidence that their subjects said anything to the effect of "Aha, I used to think one way eighteen months ago, and now I think this new way."[34] Researchers concluded that those who became "secure re parents" did so without much explicit awareness about the fact that they now thought differently about feelings associated with their relationship with their parents.

This finding supports the notion that people may "change for the better" within marital relationships.[35] Marriage may be thought of as providing a new caregiving environment. Perhaps surprisingly, those who became "secure re parents," compared to those who remained "insecure re parents," were not more likely to have a partner who was secure on either the AAI or the CRI.[36]

Having found that their study participants could move from "insecure re parents" to "secure re parents," the researchers delved deeper to see what predicted who would make this change. Those who did were distinguished by having been "secure re partner" on the CRI prior to marriage, along with having been "insecure re parents" on the AAI. This suggests that before marriage they felt greater security in their partner relationship than in their parental relationships, and that eventually this greater security allowed them to think more coherently about their childhood experiences with parents.

The participants who moved from "insecure re parents" to "secure re parents" were significantly more likely to have had a preoccupied state of mind than a dismissing one on the premarital AAI. In other words, those who had a dismissing state of mind on the AAI (that is, they were insecure-dismissing re parents) were less likely to move towards being "secure re parents."[37] The researchers theorized that this might be due to the tendency of dismissing individuals to avoid thinking about attachment-relevant information. In contrast, preoccupied individuals might have benefited from the greater closeness with a partner in marriage and their inclination to be open in discussing past experiences with partners.

Influence of Individuals on their Marital Partners

This study also provided some information regarding the third question posed at the start of the chapter: "In what ways might the attachment-related behaviors of one member of the dyad influence the other member?" Researchers examined whether there was a correlation between secure states of mind with respect to attachment and conflict in relationships. Before marriage, individuals who were "secure re parents" were less likely to threaten to abandon the relationship, and tended to report greater intimacy and feelings of dedication. After eighteen months of marriage, individuals classified as "secure re parents" reported fewer arguments with their partners and were less verbally aggressive than those classified as insecure.[38]

Secure Base Behavior during Conflict

At both the initial assessment and the six-year follow-up, couples participated in a discussion of a topic selected because both partners had reported that this issue caused relatively high degrees of conflict. One key variable that was examined by raters of videotaped conflict discussions was individuals' ability to engage in "secure base behavior." Behaviors indicative of good ability to *use* the partner as a secure base included being able to clearly communicate concern to the partner, to be increasingly clear and direct in expressing needs, to show the desire and need for a response from the partner, and the ability to be comforted. Correspondingly, behaviors evidencing good ability to *provide* secure base support included the ability to be a good listener and to encourage the partner to express feelings and thoughts, the ability to recognize distress or concern, skill in correctly understanding the partner's concern and in focusing on key elements rather than superficial aspects, plus the ability to help the partner, as evidenced by their behavior, words, and affective tone.[39]

Before marriage, individuals who were both "secure re parents" and "secure re partner" showed the highest-quality secure base behavior.[40] They also reported positive feelings about the relationship and low relationship conflict. In contrast, those who were both "insecure re parents" and "insecure re partner" had the lowest quality of observed secure base behavior. Finally, those who reported the least positive feelings about the relationship and who did not differ in reports of relationship conflict from those who were both "insecure re parents" and "insecure re partner" were those who were "secure re parents" *but* "insecure re partner."

To understand this finding, we need to think what the "secure with parents"/"insecure re partner" configuration means. Individuals with this configuration had, during the AAI, been calm, coherent, and reflective about their relationship with their parents. This implies that they had experienced their parents as sensitive and responsive, and they did not have to defend against uncomfortable feelings when talking about their childhood. In contrast, when talking about their relationship with their current partner, soon to become their spouse, they experienced more intense emotions and spoke less coherently about their partners. Something wasn't right in their current relationship, yet they were still headed for marriage. As we will see in the follow-up study, this group turned out to be particularly at risk.

Follow-up at Six Years

At the time of the six-year follow-up, the Stony Brook researchers brought as many individuals—either married or separated—back to the lab as possible, where they again completed the AAI and CRI as well as self-report questionnaires. Twenty-two percent of individuals were no longer together after six years, and researchers were able to obtain preliminary answers to the fourth question posed earlier in this chapter: "What factors predict marital break-up?" Researchers found that the configuration of security classifications on the AAI and CRI before marriage was a strong predictor of relationship status six years later.

Those who were "secure re parents" but "insecure re partner" were significantly more likely to have separated or divorced than those in other groups; about one-third of individuals with this configuration were no longer together. As discussed earlier, this group had expressed the least positive feelings about the relationship prior to marriage, and they also showed relatively poor secure base behaviors.[41]

The researchers hypothesized that this group recognized early on that they had a problematic relationship, and moved on relatively quickly in order to "cut their losses."[42] It is noteworthy that sometimes those with a secure generalized representation of attachment, as reflected in a secure AAI (that is, "secure re parents"), married partners with whom they did not experience security. This suggests that it is not enough to have a secure or coherent generalization of attachment (i.e., to be "secure re parents") to ensure that individuals make good choices in partners and establish strong relationships. The researchers concluded that there was little evidence of an "inoculation" effect of good childhood experiences or secure representations of relationships with parents.[43]

What about partnerships that involved two individuals who were each insecure on both the AAI and CRI? One might think these partnerships would be particularly vulnerable to dissolution. As it turned out, their rate of divorce was lower than that of the "secure re parents"/"insecure re partner" group discussed above, and not statistically different from the other two groups. When each partner was both "insecure re parents" and "insecure re partner," about a quarter of the marriages were no longer together. This compares with 16 percent (twelve out of seventy-seven) of the marriages where both partners were secure on both measures.

The Impact of Stressful Life Events

At the six-year-follow-up, participants were asked about stressful events, including those related to marriage, employment, family, children, finances, health, deaths, and legal events. The impact of stress on the four AAI/CRI configurations was examined. Individuals who were secure on both measures seemed able to take negative life events in their stride. Although stress did take its toll in bringing about increased conflict and less positive feelings about oneself, high levels of stress had little impact on participants' positive feelings about their relationships or on their secure base behavior. The researchers interpreted this finding as evidence that attachment security serves as a protective factor with respect to stress.

The two intermediate groups—those with either individuals who were "insecure re parents" but "secure re partner" or vice versa—showed a dramatic switch in their reported feelings about the relationship under high-stress conditions. They reported more negative feelings and also higher levels of conflict with partners.

Finally, the group who were both "insecure re parents" and "insecure re partner" were clearly vulnerable to relationship difficulties when stress increased. Members of this group reported the most conflict in their relationships and greater avoidance of closeness, compared to those who were both "secure re parents" and "secure re partner." Additionally, they showed poorer "secure base behaviors" during the videotaped discussion about an issue creating conflict. These partners were not observed to be skilled in behaviors such as clearly and directly showing their desire for a response from the partner or in their ability to be comforted.

Whether these more vulnerable individuals would likely divorce at a later point, or whether they would remain together despite unhappiness, is an unknown question. But it does remind us that using divorce as a yardstick for marital success does not tell the full story. Being able to sustain a relationship that brings security and satisfaction to both spouses may be the most important goal.

Clearly, relationships are highly complex, and the more nuanced information one can gain about each member of a partnership, the better one can understand how that partnership functions. This study showed that the two measures—the AAI and the CRI—both contribute important information. That is, individuals' generalized states of mind with respect to attachment (reflecting their degree of "security-re-parents" as assessed by the AAI) and their states of mind with respect to the current relationship (reflecting their degree of "security-re-partner" as assessed by the CRI) are both relevant to how a relationship fares over time.

SOCIAL/PERSONALITY RESEARCH: MARITAL SATISFACTION AND RELATIONSHIP FUNCTIONING

The social/personality psychology area of research has produced a great many studies looking at how romantic partners with different attachment styles influence each other. Mario Mikulincer and Phillip Shaver, two prominent leaders in the social/personality psychology field, have summarized findings from studies that examined couple effects on marital satisfaction. They conclude that studies show that when both partners have a secure attachment style, they report greater marital satisfaction than either "mixed couples" (in which only one partner is secure) or couples with two insecure individuals.

In fact, in contrast to the findings from the six-year study discussed above, no differences were found between mixed and doubly insecure couples, suggesting that attachment insecurity in one partner has a negative impact on couple satisfaction. Mikulincer and Shaver report that the negative effect of one partner having an insecure attachment style has been observed in studies assessing regulation of closeness, communication within the dyad, responses to a partner's transgressions, conflict-management strategies, and relational violence.[44]

More optimistically, these leaders in the social/personality psychology field point to some studies that have concluded that a secure partner can sometimes buffer the negative effects of an insecure partner on a relationship. The ultimate quality of dyadic relationships is not simply a consequence of the sum of two parts. Relationships are dynamic, with the behaviors of one partner influencing the behaviors of the other. How a secure partner can buffer or exert a protective effect on a relationship is an important area of inquiry, as encouragement of such behaviors may help to improve and sustain marriages.

Making a Relationship Work

What is the process by which partners manage to "buffer" each other's insecurities? Researchers have not yet been able to examine couple interactions over long periods of time to see how the behavior of one partner might permanently influence that of the other. However, we have some preliminary information from social/personality psychology studies that have looked at how one partner's behavior may buffer the other partner's response during discussions designed to touch on areas of conflict.

In one study that focused on dyads in which at least one partner had described themselves on a questionnaire as having an avoidant attachment style, 180 couples were videotaped discussing situations in which one member of the dyad was asked to discuss a change they desired in the other partner. Researchers found that some partners of avoidant individuals were able to "soften" avoidant defenses by such tactics as downplaying problem severity, validating the partner's point of view, recognizing positive aspects, and acknowledging progress made by the avoidant individual. When partners used softening communications, the avoidant partner showed less anger, less withdrawal, and reported greater success with the discussion.[45]

Another study looked at what factors might motivate a partner to be more supportive and accommodating in a discussion involving disagreement and conflict. A group of couples from a large midwestern city who had been married for an average of five years participated. In addition to assessing their self-reported attachment style, individuals independently reported their level of commitment to the relationship. Degree of commitment played an important role in the process and outcome of the discussion when one of the partners reported high attachment anxiety. When discussing an area of conflict with a very anxious partner, individuals who were more committed to the relationship behaved more constructively and experienced more positive feelings, and those who were less committed behaved less constructively and experienced more negative emotions.[46]

The researchers theorized that greater commitment may sustain vulnerable relationships long enough for both partners to learn that they can trust one another, allowing anxieties about attachment to gradually wane. They noted that "Highly committed individuals . . . may diminish an individual's insecurity over time by consistently providing a 'secure base.'"[47]

In general, the studies in the social/personality tradition examining how partners can buffer each other's insecurity might well be thought of as exploring specific approaches to secure base behaviors. By doing such things as validating the other's point of view and acknowledging progress, the partner is sensitively providing reassurance that he or she appreciates and values the other's efforts to improve a difficult issue.

DISORGANIZED ATTACHMENT AND ADULT RELATIONSHIPS

In Chapter Six, we saw that disorganization in younger years was associated with significant psychological and interactional problems. When disorganized infants reached middle childhood, many had developed controlling styles of interaction (either controlling-punitive or controlling-caregiving), while some remained behaviorally disorganized. In late adolescence, these three patterns were once again observed during interactions between young people and their parents, with the adolescent disorganized pattern linked to disorganization in infancy.[48]

What is the outcome for disorganized youngsters in later years, and how do they fare in romantic relationships? Our knowledge about these questions from the longitudinal studies is very limited. In the Minnesota study, 86 percent of children who were disorganized in the Strange Situation were insecure on the AAI at age nineteen. However, the majority of these adolescents were found to have a dismissing state of mind rather than to be unresolved. In contrast, in childhood unresolved status on the AAI is the classification most closely linked to Strange Situation disorganization.[49]

Borderline Personality Disorder in Adulthood

One psychiatric diagnostic category that is highly linked to unstable romantic relationships is Borderline Personality Disorder (BPD). There has been considerable theorizing about a relationship between attachment disturbances and BPD.[50] Clinical researchers and theorists have noted that the characteristics of impulsivity, affective lability, and self-damaging actions that are the hallmark of BPD occur in an interpersonal context and often are precipitated by real or imagined events in relationships.[51] While individuals with BPD only constitute 1 to 2 percent of the population, it is a disorder that takes a serious toll on individuals and families.[52]

Researchers with the Minnesota longitudinal study assessed for BPD when individuals who had participated in their study since infancy reached the age of twenty-eight. These individuals showed serious symptoms and problematic behaviors in a number of areas, including self-injurious behavior, dissociative symptoms, drug use, and domestic violence. The Minnesota study's rich array of data collected over decades allowed its authors to identify a broad range of factors that put individuals at risk for a serious psychiatric condition.

Childhood Antecedents of Borderline Personality Disorder

Looking at their large array of data, the researchers concluded that adult borderline personality symptoms reflect a lengthy, multi-determined developmental process beginning in the earliest years of life. Infants who grew up to have BPD were distinguished by having shown a number of both "endogenous" and environmental risk factors. Endogenous risk factors included differences in infant motor maturity at seven to ten days of age, muscle tone/ tension at three months, infant activity level at six months, and child emotionality at thirty months. Environmental risk factors included early abuse, attachment disorganization in the Strange Situation, maternal hostility and poor mother-child boundaries at forty-two months, and family disruption and maternal life stress during early years. They also found evidence of violation in generational boundaries in the parent-child relationship at thirteen years, observing such things as sexualized teasing and playfulness, intrusive touching, or holding hands.[53]

Reviewing representational drawings at eight years and projective storytelling and sentence completion tasks at twelve years, researchers were able to identify ways in which children at risk for BPD were internalizing very negative self-concepts. In family drawings, researchers identified "lack of organization of the self in relationships" through factors such as drawings in which human figures were omitted, "buried," or obscured. They also found fragmented or floating body parts, frightening depictions of the self, or chaotic scenes. In the projective storytelling tasks, there were references to unexplained or intrusive violence related to the self, unresolved feelings of guilt or fear, and bizarre images related to the self.

Overall, the Minnesota study suggested that many factors during development eventually contributed to symptoms warranting the diagnosis of Borderline Personality Disorder. Whether a temperamental component is needed along with being raised in a very harsh parenting environment is not yet known. However, this study provides a most valuable prospective view of the antecedents of BPD.

Treatment for Borderline Personality Disorder

Attachment theory has provided a framework for new developments in the psychotherapeutic treatment for BPD. The majority of these attachment-based treatments for BPD focus to a large degree in building an attachment relationship with the therapist. A second ingredient found to be important is helping improve patients' capacity to think about their own mental states, as well as those of others. Research has shown that a form of treatment called "transference-focused psychotherapy," which includes these elements, can successfully help patients to develop increased security in their working models of attachment.[54]

MOVING FORWARD

In the next chapter, we will look at practical applications of attachment theory and research, focusing on three areas. First, we will discuss the parenting philosophy known popularly as "attachment parenting," and consider the degree to which research supports this approach. Second, we will examine what is known about the long-term impact of non-parental child care, drawing upon a wealth of data collected by the National Institute of Child Health and Human Development Study of Early Child Care and Youth Development. Finally, we will consider research and theory regarding the application of attachment principles to divorce and custody decisions.

NOTES

1. Bowlby, *A Secure Base*, 62.
2. Bowlby, *Separation, Anxiety and Anger*.
3. Roisman et al., "Predictors of Young Adults' Representations of and Behavior in Their Current Romantic Relationship."
4. Ibid.
5. E.g., Fraley, Roisman, and Haltigan, "The Legacy of Early Experiences in Development"; Madigan et al., "Maternal Representations and Infant Attachment."
6. Simpson, Collins, and Salvatore, "The Impact of Early Interpersonal Experience on Adult Romantic Relationship Functioning," 358.
7. Crowell and Treboux, "Attachment Security in Adult Partnerships," 31.
8. Owens et al., "The Prototype Hypothesis and the Origins of Attachment Working Models"; Crowell, Treboux and Waters, "Stability of Attachment Representations."

9. Treboux, Crowell, and Waters, "When 'New' Meets 'Old'"; Cohn et al., "Working Models of Childhood Attachment and Couple Relationships"; Mayseless and Scharf, "Adolescents' Attachment Representations and Their Capacity for Intimacy in Close Relationships"; Roisman et al., "The Adult Attachment Interview and Self-Reports of Attachment Style."

10. While different teams of social/personality psychologists have used slightly different designations, the main styles are secure, avoidant, and anxious. Often, social/personality psychologists will not use categories, but will instead look at the *degree* to which individuals show avoidance and anxiety. This approach is described as dimensional, as opposed to categorical; rather than strictly classifying an individual as having one or another style, this approach assesses "how much" of each style an individual reports (Brennan, Clark, and Shaver, "Self-Report Measurement of Adult Attachment").

11. Differences stem from a variety of factors, including the fact that the AAI relates to parental relationships while attachment style questionnaires relate to peers and partners, the AAI taps into a general state of mind while questionnaires tap specific beliefs, and the AAI assesses less conscious aspects, while questionnaires investigate aspects of which the individual is more aware (Mayseless and Scharf, "Adolescents' Attachment Representations and Their Capacity for Intimacy in Close Relationships," 41).

12. Sroufe et al., *The Development of the Person.*

13. Simpson et al., "Attachment and Relationships across Time."

14. Simpson et al., "Attachment and the Experience and Expression of Emotions in Romantic Relationships."

15. Roisman et al., "The Coherence of Dyadic Behavior across Parent–Child and Romantic Relationships as Mediated by the Internalized Representation of Experience."

16. Roisman et al., "Predictors of Young Adults' Representations of and Behavior in Their Current Romantic Relationship."

17. Salvatore et al., "Recovering from Conflict in Romantic Relationships."

18. The Minnesota researchers have focused on whether secure infants go on to have high-quality relationships, not on length of romantic relationships, which was not viewed as a precise assessment of quality per se (personal communication, G. Roisman, June 2016).

19. Thompson, "Early Attachment and Later Development."

20. Electrodermal activity refers to all active as well as passive electrical properties which can be traced back to the skin and its appendages. Measuring electrodermal activity is popular in research studies because it is quite easy to obtain a distinct electrodermal response, and the intensity of the response is assumed to be related to the intensity and/or the psychological significance of stimuli encountered by research subjects (Boucsein, *Electrodermal Activity*, 1).

21. Roisman, "The Psychophysiology of Adult Attachment Relationships," 43.

22. Ibid.

23. Raby et al., "Greater Maternal Insensitivity in Childhood Predicts Greater Electrodermal Reactivity during Conflict Discussions with Romantic Partners in Adulthood."

24. Miller, Chen, and Parker, "Psychological Stress in Childhood and Susceptibility to the Chronic Diseases of Aging."

25. Puig et al., "Predicting Adult Physical Illness from Infant Attachment."

26. Lupiens et al., "Effects of stress throughout the lifespan on the brain, behaviour and cognition," 414–15; Albers et al., "Maternal Behavior Predicts Infant Cortisol Recovery from a Mild Everyday Stressor."

27. Karney and Bradbury, "The Longitudinal Course of Marital Quality and Stability."

28. Owens et al., "The Prototype Hypothesis and the Origins of Attachment Working Models."

29. Ibid.

30. Crowell, Treboux, and Waters, "Stability of Attachment Representations."

31. Clarke, "Advance Report of Final Divorce Statistics, 1989 and 1990."

32. Treboux et al., "When 'New' Meets 'Old.'"

33. Crowell, Treboux, and Waters, "Stability of Attachment Representations."

34. Ibid., 476.

35. Belsky and Pensky, "Developmental History, Personality, and Family Relationships."

36. Crowell, Treboux, and Waters, "Stability of Attachment Representations," 474.

37. Ibid., 473.
38. Ibid., 471.
39. Treboux et al., "When 'New' Meets 'Old.'"
40. The researchers divided participants into four groups: those who, prior to marriage, were secure on both the AAI and CRI ("secure re parents" and "secure re partner"), those who were insecure on both measures ("insecure re parents" and "insecure re partner"), those who were secure on the AAI but insecure on the CRI ("secure re parents" but "insecure re partner"), and those who were insecure on the AAI but secure on the CRI ("insecure re parents" but "secure re partner").
41. Treboux et al., "When 'New' Meets 'Old.'"
42. Ibid., 310.
43. Ibid., 308.
44. Mikulincer and Shaver, *Attachment in Adulthood.*
45. Overall, Simpson, and Struthers, "Buffering Attachment-Related Avoidance."
46. Tran and Simpson, "Prorelationship Maintenance Behaviors," 695.
47. Ibid.
48. Obsuth et al., "Disorganized Behavior in Adolescent-Parent Interaction."
49. Weinfield, Whaley, and Egeland, "Continuity, Discontinuity, and Coherence in Attachment from Infancy to Late Adolescence."
50. Fonagy et al., "The Developmental Roots of Borderline Personality Disorder in Early Attachment Relationships."
51. Levy, Beeney, and Temes, "Attachment and Its Vicissitudes in Borderline Personality Disorder."
52. Carlson, Egeland, and Sroufe, "A Prospective Investigation of the Development of Borderline Personality Symptoms."
53. Ibid.
54. Bateman and Fonagy, "The Development of an Attachment-Based Treatment Program for Borderline Personality Disorder"; Diamond et al., "The Reciprocal Impact of Attachment and Transference-Focused Psychotherapy with Borderline Patients"; Kernberg, "New Developments in Transference-Focused Psychotherapy."

REFERENCES

Albers, Esther M., J. Marianne Riksen Walraven, Fred C. G. J. Sweep, and Carolina de Weerth. "Maternal Behavior Predicts Infant Cortisol Recovery from a Mild Everyday Stressor." *Journal of Child Psychology and Psychiatry* 49, no. 1 (2008): 97–103.

Bateman, Anthony W., and Peter Fonagy. "The Development of an Attachment-Based Treatment Program for Borderline Personality Disorder." *Bulletin of the Menninger Clinic* 67, no. 3 (2003): 187–211.

Belsky, Jay, and Emily Pensky. "Developmental History, Personality, and Family Relationships: Toward an Emergent Family System." In *Relationships Within Families: Mutual Influences*, edited by Robert A. Hinde and Joan Stevenson-Hinde, 193–217.Oxford: Oxford University Press, 1988.

Boucsein, Wolfram. *Electrodermal Activity.* New York, Spring Science+Business Media, 1992.

Bowlby, John. *Separation, Anxiety and Anger.* New York: Basic Books, 1973.

———. *A Secure Base: Parent-Child Attachment and Healthy Human Development.* New York: Basic Books, 1988.

Brennan, Kelly A., Catherine L. Clark, and Phillip R. Shaver. "Self-Report Measurement of Adult Attachment: An Integrative Overview." In *Attachment Theory and Close Relationships*, edited by Jeffry A. Simpson and W. Stephen Rhodes, 46–76. New York: The Guilford Press, 1998.

Carlson, Elizabeth A., Byron Egeland, and L. Alan Sroufe. "A Prospective Investigation of the Development of Borderline Personality Symptoms." *Development and Psychopathology* 21, no. 4 (2009): 1311–34.

Clarke, Sally C. "Advance Report of Final Divorce Statistics, 1989 and 1990." *Monthly Vital Statistics Report* 43 (1995): 1–32.

Cohn, Deborah A., Daniel H. Silver, Carolyn P. Cowan, Philip A. Cowan, and Jane Pearson. "Working Models of Childhood Attachment and Couple Relationships." *Journal of Family Issues* 13, no. 4 (1992): 432–49.

Crowell, Judith, and Dominique Treboux. "Attachment Security in Adult Partnerships." In *Adult Attachment and Couple Psychotherapy: The "Secure Base" in Practice and Research*, edited by Christopher F. Clulow, 28–42. London: Brunner-Routledge, 2000.

Crowell, Judith A., Dominique Treboux, Yuan Gao, Celene Fyffe, H. Pan, and E. Waters. "Secure Base Behavior in Adulthood: Measurement, Links to Adult Attachment Representations, and Relations to Couples' Communication Skills and Self-Reports." *Developmental Psychology* 38 (2002): 679–93.

Crowell, Judith A., Dominique Treboux, and Everett Waters. "Stability of Attachment Representations: The Transition to Marriage." *Developmental Psychology* 38, no. 4 (2002): 467–79.

Diamond, Diana, Frank E. Yeomans, John F. Clarkin, Kenneth N. Levy, and Otto F. Kernberg. "The Reciprocal Impact of Attachment and Transference-Focused Psychotherapy with Borderline Patients." In *Clinical Applications of the Adult Attachment Interview*, edited by Howard Steele and Miriam Steele, 270–94. New York: The Guilford Press, 2008.

Fonagy, Peter, Mary Target, George Gergely, Jon G. Allen, and Anthony W. Bateman. "The Developmental Roots of Borderline Personality Disorder in Early Attachment Relationships: Theory and Some Evidence." *Psychoanalytic Inquiry* 23, no. 3 (2003): 412–59.

Fraley, R. Chris, Glenn I. Roisman, Cathryn Booth-LaForce, Margaret Tresch Owen, and Ashley S. Holland. "Interpersonal and Genetic Origins of Adult Attachment Styles: A Longitudinal Study from Infancy to Early Adulthood." *Journal of Personality and Social Psychology* 104, no. 5 (2013): 817–38.

Fraley, R. Chris, Glenn I. Roisman, and John D. Haltigan. "The Legacy of Early Experiences in Development: Formalizing Alternative Models of How Early Experiences Are Carried Forward over Time." *Developmental Psychology* 49, no. 1 (2013): 109–26.

Karney, Benjamin R., and Thomas N. Bradbury. "The Longitudinal Course of Marital Quality and Stability: A Review of Theory, Methods, and Research." *Psychological Bulletin* 118, no. 1 (1995): 3–34.

Kernberg, Otto F. "New Developments in Transference Focused Psychotherapy." *The International Journal of Psychoanalysis* 97, no. 2 (2016): 385–407.

Levy, Kenneth N., Joseph E. Beeney, and Christina M. Temes. "Attachment and Its Vicissitudes in Borderline Personality Disorder." *Current Psychiatry Reports* 13, no. 1 (2011): 50–59.

Lupien, Sonia J., Bruce S. McEwen, Megan R. Gunnar, and Christine Heim. "Effects of Stress throughout the Lifespan on the Brain, Behaviour and Cognition." *Nature Reviews Neuroscience* 10, no. 6 (2009): 434–45.

Madigan, Sheri, Erinn Hawkins, Andre Plamondon, Greg Moran, and Diane Benoit. "Maternal Representations and Infant Attachment: An Examination of the Prototype Hypothesis." *Infant Mental Health Journal* 36, no. 5 (2015): 459–68.

Mayseless, Ofra, and Miri Scharf. "Adolescents' Attachment Representations and Their Capacity for Intimacy in Close Relationships." *Journal of Research on Adolescence* 17, no. 1 (2007): 23–50.

Mikulincer, Mario, and Phillip R. Shaver. *Attachment in Adulthood: Structure, Dynamics, and Change, Second Edition*. New York: The Guilford Press, 2016.

Miller, Gregory E., Edith Chen, and Karen J. Parker. "Psychological Stress in Childhood and Susceptibility to the Chronic Diseases of Aging: Moving toward a Model of Behavioral and Biological Mechanisms." *Psychological Bulletin* 137, no. 6 (2011): 959–97.

Obsuth, Ingrid, Katherine Hennighausen, Laura E. Brumariu, and Karlen Lyons-Ruth. "Disorganized Behavior in Adolescent-Parent Interaction: Relations to Attachment State of Mind, Partner Abuse, and Psychopathology." *Child Development* 85, no. 1 (2014): 370–87.

Overall, Nickola C., Jeffry A. Simpson, and Helena Struthers. "Buffering Attachment-Related Avoidance: Softening Emotional and Behavioral Defenses during Conflict Discussions." *Journal of Personality and Social Psychology* 104, no. 5 (2013): 854–71.

Owens, Gretchen, Judith A. Crowell, Helen Pan, Dominique Treboux, Elizabeth O'Connor, and Everett Waters. "The Prototype Hypothesis and the Origins of Attachment Working Models: Adult Relationships with Parents and Romantic Partners." *Monographs of the Society for Research in Child Development* 60, no. 2–3 (1995): 216–33.

Puig, Jennifer, Michelle M. Englund, Jeffry A. Simpson, and W. Andrew Collins. "Predicting Adult Physical Illness from Infant Attachment: A Prospective Longitudinal Study." *Health Psychology* 32, no. 4 (2013): 409–17.

Raby, K. Lee, Glenn I. Roisman, Jeffry A. Simpson, W. A. Collins, and Ryan D. Steele. "Greater Maternal Insensitivity in Childhood Predicts Greater Electrodermal Reactivity during Conflict Discussions with Romantic Partners in Adulthood." *Psychological Science* 26, no. 3 (2015): 348–53.

Roisman, Glenn I. "The Psychophysiology of Adult Attachment Relationships: Autonomic Reactivity in Marital and Premarital Interactions." *Developmental Psychology* 43, no. 1 (2007): 39–53.

Roisman, Glenn I., W. Andrew Collins, L. Alan Sroufe, and Byron Egeland. "Predictors of Young Adults' Representations of and Behavior in Their Current Romantic Relationship: Prospective Tests of the Prototype Hypothesis." *Attachment & Human Development* 7, no. 2 (2005): 105–21.

Roisman, Glenn I., Ashley Holland, Keren Fortuna, R. Chris Fraley, Eric Clausell, and Alexis Clarke. "The Adult Attachment Interview and Self-Reports of Attachment Style: An Empirical Rapprochement." *Journal of Personality and Social Psychology* 92, no. 4 (2007): 678–97.

Roisman, Glenn I., Stephanie D. Madsen, Katherine H. Hennighausen, L. Alan Sroufe, and W. Andrew Collins. "The Coherence of Dyadic Behavior Across Parent–Child and Romantic Relationships as Mediated by the Internalized Representation of Experience." *Attachment & Human Development* 3, no. 2 (2001): 156–72.

Salvatore, Jessica E., I. Sally, Chun Kuo, Ryan D. Steele, Jeffry A. Simpson, and W. Andrew Collins. "Recovering from Conflict in Romantic Relationships: A Developmental Perspective." *Psychological Science* 22, no. 3 (2011): 376–83.

Simpson, Jeffry A., W. Andrew Collins, Allison K. Farrell, and K. Lee Raby. "Attachment and Relationships across Time: An Organizational-Developmental Perspective." In *Bases of Adult Attachment*, edited by Vivian Zayas and Cindy Hazan, 61–78. New York: Springer, 2015.

Simpson, Jeffry A., W. Andrew Collins, and Jessica E. Salvatore. "The Impact of Early Interpersonal Experience on Adult Romantic Relationship Functioning: Recent Findings from the Minnesota Longitudinal Study of Risk and Adaptation." *Current Directions in Psychological Science* 20, no. 6 (2011): 355–59.

Simpson, Jeffry A., W. Andrew Collins, SiSi Tran, and Katherine C. Haydon. "Attachment and the Experience and Expression of Emotions in Romantic Relationships: A Developmental Perspective." *Journal of Personality and Social Psychology* 92, no. 2 (2007): 355–67.

Sroufe, L. Alan, Byron Egeland, Elizabeth A. Carlson, and W. Andrew Collins. *The Development of the Person: The Minnesota Study of Risk and Adaptation from Birth to Adulthood.* New York: The Guilford Press, 2005.

Thompson, Ross A. "Early Attachment and Later Development: Reframing the Questions." In *Handbook of Attachment: Theory, Research, and Clinical Applications, Third Edition*, edited by Jude Cassidy and Phillip R. Shaver, 330–48. New York: The Guilford Press, 2016.

Tran, SiSi, and Jeffry A. Simpson. "Prorelationship Maintenance Behaviors: The Joint Roles of Attachment and Commitment." *Journal of Personality and Social Psychology* 97, no. 4 (2009): 685–98.

Treboux, Dominique, Judith A. Crowell, and Everett Waters. "When 'New' Meets 'Old': Configurations of Adult Attachment Representations and Their Implications for Marital Functioning." *Developmental Psychology* 40, no. 2 (2004): 295–314.

Weinfield, Nancy S., Gloria J. L. Whaley, and Byron Egeland. "Continuity, Discontinuity, and Coherence in Attachment from Infancy to Late Adolescence: Sequelae of Organization and Disorganization." *Attachment & Human Development* 6, no. 1 (2004): 73–97.

Chapter Eight

The Impact of Attachment Parenting, Child Care, and Post-Divorce Overnight Visitation for Young Children

What Research Tells Us

It is my hope that this book will extend understanding of the rich fund of knowledge that has accumulated about attachment patterns and their meaning. Individuals who provide child care for children of working parents, child welfare workers and administrators, those who work in the family court system, teachers in elementary, middle, and high schools—even coaches and members of the clergy—may make important decisions about children's welfare, and may also play important roles as attachment figures. All of these individuals could benefit from accurate, scientifically based information about attachment through the lifespan.

While parents typically have a basic understanding of attachment from observing the responses of their children when they feel threatened or anticipate separation, most lack an understanding of the factors that contribute to attachment security. Perhaps the most popularized information about attachment comes from advocates of "attachment parenting," a parenting philosophy/method that emphasizes the importance of extensive and frequent physical contact between infant and mother. This chapter will explore whether research supports some of the more important tenets of attachment parenting.

A concern for many parents (as well as professionals who work with young children and their families) regards the impact of non-parental child care. Whether mothers work because they value their careers or must do so to help support the family, the majority of young children today receive some regular care provided by someone other than mother. The large body of research that has accumulated on the impact of child care on children's attachment security and later development will be reviewed in this chapter.

A third practical application to be considered in this chapter concerns visitation and custody arrangements for very young children of parents who live in separate residences. In most cases, this issue involves divorcing spouses. However, as more non-traditional family structures emerge, this issue may be relevant to a variety of diverse parenting situations. The most controversy and concern regarding the impact of shared custody has focused on overnight visitation for young children, and relevant research will be reviewed here.

ATTACHMENT RESEARCH AND "ATTACHMENT PARENTING"

The philosophy termed "attachment parenting" developed outside of the walls of academia, but its proponents consistently refer to the work of John Bowlby and Mary Ainsworth. While some attachment parenting recommendations make good sense and are consistent with attachment research, other guidelines have little support from research findings.

The term "attachment parenting" came into common use in the late 1980s and early 1990s. Its best-known proponents are William and Martha Sears, a pediatrician/registered nurse couple and the co-authors of numerous parenting books. In *The Baby Book: Everything You Need to Know about Your Baby from Birth to Age Two*, first published in 1992 and still popular today, the Sears introduced aspects of attachment parenting.[1] Then, in 2001, the authors published *The Attachment Parenting Book: A Commonsense Guide to Understanding and Nurturing Your Baby*.[2] In the introduction to this volume, Dr. and Ms. Sears assert: "We believe that attachment parenting immunizes children against many of the social and emotional diseases that plague our society."[3] While such immunization is an admirable goal, the reality is that this viewpoint is not supported by research; studies indicate that while quality of early parenting is very important, it does *not* necessarily protect children from later adversity.[4]

The term "attachment parenting" is somewhat misleading. All babies raised by reliable caregivers are attached; children simply differ in degree of attachment security. With that caveat, it should be acknowledged that the philosophy of attachment parenting does include many recommendations consistent with what academic attachment theory and research have taught us about the importance of parental sensitivity. Overall, parents who follow attachment parenting guidelines are advised to be sensitive and responsive to children and to attend to verbal and non-verbal cues. They also should be appropriately protective of children, which includes being thoughtful in choosing alternative child-care providers.[5]

Where attachment parenting parts ways with traditional attachment research is in its strong emphasis on the importance of physical contact between mother and child, both day and night. To begin with, the Sears advocate "birth bonding," asserting that the hours and days after birth are a sensitive period when mothers are uniquely primed to care for the newborns.[6] They also argue for "baby-wearing," i.e., wearing babies in a sling or soft baby carrier, and "bed-sharing," the practice of having babies share the parental bed. Not surprisingly, breastfeeding is recommended, and the Sears suggest that it is advantageous to breastfeed for an extended time, into the toddler years and even beyond.

While many of these practices may be appropriate for some parent-child dyads and potentially supportive of a secure attachment, the research base that has accumulated reveals that it is primarily emotional sensitivity and responsiveness, not physical contact, that promote attachment security. In fact, the vignette at the beginning of Chapter Two describes a child observed by Mary Ainsworth in Uganda. This little boy was virtually always in extremely close physical contact with his mother. Yet he was a fussy baby, his mother was anxious and preoccupied, and later in the chapter we read that Mary Ainsworth judged this child to be insecurely attached.

In Ainsworth's Baltimore study, she concluded that *how* parents interacted with the children was more important than *how often* they did specific behaviors. Home observations showed that mothers of insecure-avoidant babies (i.e., those who appeared to maintain a "stiff upper lip" in the Strange Situation) held their babies as much as did mothers of those judged securely attached, but they held their babies in ways that were less comforting and more intrusive compared to mothers of securely attached babies.[7]

Indeed, in some cases extensive holding may be contraindicated. In the Netherlands intervention study for irritable infants discussed in Chapter Two, mothers were taught to adapt their behaviors to their infants' needs. Coaches helped mothers see that some babies liked close physical contact and some did not. When children did not respond well to close contact, their mothers were offered effective alternative ways to soothe them.[8]

Research Pertinent to Attachment Parenting

Is there any support for the notion that extensive physical contact enhances attachment security, at least for the large majority of infants? I will focus on two topics that have been examined in solid research studies. The first topic concerns the importance of breastfeeding for attachment security, and the second topic concerns the impact of infant carrying.

Breastfeeding and Attachment

A study that looked at the relationship between breastfeeding, maternal sensitivity, and attachment security found that the quality of mother's interaction with her child at six months, rather than the mode of feeding (breast or bottle), predicted attachment security. Mothers who, prior to their child's birth, expressed an intent to breastfeed to a later age (the vast majority planned to breastfeed for one year or less) had children who were more securely attached at one year. The data suggest that a mother's willingness to breastfeed may be more important to secure attachment than whether or not circumstances allowed her to actually do so. The researchers concluded that mothers who choose to breastfeed for a number of months may *also* be more likely to be sensitive in responding to the cues of their infants. The data did not support the notion that the actual experience of early breastfeeding contributes to maternal sensitivity.[9]

Other studies have shown that women who choose to breastfeed differ in significant ways from women who choose to use formula. For example, one study found both socio-demographic and personality differences in women who made the choice to breastfeed. Breastfeeding mothers were of higher socioeconomic status, more likely to be married, and better educated compared to mothers who bottle-fed. In terms of personality, breastfeeding mothers described themselves as more affectionate, friendly, optimistic, receptive to emotional experience, and willing to try new activities. The formula-feeding group described themselves as more reserved, less exuberant, less likely to try new activities, less likely to acknowledge feeling states as important, and more skeptical. The researchers noted that their results were similar to earlier studies that found mothers who breastfeed were better adjusted psychologically.[10]

The research regarding mothers' decisions to breastfeed found choices largely related to personality factors, but the economic and social context in which breast or bottle feeding occurs must be considered. The researchers reported that formula-feeding mothers were more likely to be African-American, single, unskilled, or Medicaid dependent, as compared to breast-feeding mothers. However, controlling for ethnicity and maternal insurance status did not eliminate the importance of personality factors.[11] It may be that personality factors and social challenges cannot be entirely disentangled; women who face greater financial and social stress may be less able to maintain an upbeat, outgoing attitude, which would encourage them both to breastfeed and to have the energy to respond sensitively to children. Certainly, research reviewed earlier in this book emphasizes that external stressors undermine parents' ability to provide optimally sensitive parenting.[12]

Infant Carrying and Attachment

In investigating the impact of mothers carrying or "wearing" their babies, one study cleverly managed to incentivize a group of parents to use soft baby carriers while another group used an infant seat. The soft baby carriers were of the type known as "Snuglis," and the seats were plastic infant seats that can be used for carrying babies from place to place or to position an infant near its mother. Women in this study were recruited from a low-income medical clinic. They were predominantly Latina and African-American, and approximately three-quarters of them were receiving public assistance.

Researchers made considerable effort to disguise the purpose of the study. Initially, the women were read a list of different baby items and asked whether or not they would use the items if received as a gift. Embedded in the list were a soft baby carrier and an infant seat. Women who either had already decided to use a soft baby carrier (14 percent of the sample) or who would not consider using one (46 percent of the sample) were eliminated from the study. Then, mothers who had said they would use *either* a soft baby carrier or an infant seat were told details of the study. Mothers would randomly receive one of these items, and they had to agree that they would use the item given to them and not the other. The vast majority of these mothers agreed to participate and follow the study directions. In order to get a valid estimate of the amount the soft baby carriers were used, pedometers were sewn inside them.

The mothers who received soft baby carriers and regularly carried their children in them were found to respond in a manner that was more contingent and sensitive to their children's vocalizations at age three and a half months, and also to have children who were more securely attached at age thirteen months, compared to a control group who were given an infant seat. The mothers who used soft baby carriers also reported significantly fewer periods of regular crying.[13]

In the soft baby carrier group, there were many fewer babies who were given an insecure-avoidant designation in the Strange Situation than in the infant seat group. The researchers noted that mothers of insecure-avoidant babies often have an aversion to physical contact, and they hypothesized that carriers may have helped some mothers overcome their aversion to physical contact. In the infant seat group, as in other groups composed of mothers of minority background with low socio-economic status, there were high rates of insecure-avoidant attachment.

Controversial Aspects of Attachment Parenting

One of the most controversial aspects of attachment parenting has been its recommendation for bed-sharing. The American Pediatric Association recommends against bed-sharing due to the risk to infants of death by suffocation.[14] While attachment parenting advocates have to some extent addressed safety concerns by extending sleep recommendations to include "co-sleeping" (defined as having the baby sleep in close proximity, e.g., directly beside the parent's bed), sharing the same bed is not actively discouraged.[15]

Attachment Parenting in the Media

Attachment parenting became a familiar phrase to many when *Time* magazine featured it as a cover story in 2012. In a memorable cover photo, *Time* featured a child old enough to breastfeed by standing on a chair in front of his mother, her breast easily accessible to the child's lips. The *Time* magazine article included anecdotes of parents reporting that they avoided any separations from their children. The article argued that this approach to parenting has the potential to heighten parents' anxiety and guilt:

> Attachment parenting says that the more time babies spend in their mothers' arms, the better the chances they will turn out to be well-adjusted children. It's not a big leap from there to an inference that can send anxious moms into guilt-induced panic: that any time away from their baby will have lifelong negative consequences.[16]

While the *Time* article featured some of the more extreme versions of attachment parenting, it is likely that any popularization of research that becomes a "movement" will attract zealots who misinterpret research findings.

Science and Attachment Parenting

The research reviewed in this section indicates that the impact of using attachment parenting techniques is mixed. The literature on breastfeeding mothers suggests that their babies may have advantages, but that the benefits are due, at least in large part, to qualities of the mothers who choose to breastfeed. The research conducted to date does not provide information about the attachment security of children of mothers who breastfeed for a number of years. As with the decision to breastfeed in the first place, it is likely that parental characteristics may turn out to be more important than the breastfeeding experience itself.

The research on infant carrying is intriguing. A study conducted with monkeys in the early 1970s provides some support for the idea that monkey mothers who are rejecting towards their own babies because they themselves had failed to receive adequate caregiving can become more nurturing when they were encouraged (sometimes quite forcefully) by their babies to have a great deal of physical contact. In a study conducted by Harry Harlow and Stephen Suomi, the researchers were surprised when at least some monkey mothers who had been deprived of social interaction during their own early months eventually responded positively when their babies persistently sought close body contact.[17]

In the study reviewed in this chapter, it appeared that the process of carrying a baby in a Snugli encouraged some mothers who might have had an initial aversion to physical contact to overcome it and form more responsive relationships with their children. The authors concluded that the physical contact inherent in carrying seems to have brought out latent nurturing behavior in the disadvantaged mothers in their sample.

It must be emphasized that the study which found use of soft baby carriers to be effective in increasing attachment security was conducted with a low-income sample, and caution must be used in generalizing to a more affluent sample. The study was conducted in a manner that mothers did not feel pressure to use the baby carrier "gifts," but they did have access to an item they might not have been able to afford. If an intervention as simple as providing a baby carrier reliably results in greater sensitivity and attachment security for the families who are open to trying the practice of baby-wearing, this could be an easy and inexpensive way to support mothers and their children. While the results are only based on a single study, perhaps a fair conclusion would be that for the general population of women, there is some support that baby-wearing is beneficial for children. However, if mothers are not comfortable with this practice, there are other ways that they can make efforts to be responsive and attuned to their children.

THE MOMMY WARS: WORKING MOTHERS AND CHILD CARE

Debate, bordering on warfare, about possible risks of day care erupted in the 1980s. Some preliminary studies found higher rates of insecure attachment in children who were in child care more than twenty hours per week. John Bowlby remained staunchly opposed to day care unless the family had a nanny who would stay until the child was grown.[18] Yet, women who wished to work or who needed to do so to support themselves and their families were hearing encouragement that substitute care would not hurt children.[19]

It remains a very sensitive issue to consider the impact of regular child care on children's attachment security and on their subsequent development. While guilt about leaving children in child care may be less common than it was in previous decades,[20] a perusal of the Internet indicates that mothers who work continue to feel guilty leaving care of their children to others. However, mothers working outside the home is a fact of life in the twenty-first century, so rather than asking whether non-maternal child care is good for children, perhaps the more important question to ask is what forms, as well as amounts, of child care are best for children's attachment security and later emotional development.

Non-maternal care arrangements sometimes involve care by relatives, most commonly grandparents or fathers. Alternatively, in-home nannies may be hired, children may go to small family day care homes, or receive center-based care, where they typically are grouped with children of roughly the same age. In most of these settings there is the possibility of changes in caregivers. Most child-care workers are not well-reimbursed for their hard work, which increases the likelihood of turnover.[21] And, in centers, children typically "move up" to a new classroom every year, thus changing caregivers at least annually.

The National Institute of Child Health and Human Development (NICHD) Study

Earlier chapters have discussed various findings of the major longitudinal study that was launched in the early 1990s by the National Institute of Child Health and Human Development (NICHD). This study, which recruited over 1,300 families living in ten states, was initiated to address the controversies regarding whether experiences in non-maternal care influenced children's development.[22]

The NICHD study investigated a number of aspects of care, including the impact of quality of care, type, and stability on children's development. It also looked at whether quality of parenting, as assessed by home observations, was in any way associated with the effects of non-maternal care. This study has now followed children from infancy until the age of fifteen. In 2007, when much of the research had been conducted and published, a reviewer for a book summarizing the study's findings described the data gathered as "a treasure, a data set for the ages."[23]

Because of the size of this study and the amount of data collected over a number of years (indeed, the study actually had a fifteen-year follow-up), this study's findings are generally viewed as the most important summary of the impact of child care. Researchers working with the NICHD study were careful to note that what is referred to as the "effects" of child care are only statistical associations.[24] These associations do not prove causation; it is possible that some additional factor that isn't accounted for explains the observed statistical correlations.

For example, in considering the "effects" of quality of child care, we must assume that choice of child-care placement is not a totally random event; some parents may be more willing or able to pay for, or to commute further to, a child-care setting that seems of higher quality. It is possible that these parents may provide other advantages for their children during their early years. Yet, statistical associations are typically referred to as "effects," and, indeed, they may well reflect causation rather than simply correlation.

The NICHD Study and Mother-Child Attachment

While the NICHD study was not primarily an investigation of attachment, children did participate in the Strange Situation Procedure at age fifteen months. Researchers found no relationship between attachment security at fifteen months and any of the child-care factors they looked at, including quality of care, amount of care, age of entry, and the number of different arrangements the child experienced during the first fifteen months.[25] As has been found consistently in the studies discussed in this book, children's attachment security was related to mothers' sensitivity as well as to mothers' psychological adjustment. Thus, for the sample as a whole, child care by individuals other than mother did not change mothers' influence on children's security, which was certainly a reassuring finding.[26]

When the researchers probed the data further, it was discovered that the influence of the mother depended on several factors related to child care. For children in high-quality child care, time in care did not influence the relationship between maternal sensitivity and attachment security.[27] But, when children were in low-quality child care yet had mothers who were *highly* sensitive, children were more likely to be judged securely attached to mother in the Strange Situation. It seems that some mothers were able to compensate for lower-quality care by being highly responsive to their children when with them.[28]

Also, boys seemed to be more vulnerable to larger amounts of non-maternal child care than were girls. The proportion of boys who were secure was lowest among boys in more than thirty hours of child care per week. The authors attributed this to the fact that boys in general tend to be more vulnerable than girls to psychosocial stress.[29]

Factors Contributing to Quality of Care

In determining quality of care, researchers spent several hours observing the behaviors of caregivers with each study child, looking at things such as caregivers' positive affect and positive physical contact, their response to children's distress and to their communications, and caregivers' stimulation of children's cognitive and social development. Researchers found several factors that correlated with positive caregiving, and they were important regardless of setting, whether center-based, child-care homes, care by in-home sitters, or grandparents and fathers.

For infants aged six months, caregivers provided more positive and sensitive care when group sizes were smaller and child-adult ratios were lower. Sensitive caregiving was also more likely when caregivers had higher levels of education and experience and when the environment was safer and more stimulating.

The lower the child-adult ratio was, the more likely care was to be highly sensitive. While some providing one-on-one care were relatives, this finding held with unrelated in-home sitters as well. With one-to-one ratios, almost 40 percent of caregivers were rated as highly sensitive; 17 percent were highly sensitive when the ratio was two-to-one, and only 8 percent with four-to-one ratios. Child-adult ratios and group sizes were larger in child-care centers than in private child-care homes.[30] While this finding is sobering, having a caretaker solely devoted to one infant is a luxury that is out of reach for many parents. Even a mother who stays home may not be able to provide one-on-one child care, as there may be other siblings needing mother's attention.

With children aged one to three, child-adult ratios and group sizes continued to be significantly related to positive caregiving behaviors. However, by thirty-six months, lower child-adult ratios became somewhat less important.[31]

Weekly Hours in Care—Impact on Attachment

In the sample as a whole, the amount of time children spent in non-maternal care did not impact their attachment security. However, there were two findings that suggest circumstances where larger quantity of care appears to pose risks. First, children were more likely to be insecure if they were in child care more than minimal amounts, i.e., more than ten hours a week, *and* if they also had mothers with low levels of sensitivity.[32] Second, when children six months and older received long hours of child care—sixty or more hours per week—they were significantly more likely to have a disorganized attachment style. When hours increased beyond sixty hours per week, the risk of disorganized attachment increased dramatically. This finding of higher rates of disorganized attachment was also replicated in another study that included a relatively large number of children who spent sixty or more hours weekly in child care.[33]

As disorganized attachment is a risk factor for later psychopathology, the finding that very long hours of care increases the likelihood of disorganization is concerning. Differences in quality of alternative care could not explain this finding, nor could mothers' sensitivity during videotaped play sessions or other factors such as the child's temperament or family income.

At this point, research can't explain whether it is that sixty or more hours per week of care leaves children too little time to develop an organized attachment with their mothers, or whether the long working hours that require this level of care leave mothers too sleep deprived or stressed to be sufficiently emotionally responsive to their children. Even though mothers may be able to be sensitive with their children under non-stressful conditions, as they were observed to be in one of the research studies, the pressures of either working two jobs or working one very demanding job likely make interactions at the end of a long day very difficult for parents.[34]

Certainly, not all children who are in child care for very long hours develop disorganized attachments. Research has not yet identified specific factors that either increase risk or that are protective. And the long-term adjustment of these children is unknown. Further research in this area would be very important to provide guidance for families.

NICHD Follow-up Studies

The NICHD cohort of children in child care were followed until the age of fifteen, and their cognitive functioning and behavioral adjustment were intensively evaluated at a number of points in time. Children's cognitive, academic, and language abilities were assessed when they were four and a half years old, several times during elementary school, and again when they were fifteen years old. For information about behavioral adjustment, parents and teachers completed questionnaires at four and a half years, then annually through sixth grade. At fifteen years, youngsters themselves reported on their behavior as well as their risk taking and impulsiveness.

First, it is important to note that parenting quality was a far stronger and more consistent predictor of both tested achievement and teacher-reported social functioning than was the child's experience in child-care. The "effects" of child care that were discovered were relatively small in comparison to the influence of parents' relationships with their children. However, the impact of child care experience did make some difference. Overall, the follow-up studies indicate that child care appeared to offer both risks and benefits.

Benefits of child care were in the academic/cognitive area. For example, quality, quantity, and type of care were correlated with children's school readiness. At four and a half years, higher-quality child care predicted higher levels of pre-academic skills and language ability. In subsequent years, higher-quality care continued to be linked to higher scores in math, memory, and vocabulary skills. Even at fifteen years of age, higher-quality care predicted higher academic achievement.

In contrast, the NICHD data showed that children's behavioral adjustment and social skills had the potential to be negatively affected by *quantity* of child care. At four and a half years, children who had spent more time in any of a variety of non-maternal care arrangements were rated by mothers, caregivers, and teachers as having higher rates of externalizing problems, such as disobedience and aggression, and more conflict with teachers. When taking into account variations in quality, type, and instability of arrangements, these findings were slightly weakened, but they did remain significant.[35] Similar findings continued to be obtained during elementary school.

When these children were assessed at age fifteen (over ten years since they left non-maternal care), higher quality of care continued to predict higher academic functioning. While the magnitude of this effect was small, it remained consistent with the results found at four and a half years. Additionally, youngsters reported fewer externalizing behaviors if they had been in higher-quality care, and they reported higher levels of risk taking and impulsivity when they had had a greater quantity of nonrelative care.[36]

The study authors emphasized that elementary school teacher reports of greater externalizing problems did not reflect levels of problems that would be considered in the "clinical" range. Thus, it is important to note that non-maternal care does not predict psychopathology, but only that it appears to result in slightly, but significantly, higher levels of externalizing behaviors in what is considered the normal range.[37]

What Explains Effects of Early Child Care?

When children who have received varying "doses" of quality and quantity are compared, both factors contribute to the small but significant differences found. The positive effect of higher-quality child care on academic functioning is heartening, but the negative effect on behavioral adjustment when child care is of poorer quality and when more hours are spent in child care are a concern.

Is the finding that children who spend longer hours in child care have higher levels of externalizing behaviors related to the fact that they are separated from their mothers (who are assumed to be their primary caregivers) for longer periods? Other areas of research on child-care effects suggest that longer hours do not simply reflect the fact that children are "missing Mommy." A number of studies have investigated whether social stress experienced by children in child care might explain the findings.[38]

Physiological Assessment of Stress

A method of assessing stress that is increasingly used in research is measuring levels of the hormone cortisol. Cortisol is released in response to stress, and there is good evidence that assessing saliva cortisol validly provides an indication of stress in humans.[39] Additionally, it is very easy to measure cortisol levels, as they can be reliably measured from saliva samples. The normal pattern of cortisol production, for children as well as adults, is for there to be the highest levels of cortisol on awakening in the morning, and for levels to decrease over the day. Any changes from this pattern may indicate effects of stress. Laboratory studies investigating the kinds of acute psychological tasks that most impact levels of cortisol have shown that two factors—when stress is uncontrollable, and when task performance could be judged negatively by others—stand out as most influential in stimulating production of cortisol.[40]

Social interactions in child-care settings may be stressful for children. When young children have immature self-regulatory and social skills, they may feel vulnerable and threatened, and may experience rejection by peers.[41] Research reviewing literature on cortisol levels in children in child care found that the age of children mattered. Children showed greater evidence of stress when they were toddlers and young preschoolers than when they were infants or older children (e.g., three and a half to five years of age).[42] Researchers noted that younger children do not have the capacity to handle various social situations, e.g., to argue and negotiate over toys and play activities. This effect was larger in low-quality than high-quality care centers, and there was also evidence of larger effects when children were identified as having difficult temperaments. It is likely that in higher-quality centers, teachers can more often intervene to help children negotiate difficult social interactions.

In the NICHD study, when fifteen-year-olds were interviewed, researchers also collected cortisol saliva samples. The researchers found that, when they had a history of their mothers being less sensitive *or* when they had spent more time in child-care centers in the first three years of life, the fifteen-year-olds differed slightly but significantly in the patterning of morning cortisol, in a way that was suggestive of exposure to stress. Maternal insensitivity and greater time in child-care centers each contributed separately, and when both were present, they added together.[43] So, once again, there is evidence of small but persistent effects of child care into adolescence.

Attachment Theory and Child Care

When the NICHD study was launched, many developmental psychologists would have predicted that non-maternal care would reduce the likelihood of children having a secure attachment to their mothers.[44] This was definitely not the case. However, while children in this US-based study of child care did not have increased rates of attachment insecurity in the Strange Situation, children studied in Israel did. Infant-caregiver ratios in Israeli child-care centers are very high (average of 8:1), and in a very large study, Israeli children in center care were found to have less secure attachments to their mothers compared to those in maternal care or other settings with paid individual care.[45] Children in these poorly staffed centers were found to be significantly more likely to be insecure-resistant (that is, they resisted consolation when experiencing stress in the Strange Situation) than were children in either maternal care or other care settings.

While attachment theory in general has been proven wrong to uphold the importance of children being exclusively cared for by their mothers, it has offered useful perspectives on the important ingredients of alternative care. No matter what the setting, children benefit from sensitive, supportive caregiving. When they are stressed by social challenges, they need a familiar figure to be available to help calm their distress and support them in finding ways of overcoming challenges.

Child Care, Quality, and Cost

Unfortunately, few child-care settings provide optimal support for children's development. In a paper published in the year 2000, researchers with the NICHD study extrapolated from their population to estimate quality of caregiving in the entire United States. When looking to what extent caregiving could be characterized as "positive," only 9 percent of children were receiving clearly positive caregiving, and another 30 percent were receiving caregiving that had some positive characteristics. The rest of the children were either receiving caregiving that was clearly not positive (8 percent) or that had few aspects of sensitive, supportive caregiving.[46] As researchers believe the NICHD study did not manage to include settings of the poorest quality, US children may face somewhat greater risk than suggested by the NICHD findings.

Ideally, all child-care settings would have low adult-child ratios, small group size, and caregivers who were positive and sensitive. But it is very expensive to provide this level of care. The National Association for the Education of Young Children recommends, for best practices, that the adult-child ratios for infants and toddlers through twenty-eight months not exceed four-to-one, and for preschoolers age thirty to fifty-eight months not exceed nine-to-one.[47] Recall that the NICHD study found that with infants who were cared for in settings with four-to-one ratios, only 8 percent of caregivers were judged to be highly sensitive. These ratios are certainly not ideal for providing a setting in which caregivers can meet each child's needs, but they may be the most realistic goals that many care settings, and the parents they serve, can afford.

Parents seeking child care, and those advising them on this process, should understand what aspects of care are the most important for their children. Unfortunately, parents have been found to overestimate the quality of care their own children receive.[48] And studies have suggested that typically, parents place cost and convenience above aspects of quality considered important by child development professionals. Since child-care fees often consume significant proportions of some families' incomes, of necessity, cost must be a consideration.[49]

Readers may find this review of research on the effects of non-maternal child care sobering, but giving policy-makers solid information is a first step towards considering ways to improve the quality of life for young children and their families. In the final chapter of this book, I will discuss possible ways in which society's resources might be better allocated, in the best interests of our children.

WHEN PARENTS LIVE APART:
ATTACHMENT, VISITATION, AND CUSTODY

Several studies raise concerns about the impact of shared custody with over-nights for young children. At what point do the benefits of extensive time with each parent outweigh the benefits of consistent routines? While we do not yet have longitudinal data about the impact of frequent home changes on very young children, current research suggests caution is warranted.

Overnight Custody Arrangements for Infants and Toddlers

For infants and young toddlers, the wisdom of visits that include overnight stays at the home of a parent who is not the primary attachment figure has been an area of disagreement among professionals in past years. However, with more research there is increasing consensus. Historically, attachment theory has been used as an argument for the importance of continuity of caregiving for the young child, with an emphasis on the importance of mothers. In contrast, the value of sustaining joint parental involvement, par-ticularly including fathers in regular caregiving, has supported arguments for sharing nights as well as days.[50] With these two contradictory viewpoints, families and decision-makers have not had clear guidelines.

In an influential 2000 paper published in the *Family Court Review*, Joan Kelly and Michael Lamb asserted that evening and overnight periods were especially important psychologically for infants, toddlers, and young chil-dren. They argued that overnight periods provide opportunities for nurturing activities, including bathing, soothing hurts and anxieties, bedtime rituals, comforting in the middle of the night, and the reassurance and security of snuggling in the morning after awakening.[51] High parental conflict at the time of transition may heighten children's anxiety about separation, but even without conflict, transitions that involve moving from one set of routines or one parental style to another can cause unsettled behavior. Kelly and Lamb suggested that with high levels of conflict, transitions should take place in neutral places, such as with babysitters or at day-care centers.

Accumulating Research Data

Since the publication of this influential paper, there have been several research studies that indicate increased risk for emotional dysregulation and/or insecure or disorganized attachments when infants and young toddlers spend regular overnights. An early study raised concerns about increased rates of disorganized attachments in separated or divorced families with regular overnights, particularly when parents were unable to provide adequate psychological support for the child.[52] These researchers found that intense conflict or frigid avoidance of all communication were common occurrences during transitions, resulting in an atmosphere of tension and hostility that likely heightened infants' anxiety and need for reassurance. In this atmosphere, many mothers reported feeling helpless or unable to provide protection, and the children of these mothers were more likely to develop disorganized attachments.

Two more recent studies provided additional reason for concern about overnights for infants and toddlers. An Australian study distinguished between "some overnights" and "substantial overnights" for infants, with "substantial overnights" including one or more per week and "some overnights" included one to three nights per month. This study looked at a variety of factors related to emotional regulation. Infants in the "substantial overnights" group were more fretful on waking up and/or going to sleep, had greater difficulty amusing themselves for a length of time, more often cried continuously in spite of several minutes of soothing, and more often cried when left to play alone, compared to infants in the "some overnights" group.[53]

These researchers also found that children aged two to three with "substantial overnights" (now defined as 35 to 65 percent of nights per week with each parent) had significantly lower persistence scores on tasks as reported by parents, and also more behavior problems on a parent report scale, compared to those with either some overnights or daytime-only contact. The Australian researchers noted that young infants and toddlers lack memory or language capacities to support an understanding of repeated separations, or to anticipate, predict, or control events such as reunions. But, by age four or five, children have a much greater ability to understand absence and to predict reunion.

A third group of researchers studied children from low-income families. This study found higher rates of attachment insecurity when infants spent one or more nights a week with the other parent. The relationship between frequent overnights and attachment security was less clear for toddlers aged one to three.[54]

Reaching Consensus on Overnights for Very Young Children

In 2014, three researchers who had in the past taken positions on different sides of the debate about overnight care—Marsha Kline Pruett, Jennifer McIntosh, and Joan Kelly—wrote two consensus papers to provide guidelines for courts. They noted that while evidence had grown that frequent overnights could be problematic for at least some children, it is not yet known which infants fare better with more frequent overnight arrangements and what aspects of development may be enhanced by including overnight care in parenting schedules from an early age. But, given increasing legislative support for shared-time parenting following separation, there is great need for guidance about appropriate plans for very young children. [55]

These researchers provided specific recommendations as to when rare or no overnights were indicated, when lower-frequency overnights were appropriate, and when higher-frequency overnights could be considered. Their guidelines include consideration of a variety of factors, including children's trust and security with each parent, the parents' mental health, children's physical health and behavioral adjustment, the quality of the co-parental relationship, the existence of pragmatic resources to support sharing of overnights, and consideration of family factors. Overall, the guidelines emphasized the importance that parents communicate well and be alert to specific physical and psychological needs of their children. [56]

In concluding, the researchers recommended that, when a young child shows he or she cannot master both attachment security and the developmental demands of overnight stays, delaying overnights may simply allow development to catch up with the challenge of the new situation. This view was succinctly described by a father who wrote a letter describing his co-parenting experiences during the first three years:

> Our son is nearly three. We separated shortly after he was born, and had court orders for increasing overnights, which would have led to 50/50 by the time he was two. He started to stay overnights with me when he turned one but was clearly distressed with the separations. I couldn't have him be distressed. I chose (despite friends believing otherwise) to work with his desires and wants. So we discontinued the overnights for a while. . . . Over time, through his own volition he became comfortable with staying overnight. . . . He often now wants to stay on longer with me and transition times are joyfully undertaken. We are on a roll. So, needless to say I'm happy with the decision to allow him to come to this in his own time. [57]

Undoubtedly, this father demonstrated sensitive, responsive parenting at its best, and we would expect he will have a very solid relationship with his son as he grows.

In the concluding chapter, I will bring together many of the important findings from attachment research that have been covered in this book. I will look particularly at the evidence that the early attachment bond is important in the development of affect regulation and stress physiology. Additionally, I will complete consideration of attachment security through the entire life-span, looking specifically at relationships between mothers with dementia and their caregiving daughters.

NOTES

1. Sears et al., *The Baby Book.*
2. Sears and Sears, *The Attachment Parenting Book.*
3. Ibid., ix.
4. Belsky and Fearon, "Early Attachment Security, Subsequent Maternal Sensitivity, and Later Child Development."
5. Sears and Sears, *The Attachment Parenting Book.*
6. Ibid., 4.
7. Ainsworth et al., *Patterns of Attachment.*
8. van den Boom, "The Influence of Temperament and Mothering on Attachment and Exploration."
9. Britton, Britton, and Gronwaldt, "Breastfeeding, Sensitivity, and Attachment."
10. Wagner et al., "The Role of Personality and Other Factors in Mother's Decision to Initiate Breastfeeding."
11. Ibid., 23.
12. Belsky and Fearon, "Early Attachment Security, Subsequent Maternal Sensitivity, and Later Child Development."
13. Anisfeld et al., "Does Infant Carrying Promote Attachment?"
14. Colvin et al., "Sleep Environment Risks for Younger and Older Infants." The risk of Sudden Infant Death during bed-sharing is highest for infants less than four months old and with mothers who smoked during pregnancy (Moon and AAP TASK FORCE, "SIDS and Other Sleep-Related Infant Deaths").
15. Nicholson and Parker, *Attached at the Heart.*
16. Pickert, "The Man Who Remade Motherhood."
17. Harlow and Suomi, "Social Recovery by Isolation-Reared Monkeys."
18. Karen, *Becoming Attached.*
19. Scarr, *Mother Care/Other Care.*
20. Sroufe, "Developmental Perspective on Day Care."
21. Kisker and Maynard, "Quality, Cost, and Parental Choice of Child Care."
22. NICHD Early Child Care Research Network, "Characteristics and Quality of Child Care for Toddlers and Preschoolers."
23. Newcombe, "Developmental Psychology Meets the Mommy Wars."
24. Belsky et al., "Are There Long-Term Effects of Early Child Care?," 681.
25. NICHD Early Child Care Research Network, "The Effects of Infant Child Care on Infant-Mother Attachment Security," 865.
26. Ibid., 868.
27. Ibid., 871–73.
28. Ibid., 873.
29. Ibid., 876.
30. NICHD Early Child Care Research Network, "Characteristics of Infant Child Care."
31. NICHD Early Child Care Research Network, "Characteristics and Quality of Child Care for Toddlers and Preschoolers."
32. Ibid.; NICHD Early Child Care Research Network, "The Effects of Infant Child Care on Infant-Mother Attachment Security."

33. Hazen et al., "Very Extensive Nonmaternal Care Predicts Mother–Infant Attachment Disorganization."

34. There is no information about the long-term adjustment of children who experienced more than sixty hours per week of child care. In the NICHD study, there were too few participants with long-term follow-up data who were both disorganized and had experienced very extensive nonmaternal care (over sixty hours per week) during their infancy (personal communication, Nancy Hazen, May 2016).

35. NICHD Early Child Care Research Network, "Does Amount of Time Spent in Child Care Predict Socioemotional Adjustment during the Transition to Kindergarten?"

36. Vandell et al., "Do Effects of Early Child Care Extend to Age 15 Years?"

37. Belsky et al., "Are There Long-Term Effects of Early Child Care?," 697.

38. Geoffroy et al., "Daycare Attendance, Stress, and Mental Health"; Vermeer and van IJzendoorn, "Children's Elevated Cortisol Levels at Daycare."

39. Vermeer and van IJzendoorn, "Children's Elevated Cortisol Levels at Daycare."

40. Dickerson and Kemeny, "Acute Stressors and Cortisol Responses."

41. Vermeer and van IJzendoorn, "Children's Elevated Cortisol Levels at Daycare," 391; Gunnar et al., "Peer Rejection, Temperament, and Cortisol Activity in Preschoolers."

42. Vermeer and van IJzendoorn, "Children's Elevated Cortisol Levels at Daycare"; Geoffroy et al., "Daycare Attendance, Stress, and Mental Health."

43. Roisman et al., "Early Family and Child-Care Antecedents of Awakening Cortisol Levels in Adolescence."

44. Newcombe, "Developmental Psychology Meets the Mommy Wars."

45. Sagi et al., "Shedding Further Light on the Effects of Various Types and Quality of Early Child Care on Infant-Mother Attachment Relationship."

46. NICHD Early Child Care Research Network, "Characteristics and Quality of Child Care for Toddlers and Preschoolers."

47. http://www.naeyc.org/academy/files/academy/file/Teacher_Child_Ratio_Chart.pdf.

48. Helbern and Howes, "Child Care Cost and Quality."

49. Kisker and Maynard, "Quality, Cost, and Parental Choice of Child Care."

50. Pruett, McIntosh, and Kelly, "Parental Separation and Overnight Care of Young Children, Part I."

51. Kelly and Lamb, "Using Child Development Research to Make Appropriate Custody and Access Decisions for Young Children."

52. Solomon and George, "The Development of Attachment in Separated and Divorced Families."

53. McIntosh, Smyth, and Kelaher, "Overnight Care Patterns Following Parental Separation."

54. Ibid.

55. Pruett, McIntosh, and Kelly, "Parental Separation and Overnight Care of Young Children, Part I."

56. McIntosh, Pruett, and Kelly, "Parental Separation and Overnight Care of Young Children, Part II."

57. Ibid., 261.

REFERENCES

Ainsworth, Mary D. Salter, Mary C. Blehar, Everett Waters, and Sally N. Wall. *Patterns of Attachment: A Psychological Study of the Strange Situation.* New York and London: Psychology Press, 1978/2015.

Anisfeld, Elizabeth, Virginia Casper, Molly Nozyce, and Nicholas Cunningham. "Does Infant Carrying Promote Attachment? An Experimental Study of the Effects of Increased Physical Contact on the Development of Attachment." *Child Development* 61, no. 5 (1990): 1617–27.

Belsky, Jay, and R. M. Pasco Fearon. "Early Attachment Security, Subsequent Maternal Sensitivity, and Later Child Development: Does Continuity in Development Depend Upon Continuity of Caregiving?" *Attachment & Human Development* 4, no. 3 (2002): 361–87.

Belsky, Jay, Deborah Lowe Vandell, Margaret Burchinal, K. Alison Clarke-Stewart, Kathleen McCartney, and Margaret Tresch Owen. "Are There Long-Term Effects of Early Child Care?" *Child Development* 78, no. 2 (2007): 681–701.

Britton, John R., Helen L. Britton, and Virginia Gronwaldt. "Breastfeeding, Sensitivity, and Attachment." *Pediatrics* 118, no. 5 (2006): 1436–43.

Colvin, Jeffrey D., Vicki Collie-Akers, Christy Schunn, and Rachel Y. Moon. "Sleep Environment Risks for Younger and Older Infants." *Pediatrics* 134, no. 2 (2014): 406–12.

Dickerson, Sally S., and Margaret E. Kemeny. "Acute Stressors and Cortisol Responses: A Theoretical Integration and Synthesis of Laboratory Research." *Psychological Bulletin* 130, no. 3 (2004): 355–91.

Geoffroy, Marie-Claude, Sylvana M. Côté, Sophie Parent, and Jean Richard Séguin. "Daycare Attendance, Stress, and Mental Health." *The Canadian Journal of Psychiatry* 51, no. 9 (2006): 607–15.

Gunnar, Megan R., Anne M. Sebanc, Kathryn Tout, Bonny Donzella, and Manfred M. H. van Dulmer. "Peer Rejection, Temperament, and Cortisol Activity in Preschoolers." *Developmental Psychobiology* 43, no. 4 (2003): 346–68.

Harlow, Harry F., and Stephen J. Suomi. "Social Recovery by Isolation-Reared Monkeys." *Proceedings of the National Academy of Sciences* 68, no. 7 (1971): 1534–38.

Hazen, Nancy L., Sydnye D. Allen, Caroline Heaton Christopher, Tomotaka Umemura, and Deborah B. Jacobvitz. "Very Extensive Nonmaternal Care Predicts Mother–Infant Attachment Disorganization: Convergent Evidence from Two Samples." *Development and Psychopathology* 27, no. 3 (2015): 649–61.

Helburn, Suzanne W., and Carollee Howes. "Child Care Cost and Quality." *The Future of Children* 6, no. 2 (1996): 62–82.

Karen, Robert. *Becoming Attached: First Relationships and How They Shape Our Capacity to Love.* New York: Oxford University Press, 1998.

Kelly, Joan B., and Michael E. Lamb. "Using Child Development Research to Make Appropriate Custody and Access Decisions for Young Children." *Family Court Review* 38, no. 3 (2000): 297–311.

Kisker, Ellen, and Rebecca Maynard. "Quality, Cost, and Parental Choice of Child Care." In *Economics of Child Care,* edited by David M. Blau, 127–43. New York: Russel Sage Foundation, 1991.

McIntosh, Jennifer E., Marsha Kline Pruett, and Joan B. Kelly. "Parental Separation and Overnight Care of Young Children, Part II: Putting Theory into Practice." *Family Court Review* 52, no. 2 (2014): 256–62.

McIntosh, Jennifer E., Bruce M. Smyth, and Margaret Kelaher. "Overnight Care Patterns Following Parental Separation: Associations with Emotion Regulation in Infants and Young Children." *Journal of Family Studies* 19, no. 3 (2013): 224–39.

Moon, Rachel Y., and AAP TASK FORCE ON SUDDEN INFANT DEATH SYNDROME. "SIDS and Other Sleep-Related Infant Deaths: Evidence Base for 2016 Updated Recommendations for a Safe Infant Sleeping Environment." *Pediatrics* 138, no. 5 (2015): e20162940.

Newcombe, Nora S. "Developmental Psychology Meets the Mommy Wars." *Journal of Applied Developmental Psychology* 28, no. 5 (2007): 553–55.

NICHD Early Child Care Research Network. "Characteristics of Infant Child Care: Factors Contributing to Positive Caregiving." *Early Childhood Research Quarterly* 11 (1996): 269–306.

———. "The Effects of Infant Child Care on Infant-Mother Attachment Security: Results of the NICHD Study of Early Child Care." *Child Development* 68, no. 5 (1997): 860–79.

———. "Characteristics and Quality of Child Care for Toddlers and Preschoolers." *Applied Developmental Science* 4, no. 3 (2000): 116–35.

———. "Does Amount of Time Spent in Child Care Predict Socioemotional Adjustment during the Transition to Kindergarten?" *Child Development* 74, no. 4 (2003): 976–1005.

Nicholson, Barbara, and Lysa Parker. *Attached at the Heart: Eight Proven Parenting Principles for Raising Connected and Compassionate Children.* Deerfield Beach, FL: Health Communications, Inc., 2013.

Pickert, Kate. "The Man Who Remade Motherhood." *Time Magazine*, May 21, 2012.
Pruett, Marsha Kline, Jennifer E. McIntosh, and Joan B. Kelly. "Parental Separation and Overnight Care of Young Children, Part I: Consensus through Theoretical and Empirical Integration." *Family Court Review* 52, no. 2 (2014): 240–55.
Roisman, Glenn I., Elizabeth Susman, Kortnee Barnett-Walker, Cathryn Booth-LaForce, Margaret Tresch Owen, Jay Belsky, Robert H. Bradley, Renate Houts, and Laurence Steinberg. "Early Family and Child-Care Antecedents of Awakening Cortisol Levels in Adolescence." *Child Development* 80, no. 3 (2009): 907–20.
Sagi, Abraham, Nina Koren-Karie, Motti Gini, Yair Ziv, and Tirtsa Joels. "Shedding Further Light on the Effects of Various Types and Quality of Early Child Care on Infant-Mother Attachment Relationship: The Haifa Study of Early Child Care." *Child Development* 73, no. 4 (2002): 1166–86.
Scarr, Sandra. *Mother Care/Other Care*. New York: Basic Books, 1984.
Sears, William, and Martha Sears. *The Attachment Parenting Book: A Commonsense Guide to Understanding and Nurturing Your Baby*. New York: Little, Brown and Co., 2001.
Sears, William, Martha Sears, Robert Sears, and James Sears. *The Baby Book: Everything You Need to Know about Your Baby from Birth to Age Two*. New York: Little, Brown and Co., 1992.
Solomon, Judith, and Carol George. "The Development of Attachment in Separated and Divorced Families: Effects of Overnight Visitation, Parent and Couple Variables." *Attachment & Human Development* 1, no. 1 (1999): 2–33.
Sroufe, L. Alan. "A Developmental Perspective on Day Care." *Early Childhood Research Quarterly* 3, no. 3 (1988): 283–91.
van den Boom, Dymphna C. "The Influence of Temperament and Mothering on Attachment and Exploration: An Experimental Manipulation of Sensitive Responsiveness among Lower-Class Mothers with Irritable Infants." *Child Development* 65, no. 5 (1994): 1457–77.
Vandell, Deborah Lowe. "Characteristics of Infant Child Care: Factors Contributing to Positive Caregiving: NICHD Early Child Care Research Network." *Early Childhood Research Quarterly* 11, no. 3 (1996): 269–306.
Vandell, Deborah Lowe, Jay Belsky, Margaret Burchinal, Laurence Steinberg, and Nathan Vandergrift. "Do Effects of Early Child Care Extend to Age 15 Years? Results from the NICHD Study of Early Child Care and Youth Development." *Child Development* 81, no. 3 (2010): 737–56.
Vermeer, Harriet J., and Marinus H. van IJzendoorn. "Children's Elevated Cortisol Levels at Daycare: A Review and Meta-Analysis." *Early Childhood Research Quarterly* 21, no. 3 (2006): 390–401.
Wagner, Carol L., Mark T. Wagner, Myla Ebeling, Katreia Gleaton Chatman, Millicent Cohen, and Thomas C. Hulsey. "The Role of Personality and Other Factors in Mother's Decision to Initiate Breastfeeding." *Journal of Human Lactation* 22, no. 1 (2006): 16–26.

Conclusion

Putting It All Together:
The Role of Attachment through the Lifespan

Early-care experiences, and the attachment bonds they foster, matter. More than expected by chance, longitudinal studies have now shown that individuals who have the luxury of sensitive care in infancy are more likely to grow to adulthood prepared for romantic relationship success.

But early-childhood experience is not destiny. Later experiences matter, too. A secure and harmonious relationship with mother and/or father during the first year is important, but not necessarily formative. As we saw in Chapter Three, theory and research are now providing evidence that the human brain is considerably "plastic," at least during the first decade of life. Even experiences in adulthood, such as forming a relationship with a partner who is able to reflect on feelings in a coherent manner and to deal with conflict constructively, can bring about positive changes. A secure partner, one who can be relied upon as a secure base, can help an insecure individual move from a "state of mind" marked by insecurity towards one that is more secure. Emotionally salient experiences that influence our attachment behavior accumulate over time, even as memories of specific events are forgotten.

When emotional interactions have been sensitive and largely positive, we expect that individuals will reach adulthood well positioned to establish a solid romantic relationship and become sensitive, supportive parents themselves. Conversely, as we saw in Chapter Seven, when harsh and very negative experiences accumulate, in the most severe cases, the ultimate result can be the development of psychiatric disorders such as Borderline Personality Disorder, which brings great individual anguish as well as significant cost to society. However, it is important to recognize that many people fall between

193

these two extremes, and these individuals may suffer various degrees of disappointment, hurt, or a sense of failure in intimate relationships.

Bowlby's Theory and Working Models: The Debate on Continuity versus Discontinuity

Bowlby's "prototype hypothesis"—that early experiences result in working models being established that become influential, though often unconscious, cognitive brain structures—has been subjected to considerable examination in studies that have followed individuals over time. Based on the results of the major longitudinal studies, Marinus van IJzendoorn, a very prominent figure in the field, concluded that there was only support for a "weak" version of the prototype hypothesis. He concluded that there is considerable evidence that major changes, such as divorce, parental psychiatric illness, or serious illnesses in the parents or the child, lead to changes in attachment security. Whether more minor changes, e.g., a change in a parent's job that decreases their sensitivity to the child, lead to modifications in a child's working models has not been tested. [1]

Might there be some areas in which early experiences are particularly important for later emotional adjustment? In Chapter Six, we saw that the Minnesota researchers found a strong correlation between fifteen-year-olds' capacity to be vulnerable and their early attachment status. It is certainly plausible that the capacity for intimacy might be particularly influenced by early experiences. Alan Sroufe, one of the chief researchers with the Minnesota longitudinal study, has argued that traces of early experiences persist, and even if circumstances change, the early experiences always can be reactivated. [2] While this notion seems quite reasonable, solid data to support this are not yet available.

Attachment Security: A Family Affair

Much of the literature on attachment focuses on the role of the mother. However, I have striven to emphasize the importance of fathers, both in directly influencing their children through sensitive interactions and in providing emotional support for their partners. The early attachment research emphasized that fathers' play sensitivity is a key contribution to children's development. However, as men increasingly adopt less traditional roles, their ability to sensitively soothe and nurture children is undoubtedly becoming more important.

Parental classifications on the Adult Attachment Interview—indicating their "states of mind with respect to attachment"—have been shown to be strongly predictive of children's attachment classifications. [3] Mothers' states of mind tends to be more strongly related to children's attachment security than is the case with fathers, but fathers' attachment-related states of mind also correlate with their children's attachment security. And, as we saw in the German study in Chapter Four, when security of attachment is the same with both parents, it may have a cumulative effect. In Germany, children who had had two secure attachment relationships in the first year of life were doing particularly well in preschool, and children with two insecure relationships were doing the least well.

The relationship between security in the parental state of mind and child attachment security appears to be a fairly universal phenomenon. Research conducted in West European, Scandinavian, Asian, and Middle Eastern cultures has found correlations between child attachment security and parents' "states of mind with respect to attachment."[4] And, as we saw in Chapter Five, two studies that looked at security of attachment in three generations—in mother, her child, and in mother's own mother—also have found at least moderate stability in states of mind with respect to attachment across generations.[5] Degree of parental sensitivity in caregiving has been shown to be particularly important for children who face greater-than-ordinary risks. For example, in Chapter Two, the Netherlands study found irritable infants were at greater risk of developing an insecure attachment. However, their mothers could be coached to interact more sensitively with these infants, with the result that the children showed significantly greater attachment security at one year than a control group.

A second at-risk group where degree of parenting sensitivity (as inferred from mothers' states of mind with respect to attachment) has been shown to influence adjustment is with "late-adopted children." A London study with children with histories of multiple changes in foster homes in their first four or more years, who are at high risk of emotional disturbance and behavioral problems, showed that with this group of children, parenting sensitivity made a clear difference in how well these children fared post-adoption.[6]

Attachment Security and Marital Success

Research is only beginning to provide data about the impact of attachment security on the course of long-term relationships in adulthood. In Chapter Seven, we saw that in some cases the move to marriage can be conceptualized as providing a new caregiving environment, and that one secure partner can help their insecure spouse achieve a greater sense of security. In laboratories, researchers have observed that during discussions designed to touch on areas of conflict, sensitive partners can "buffer" the insecurities of their partner. In the future, research findings may be translated into intervention programs that strengthen marital relationships.

The role of attachment security in marriages that dissolve has to date not been well researched. One study discussed in Chapter Seven showed that in marriages that end during the first two years, individuals who generally have a secure state of mind with respect to attachment, but enter into relationships in which they do not experience their partners as providing a secure base, are the most likely to divorce early on. However, the role of attachment security in marriages in which partners separate after many years is not yet known. Only prospective longitudinal studies can accurately address that question, and such studies have yet to be done.

Attachment Security and Mental Health

Security in attachment predicts the best outcomes for mental health. However, insecure forms of attachment should not necessarily be interpreted as indications of psychopathology. The 35 percent or so of youngsters in middle-class samples who have insecure attachments and the 45 percent of adults who have insecure or unresolved states of mind with respect to attachment (as reported in Chapters Two and Five) do constitute a large minority of the population. These individuals may be a more vulnerable group, but we would be hard-pressed to consider them as truly deviant. We must recognize that a good proportion of these individuals lead productive lives. "Insecurity of attachment" is not equivalent to mental illness, by any means.

Affect Regulation and Mental Health

In Chapter Three, we saw that more recent attachment theorists such as Allan Schore have argued that the attachment bond evolved not only to keep children close to caregivers, and thus avoid predators, but also to assist in the development of emotion regulation skills.[7] In the early months of an infant's life, the caregiver has an important role in regulating the child's affect by interpreting his or her signals and striving to satisfy the child's needs. With repeated interactions, parents begin to influence how children themselves cope with emotionally arousing events. If parents are sensitive, particularly in response to children's distress, children are helped to learn to self-regulate.

Some support for the theory that security of attachment has a relationship with affect regulation and the underlying physiological processes for regulating emotions was found in two studies discussed in Chapter Three that found that in the Strange Situation, children in the insecure-avoidant group did not show much distress during separation despite the fact that their heart rates increased.[8] And in one study, measurement of a stress hormone (cortisol) after the Strange Situation Procedure indicated that the laboratory procedure was *more* stressful for avoidant than for secure babies. But, unlike secure babies, insecure-avoidant children (i.e., those who appeared to maintain a "stiff upper lip") did not turn to their mothers when heart rate measures showed they were highly aroused. These findings suggested that insecure-avoidant children were inhibiting behavioral reactions of distress, and also were not inclined to try to use their mothers to be soothed.

In Chapter Five, evidence that such variations may continue into adulthood were found in an Israeli study in which individuals with known attachment styles were asked to judge degree of hostile intent in a number of imaginary scenarios. This study found an odd pattern of anger arousal and hostility attribution among individuals with an avoidant style. These individuals, as a group, attributed hostile intent even in the non-hostile scene, but they did not report feeling anger in any of the scenes, including the hostile scene. However, while they did not report feeling anger, avoidant individuals had increased heart rate, thus showing physiological arousal.[9]

Further evidence for the impact of attachment security on affect regulation processes was found in a follow-up of members of the Minnesota longitudinal study when they were in their thirties. In Chapter Seven, we saw that participants who had partners at the time of this follow-up engaged in conflict-arousing discussions with partners, during which their electrodermal reactivity responses were measured. Electrodermal reactivity indicates activity in the behavioral inhibition system and has been shown to be involved in the effortful inhibition of behavior. Results showed that those who had experienced greater maternal sensitivity, as measured at various points across the childhood years, showed significantly lower electrodermal reactivity during the conflict discussion. The researchers concluded that early parent-child relationships may have a unique contribution in shaping autonomic responses during partner interactions, and that any contribution is largely outside conscious control.[10]

The finding that adults with different attachment classifications show different autonomic response patterns in situations that involve interpersonal conflict raises questions about possible attachment-related health effects. Indeed, researchers following the Minnesota cohort found significant correlations between infant attachment security and adult health outcomes. As discussed in Chapter Seven, children who had been judged insecure-resistant or insecure-avoidant grew up to report significantly elevated levels of inflammation-related illnesses.

It is highly unlikely that the researchers who began studying the Minnesota infants in the 1970s ever dreamed that thirty years later researchers would find correlations between the twenty-minute Strange Situation assessments at eighteen months and major adult health variables! These findings raise questions as to whether one important legacy of insensitive and unresponsive care may be heightened stress reactivity, with the possible result that a biological and/or behavioral process is initiated that may culminate in poor health in adulthood. This area needs more investigation, but the research on health outcomes provides further reason to believe that early relationships matter, and perhaps may matter for more outcomes than had ever been anticipated.

Disorganized Attachment

Studies have shown that children with disorganized attachments may have the most serious psychological problems as they grow.[11] As noted in Chapter Two, in very high risk samples and those where children are known to have been maltreated, the majority of children show disorganized attachment.[12] However, even if there has been no documented history of maltreatment, children in families with multiple risk factors also show high levels of disorganized attachment.[13]

Additionally, in more affluent families, about 15 percent of children show disorganized attachment, and in these families, parents often have a history of personal loss or trauma.[14] Further, in Chapter Eight we saw that disorganized attachments are found disproportionately more often when children spend sixty or more hours a week in non-maternal child care, and also when very young children regularly move between parental homes post-divorce.

Mary Main and colleagues have expressed concern that there is a widespread perception that disorganized attachment in the Strange Situation Procedure indicates maltreatment.[15] As noted in Chapter Two, a 2012 paper that appeared in the *Journal of Social Work Practice* argued that child protection workers should be trained to assess disorganized attachment since *"disorganized attachment is not just associated with child maltreatment but is indicative of it"* (italics added).[16] Given that other bases for disorganized attachment have been identified, assumptions of maltreatment are clearly not warranted. However, the finding of disorganized attachment may well indicate that a therapeutic intervention with mother and child should be implemented.

Based on the information provided in Chapter Eight, individuals making decisions about post-divorce visitation schedules should certainly attend to research suggesting that infants and toddlers may be stressed by spending nights away from a primary attachment figure. Delaying overnight visitation until children are somewhat older need not undermine a child's attachment relationship with either parent. And, if for one reason or another mothers must place their children in non-parental child care for more than sixty hours per week, parents should be knowledgeable about potential risks for disorganized attachment and make efforts to reduce stresses that might exacerbate attachment difficulties.

Child Care for Working Parents

Some readers may have found the research on non-maternal child care reviewed in Chapter Eight a bit sobering. The National Institute of Child Health and Human Development (NICHD) Early Child Care Research Network study was very large, thorough, and it included regular follow-up assessments until the age of fifteen. One important and positive finding of the NICHD study was that, contrary to the expectation of many developmental psychologists, day-time non-maternal child care did not reduce the likelihood of children having a secure attachment to their mothers. [17]

Overall, this major longitudinal study indicated that child care appears to offer both benefits and risks. Higher-quality child care has a positive impact on academic and cognitive skills. But the finding that quantity of child care appears to have a small but persistent negative impact on behavioral adjustment and social skills through the age of fifteen raises some concerns.

The researchers who followed the large NICHD cohort emphasized that elementary school teacher reports of greater externalizing problems such as aggression or disobedience did not reflect levels of problems that would be considered in the "clinical" range. Thus, it is important to note that non-maternal care does not predict psychopathology, but only that it appears to result in slightly but significantly higher levels of externalizing behaviors in what is considered the normal range. [18]

Also, it is important to emphasize that parenting quality was a far stronger and more consistent predictor of both tested achievement and teacher-reported social functioning than was the child's experience in child care. The "effects" of child care that were discovered were relatively small in comparison to the influence of parents' relationships with their children. However, the impact of child-care experience did make some difference.

In considering the reason for reports of slightly increased behavior problems, other research studies suggest that separation from mother may not be the main source of difficulty. Social interactions in child-care settings may be stressful for children; and researchers have noted that younger children do not have the capacity to handle various social situations, e.g., to argue and negotiate over toys and play activities. [19] It is likely that in higher-quality centers, teachers can more often intervene to help children negotiate difficult social interactions.

Quality, Cost, and Society's Priorities

Particularly for young children, the adult-child caretaker ratio was found to strongly relate to the observed sensitivity of alternative-care providers. While guidelines of the National Association for the Education of Young Children allow for a maximum of eight infants to two teachers in one group, and with toddlers, a maximum of twelve children with two teaching staff, these ratios may make it difficult for teachers to provide sensitive, individualized care. These caretaking ratios are much better than those in Israel, where one teacher may care for eight infants. However, observations in the United States of teachers working in groups with four-to-one ratios indicated that only a small minority were observed to be sensitive.

The greatest concern is probably for the children of the least advantaged parents, many of whom are likely to be forced to place children in day-care arrangements where there are many children and poorly paid providers. Researchers believe that the NICHD study did not manage to include settings of the poorest quality, so the general population of US children whose parents work and who are placed in non-parental child-care settings may face somewhat greater risk than suggested by the NICHD findings. And, given the general conclusion of many studies on child outcome that risks go up when more stressors are present, adding the experience of poor-quality child care when children are already experiencing multiple stressors due to their disadvantaged status likely increases risks for children's development.

Child development research has an important role in providing scientific data about the psychological consequences of different configurations of non-parental care. Policy-makers could certainly decide that subsidizing child care and thus investing in the well-being of the next generation would be a wise and forward-thinking move. It is hoped that the information in this book will provide support for stronger societal support for young families.

COMING FULL CIRCLE: AGING MOTHERS' ATTACHMENT TO CAREGIVING DAUGHTERS

As we come to the end of this book, it seems appropriate to consider attachment relationships at the end of the lifespan. While this area of research is quite new and the results only suggestive, it provides an intriguing view of the life-long importance of attachment security.

It has been argued that those who live with dementia inhabit a world that has become a permanent "strange situation." When family members visit, their appearance is at least as unexpected as the return of parents in the Strange Situation Procedure. When family members depart, the aging parent may experience loss and a sense of being unsafe. [20]

In an experimental study, researchers brought caretaking daughters and their mothers with dementia to the laboratory. Daughters met separately to participate in the Adult Attachment Interview, and their mothers met with a female researcher who engaged them in conversations about family members. After about forty-five minutes, mothers and daughters were reunited.

The mothers' emotional responses to reunion were coded for positive facial expressions, proximity-seeking and contact-maintaining behavior, and responsiveness. The overall emotional attunement of the dyad was also rated. Ratings of daughters' coherence on the AAI, which is a hallmark of a secure-autonomous state of mind, were predictive of their mothers' reunion behavior. The more coherence the daughter showed on the AAI, the greater the joy and relatedness the mother showed during reunion. Severity of dementia did not influence these findings.[21]

Here, the roles of caregiver and care provider have been reversed. Based on research with the AAI, we would expect that daughters who are more coherent on the AAI are more sensitive and responsive to their mothers' attachment needs. Now it has become the daughter who potentially provides joy and a secure base to a mother living in a world that, sadly, has become a strange situation.

NOTES

1. van IJzendoorn, "Commentary."
2. Sroufe, "Attachment and Development."
3. van IJzendoorn, "Adult Attachment Representations, Parental Responsiveness, and Infant Attachment."
4. Bernier et al., "Taking Stock of Two Decades of Attachment Transmission Gap."
5. Hautamäki et al., "Transmission of Attachment across Three Generations"; Benoit and Parker, "Stability and Transmission of Attachment across Three Generations."
6. Steele et al., "Attachment Representations and Adoption."
7. Schore, "Attachment, Affect Regulation, and the Developing Right Brain"; Schore and Sieff, "On the Same Wave-Length."
8. Spangler and Grossmann, "Biobehavioral Organization in Securely and Insecurely Attached Infants"; Zelenko et al., "Heart Rate Correlates of Attachment Status in Young Mothers and Their Infants."
9. Mikulincer, "Adult Attachment Style and Individual Differences in Functional versus Dysfunctional Experiences of Anger."
10. Raby et al., "Greater Maternal Insensitivity in Childhood Predicts Greater Electrodermal Reactivity during Conflict Discussions with Romantic Partners in Adulthood."
11. van IJzendoorn, Schuengel, and Bakermans-Kranenburg, "Disorganized Attachment in Early Childhood"; Carlson, "A Prospective Longitudinal Study of Attachment Disorganization/Disorientation"; Fearon et al., "The Significance of Insecure Attachment and Disorganization in the Development of Children's Externalizing Behavior."
12. Cyr et al., "Attachment Security and Disorganization in Maltreating and High-Risk Families."
13. Carlson et al., "Disorganized/Disoriented Attachment Relationships in Maltreated Infants"; Cyr et al., "Attachment Security and Disorganization in Maltreating and High-Risk Families."
14. Hesse and Main, "Frightened, Threatening, and Dissociative Parental Behavior in Low-Risk Samples."
15. Main, Hesse, and Hesse, "Attachment Theory and Research."
16. Wilkins, "Disorganised Attachment Indicates Child Maltreatment."
17. Newcombe, "Developmental Psychology Meets the Mommy Wars."
18. Belsky et al., "Are There Long-Term Effects of Early Child Care?"
19. Vermeer and van IJzendoorn, "Children's Elevated Cortisol Levels at Daycare"; Gunnar et al., "Peer Rejection, Temperament, and Cortisol Activity in Preschoolers."
20. Miesen, "Alzheimer's Disease, the Phenomenon of Parent Fixation and Bowlby's Attachment Theory."
21. Steele, Phibbs, and Woods, "Coherence of Mind in Daughter Caregivers of Mothers with Dementia."

REFERENCES

Belsky, Jay, Deborah Lowe Vandell, Margaret Burchinal, K. Alison Clarke-Stewart, Kathleen McCartney, and Margaret Tresch Owen. "Are There Long-Term Effects of Early Child Care?" *Child Development* 78, no. 2 (2007): 681–701.

Benoit, Diane, and Kevin C. H. Parker. "Stability and Transmission of Attachment across Three Generations." *Child Development* 65, no. 5 (1994): 1444–56.

Bernier, Annie, Célia Matte-Gagné, Marie-Ève Bélanger, and Natasha Whipple. "Taking Stock of Two Decades of Attachment Transmission Gap: Broadening the Assessment of Maternal Behavior." *Child Development* 85, no. 5 (2014): 1852–65.

Carlson, Elizabeth A. "A Prospective Longitudinal Study of Attachment Disorganization/Disorientation." *Child Development* 69, no. 4 (1998): 1107–28.

Carlson, Vicki, Dante Cicchetti, Douglas Barnett, and Karen Braunwald. "Disorganized/Disoriented Attachment Relationships in Maltreated Infants." *Developmental Psychology* 25, no. 4 (1989): 525–31.

Cyr, Chantal, Eveline M. Euser, Marian J. Bakermans-Kranenburg, and Marinus H. van IJzendoorn. "Attachment Security and Disorganization in Maltreating and High-Risk Families: A Series of Meta-Analyses." *Development and Psychopathology* 22, no. 1 (2010): 87–108.

Fearon, R. Pasco, Marian J. Bakermans-Kranenburg, Marinus H. van IJzendoorn, Anne-Marie Lapsley, and Glenn I. Roisman. "The Significance of Insecure Attachment and Disorganization in the Development of Children's Externalizing Behavior: A Meta-Analytic Study." *Child Development* 81, no. 2 (2010): 435–56.

Gunnar, Megan R., Anne M. Sebanc, Kathryn Tout, Bonny Donzella, and Manfred M. H. van Dulmen. "Peer Rejection, Temperament, and Cortisol Activity in Preschoolers." *Developmental Psychobiology* 43, no. 4 (2003): 346–68.

Hautamäki, Airi, Laura Hautamäki, Leena Neuvonen, and Sinikka Maliniemi-Piispanen. "Transmission of Attachment across Three Generations." *European Journal of Developmental Psychology* 7, no. 5 (2010): 618–34.

Hesse, Erik, and Mary Main. "Frightened, Threatening, and Dissociative Parental Behavior in Low-Risk Samples: Description, Discussion, and Interpretations." *Development and Psychopathology* 18, no. 2 (2006): 309–43.

Main, Mary, Erik Hesse, and Siegfried Hesse. "Attachment Theory and Research: Overview with Suggested Applications to Child Custody." *Family Court Review* 49, no. 3 (2011): 426–63.

Miesen, Bère M. L. "Alzheimer's Disease, the Phenomenon of Parent Fixation and Bowlby's Attachment Theory." *International Journal of Geriatric Psychiatry* 8, no. 2 (1993): 147–53.

Mikulincer, Mario. "Adult Attachment Style and Individual Differences in Functional versus Dysfunctional Experiences of Anger." *Journal of Personality and Social Psychology* 74, no. 2 (1998): 511–24.

Newcombe, Nora S. "Developmental Psychology Meets the Mommy Wars." *Journal of Applied Developmental Psychology* 28, no. 5 (2007): 553–55.

Raby, K. Lee, Glenn I. Roisman, Jeffry A. Simpson, W. A. Collins, and Ryan D. Steele. "Greater Maternal Insensitivity in Childhood Predicts Greater Electrodermal Reactivity during Conflict Discussions with Romantic Partners in Adulthood." *Psychological Science* 26, no. 3 (2015): 348–53.

Schore, Allan N. "Attachment, Affect Regulation, and the Developing Right Brain: Linking Developmental Neuroscience to Pediatrics." *Pediatrics in Review* 26, no. 6 (2005): 204–17.

Schore, Allan N., and Daniella Sieff. "On the Same Wave-Length: How Our Emotional Brain Is Shaped by Human Relationships." In *Understanding and Healing Emotional Trauma: Conversations with Pioneering Clinicians and Researchers*, edited by Daniella F. Sieff, 11–136. London: Routledge, 2015.

Spangler, Gottfried, and Klaus E. Grossmann. "Biobehavioral Organization in Securely and Insecurely Attached Infants." *Child Development* 64, no. 5 (1993): 1439–50.

Sroufe, L. Alan. "Attachment and Development: A Prospective, Longitudinal Study from Birth to Adulthood." *Attachment & Human Development* 7, no. 4 (2005): 349–67.

Steele, Howard, Emily Phibbs, and Robert Woods. "Coherence of Mind in Daughter Caregivers of Mothers with Dementia: Links with Their Mothers' Joy and Relatedness on Reunion in a Strange Situation." *Attachment & Human Development* 6, no. 4 (2004): 439–50.

Steele, Miriam, Jill Hodges, Jeanne Kaniuk, Saul Hillman, and Kay Henderson. "Attachment Representations and Adoption: Associations between Maternal States of Mind and Emotion Narratives in Previously Maltreated Children." *Journal of Child Psychotherapy* 29, no. 2 (2003): 187–205.

van IJzendoorn, Marinus H. "Adult Attachment Representations, Parental Responsiveness, and Infant Attachment: A Meta-Analysis on the Predictive Validity of the Adult Attachment Interview." *Psychological Bulletin* 117, no. 3 (1995): 387–403.

———. "Commentary." *Human Development*, 39 no. 4 (1996): 224–31.

van IJzendoorn, Marinus H., Carlo Schuengel, and Marian J. Bakermans-Kranenburg. "Disorganized Attachment in Early Childhood: Meta-Analysis of Precursors, Concomitants, and Sequelae." *Development and Psychopathology* 11, no. 2 (1999): 225–50.

Vermeer, Harriet J., and Marinus H. van IJzendoorn. "Children's Elevated Cortisol Levels at Daycare: A Review and Meta-Analysis." *Early Childhood Research Quarterly* 21, no. 3 (2006): 390–401.

Wilkins, David. "Disorganised Attachment Indicates Child Maltreatment: How Is This Link Useful for Child Protection Social Workers?" *Journal of Social Work Practice* 26, no. 1 (2012): 15–30.

Zelenko, Marina, Helena Kraemer, Lynne Huffman, Miriam Gschwendt, Natalie Pageler, and Hans Steiner. "Heart Rate Correlates of Attachment Status in Young Mothers and Their Infants." *Journal of the American Academy of Child & Adolescent Psychiatry* 44, no. 5 (2005): 470–76.

Index

adolescents: AAI, measuring security of, 109, 134, 140, 163; Bowlby, interaction with teenagers, 8; child care, later effects of, 182, 183; continuity in attachment status, 141; disoriented/distracted behavior in adolescent-parent interactions, 138; gender boundaries in pre-teens, 130–131; maternal buffering effect in, 62; in Minnesota study, 129–130; self-reported avoidance of eighteen-year-olds, 113; vulnerability, capacity for linked to early attachment status, 194

adoption of older children, 195

adult attachment. *See* romantic relationships

Adult Attachment Interview (AAI): adolescent security, measuring, 109, 134, 140, 163; of caretaking daughters, 200–201; classification shift after marriage, 157–158; correspondence in security for partner pairs, 156; CRI, correlation with, 155, 156, 157; defensive exclusion, influencing responses, 109–110; ECR scale, compared to, 104; London Parent-Child Project, administering, 132, 133; Main, developed by, 16, 88–89, 90, 94–95; parental classifications as predictive of children's AAI classifications, 194–195; sample questions and

responses, 91–94; secure with parents/insecure re partner configuration, mixed responses of, 159; state of mind classifications, 92–95, 98–99, 112, 139; in Stony Brook marriage study, 159–161; Strange Situation, AAI administered to child veterans of, 139–140; Strange Situation, parallels with, 94–96; subscales of, 111; training requirements, 114n16; unresolved loss and trauma, 96–98. *See also* developmental psychology; state of mind with respect to attachment

affect regulation, 16, 17, 54–55, 56, 63, 152, 188, 196–197

Ainsworth, Mary: AAI institutes, attending, 115n40; attachment parenting proponents, referring to work of, 172; attachment patterns in infants, identifying, 88, 89; Baltimore study, heading, 25–26, 173; behaviorism, not aligning with, 40; early childhood, focus on, 59; Hazan and Shaver, relational style descriptions paralleling those of Ainsworth, 102, 103; on key parenting qualities, 29; lapse in reasoning example, providing, 97; MRI technology, guided by research of, 41; parental state of mind and child's attachment security, studying, 99; on parenting behaviors, 28, 90;

importance of, 185; criticisms towards, 35–36, 155; early quality of attachment as meaningful, 73; emotional and bodily regulation, 55; ethology as a theoretical foundation, 12; evolution and, 59–61, 196; love relationships, early attachment as foundation for, 148; misconceptions in, 57; psychoanalysis, influence of, 13, 64n2; representations of attachment, 15; scientific research and, 41; self-report approach in adult attachment, 103–104; sensitivity in parenting, importance of, 172; traditional emphasis, 123; working models of relationships, 50, 51–54
autonomic nervous system, 54, 197
autonomy support, 102

Baltimore Study, 25–26, 30, 173
Bayley Test of Mental Development, 138–139
bed-sharing, 173, 175, 188n14
behavioral adjustment and attachment histories, 80, 126, 127, 137
behaviorism, 3, 8, 40
Belsky, Jay, 36, 60
Berkeley Longitudinal Study, 69, 135, 139, 140–141
borderline personality disorder (BPD), 163–165, 193
bottle feeding, 174
Bowlby, John: on attachment figures, 88, 147; attachment parenting proponents, referring to work of, 172; conflict between feelings of love and hate, 132; critical theory, misconception regarding, 57; day care, against, 177; on defensive exclusion, 109; diversity in personality inclinations, seen as positive, 99; ethological viewpoint, 12–13, 24; evolution and attachment theory, 59; *Forty-four Juvenile Thieves*, 9–10; Hazan and Shaver, applying Bowlby's theory to romantic love, 89; Hinde, influenced by, 59; *The Making and Breaking of Affectional Bonds*, 7–8; *Maternal Care and Mental Health*, 11; as mentor of Miriam Steele, 100; prototype hypothesis, 148, 194;

psychoanalysis and, 13, 14, 15, 16, 90; *Separation: Anxiety and Anger*, 51–52; working models theory, 16, 51–52, 53, 106, 148
brain: architecture of, shaped by early experiences, 55; Bowlby on working models in the brain, 148, 194; brain functioning, influence of responsive parenting on, 39; interpersonal neurobiology, 55; patterns in activation of brain structures with different attachment representations, 115n53; plasticity in, 16, 62–63, 193; prolonged childhood and brain shaping, 63; slow brain growth in children, 59
breastfeeding, 6, 23, 173–174, 176
Brennan, Kelly, 103, 166n10
bullying, 16, 75–78

Chess, Stella, 37
child care: adult-child caretaker ratios, 179–180, 183, 184, 199; attachment security and child-care factors, no relationship between, 179; disorganized attachment, potential risks for, 180–181, 198; Israeli children in day care, 183, 199; quality of care, 179–180, 181, 182, 183, 184–185, 199, 200; transitions in parental custody at day care centers, 185; weekly hours in care, 177, 180–181, 182, 189n34, 198
Clark, Catherine, 103, 166n10
clinging instinct in mammals, 13, 14
cloth-monkey studies, 13
The Common Sense Book of Baby and Child Care (Spock), 5
conditioning, 3, 18n11
continuity and discontinuity of attachment security, 55–59, 124, 128, 140–141, 194
controlling-caregiving and controlling-punitive behavior, 135, 137, 138, 163
cortisol levels in children, 182–183, 196
co-sleeping, 176
Cowan, Philip and Carolyn P., 35–36
critical period hypothesis, 57
Crowell, Judith, 148–149
Current Relationships Interview (CRI), 155–156, 157, 158, 159–161, 167n40

marital satisfaction, 36; personal histories, differences in affecting development of marriage, 155; secure base behavior during conflict, 159; self-reporting on, 105–106; sixth year follow-up study, 159–161; social/personality research on marital satisfaction, 161–162; Stony Brook study on, 156–158

maternal sensitivity: autonomy in child problem-solving, supporting, 72–73; breastfeeding, relationship to, 174; coaching intervention, increasing sensitivity, 40; cortisol levels of children, affecting, 183; evolutionary adaptations, 61; in German Longitudinal study, 134; irritable infants, sensitivity towards, 38; low levels of, link with insecurity in child, 180; in Minnesota cohort study, 153, 197; mothers of secure children and high sensitivity scores, 29; in NICHD studies, 58–59, 112, 179; self-soothing in infants, promoting, 55; social competence, influence on, 128; Strange Situation, correlation with, 70

maternity leave, 38

McIntosh, Jennifer, 187

menstruation and maternal harshness, 60

Mikulincer, Mario, 106, 161–162

Minnesota Longitudinal Study: at-risk children, studying, 69–70, 71–73, 137, 140; attachment security and physical health, study on link between, 154–155, 197; BPD, assessing, 164–165; continuity in attachment security, research on, 128, 140–141, 194; disorganized behavior, observing, 135, 142n33, 163; early signs of problems in children, 73–74; early social experiences and adult relationship outcomes, 148; mother-toddler interactions, correlation with adult self-reports, 113; name change of cohort project, 83n7, 150–151; peer relationships of middle childhood and adolescence, 127, 132; physiological responses of adult participants, 153–154, 197; preschool bullying,

75–78; romantic relationships study, 150–152, 166n18; summer camp observations, 128–129, 130–131; tool-using problem-solving task, 70–71

monkey research, 13, 176

mothers: AAI interviews of pregnant mothers, 100, 132, 133; amygdala function and pictures of mother, 62; Bowlby on emotional attitudes of, 9; caregiving challenges, 28, 29–30, 180; custody transitions, feeling helpless during, 186; depression in, 40, 136, 140; descriptions of mothers in AAI interviews, 92–94, 96; elderly mothers' attachment to caregiving daughters, 200–201; evolution, behaviors shaped by, 59, 60; frightening episodes with, 32; guilt over day care accommodations, 177; insecure-avoidant infants, not expecting comfort from, 79, 101–102, 197; irritable children and, 38–40; maternal behavior changes and changes in child adjustment, 72; maternal deprivation, 11–12; maternal harshness and hostility, 60, 164; in Minnesota Longitudinal study, 113; in *Patterns of Child Rearing*, 6–7; physical contact, maternal discomfort with, 29–30, 175, 177; reflective functioning capacity, 101; secure infant relationship with mother leading to child self-confidence, 148; secure mothers as responsive and encouraging, 102; seductive behavior of mothers in Minnesota camp study, 131; social supports, importance of, 30–31; state of mind classifications, 98; Ugandan mother-infant interactions, 23, 24–25. *See also* child care; maternal sensitivity

National Association for the Education of Young Children, 184, 199

National Institute of Child Health and Human Development (NICHD) study: behavioral adjustment research, 80; changes in child adjustment and maternal behavior, 72; child care studies, 178, 181–182, 183, 184,

189n34, 198–199, 200; language skills
findings, 58, 79, 181; mid-adolescence,
following youngsters to, 123; mothers'
sensitivity, study on, 58, 112; social
competence through age 15, analysis of,
127–128
Netherlands intervention study, 39–40,
173, 195
neuroscience and attachment, 15, 41
non-parental child care. *See* child care

oral drive, 5
orphanages, lack of attachment figures in,
63
overnight stays, 185–188, 198

Patterns of Attachment (Ainsworth et al),
35
Patterns of Child Rearing (Sears et al), 2,
5–7
Pennsylvania Infant and Family
Development Project, 36
physical contact: attachment parenting,
emphasis on physical contact, 171, 173;
breastfeeding and attachment, 174–175;
child care, positive physical contact in,
179; close physical contact, infant
dislike of, 39, 173; infant carrying and
attachment, 175; maternal discomfort
with, 29–30, 175, 177; sensual physical
contact of mothers, 131; Uganda
example, 23, 173
physical punishment, 4, 6, 83n6
physiological responses in Minnesota
cohort study, 153–154, 166n20, 197
plasticity of brain, 16, 62–63, 193
preoccupied state of mind: AAI
classification, shift after marriage, 158;
anxiety and, 104, 116n67, 156; Bowlby
on, 99; emotional and confusing
responses to AAI questions, 93–94, 96,
110; insecure-resistance, link with, 139;
romantic partners, emotional over-
involvement with, 153
preschoolers: behavioral adjustment in,
126; bullying and victimization of,
75–78; follow-up study at summer
camp, 128; German research on, 73,
74–75; hostility of disorganized

attachment preschoolers, 81; language
development and attachment histories,
79–80; Minnesota study of high-risk
preschool children, 71–72; prediction of
later adjustment, 129; social
competence of mid-teen years,
established in preschool period, 130;
stress levels in, 183; success in
preschool when two parents are
securely attached, 195; teachers,
relationship with, 78–79
Probable Experience scale, 94, 111
prototype hypothesis, 148, 149, 151, 156,
194
Pruett, Marsha Kline, 187
psychoanalysis, 8, 12–16, 64n2, 90
Psychological Care of Infant and Child
(Watson), 3

reflective functioning, 101
Robertson, James, 10, 11, 12, 24
Robertson, Joyce, 11
romantic relationships: attachment styles
and, 17, 103, 105–106; BPD, link to
instability in, 163; as challenging prior
attachment conceptions, 149; conflict
encounters with romantic partners, 107,
153; CRI as measure of, 155–156; dual
methods of determining adult
attachment security, 150; early
attachment experiences as foundation
for love relationships, 148; Hazan and
Shaver, research on, 89, 102–103; in
Minnesota cohort study, 150–152,
166n18; romantic love as an attachment
process, 15; secure base support,
148–149; self-reporting on, 105;
sensitive care in infancy leading to
success in, 195; social/personality
psychology tradition, research on, 17,
89, 107, 162–163; of Strange Situation
child veterans, 108. *See also* marriage

Sagi, Abraham, 96
Schore, Allan, 54–55, 59, 196
Sears, Robert, 2, 5–7
Sears, William and Martha, 172, 173
secure attachment: adult health outcomes
of securely attached individuals,

About the Author

Virginia M. Shiller, PhD, is a licensed clinical psychologist and an assistant clinical professor, Yale University Child Study Center. She trained at The Cambridge Hospital, Department of Psychiatry, Harvard Medical School and at The Bush Center for Child Development and Social Policy, Yale University (now The Cambridge Alliance and Zigler Center, respectively). Dr. Shiller has a strong commitment to writing for a broad audience and for making research findings accessible to those outside of specialty fields. Throughout her thirty-five-year career, she has maintained an interest in parent-child attachment and couple and family functioning. Dr. Shiller has a private practice in New Haven, Connecticut.

CPSIA information can be obtained
at www.ICGtesting.com
Printed in the USA
BVHW030547230121
R11779200001B/R117792PG598302BVX00007B/7